Marketing Strategy in the Pharmaceutical Industry

Marketing Strategy in the Pharmaceutical Industry

Marcel Corstjens

Professor of Marketing, INSEAD, France.

CHAPMAN & HALL

London · New York · Tokyo · Melbourne · Madras

UK	Chapman & Hall, 2–6 Boundary Row, London SE1 8HN
USA	Chapman & Hall, 29 West 35th Street, New York NY10001
JAPAN	Chapman & Hall Japan, Thomson Publishing Japan, Hirakawacho Nemoto Building, 7F, 1-7-11 Hirakawa-cho, Chiyoda-ku, Tokyo 102
AUSTRALIA	Chapman & Hall Australia, Thomas Nelson Australia, 102 Dodds Street, South Melbourne, Victoria 3205
INDIA	Chapman & Hall India, R. Seshadri, 32 Second Main Road, CIT East, Madras 600 035

First edition 1991

338.4761519
C82m

© 1991 M. Corstjens

Typeset in 11/13 Garamond Light by
Rowland Phototypesetting Ltd
Bury St Edmunds, Suffolk

Printed in Great Britain by the University Press, Cambridge

ISBN 0 412 38980 0

British Library Cataloguing in Publication Data

Corstjens, Marcel
    Marketing strategy in the pharmaceutical industry.
    1. Pharmaceutical products. Marketing. Planning
    I. Title
    615.10688

    ISBN 0-412-38980-0

Library of Congress Cataloging in Publication Data

Corstjens, Marcel.
    Marketing strategy in the pharmaceutical industry / Marcel Corstjens.—1st ed.
        p.   cm.
    Includes bibliographical references and index.
    ISBN 0-412-38980-0
    1. Drugs—Marketing.   2. Pharmaceutical industry.   I. Title
HD9665.5.C67   1991
380.1′456151—dc20   90-2573
                                                      CIP

Contents

Acknowledgements

My first debt is to all the pharmaceutical executives I have worked with throughout the years: those who have involved me in their strategic problems and shared their insights and experience with me, and those who have participated in my courses. The learning process has rarely been one way. I hope you will forgive me for not trying to list all your names. However, for their comments, contributions and encouragement, I must mention: R. Abt, P. Baehr, E. Cordes, R. Doliveux, B. Fullagar, B. James, K. McDaniels and V. Troupp.

My thanks to INSEAD, who provided financial support for the project, and enabled me to benefit from the diligent assistance of M. J. Walker. Many thanks are also due to the three patient women who struggled heroically with the secretarial task: Susan Damesin, Helen Hunter and Marie-Louise Berry.

My greatest debt however is to my beloved wife Judy. She read every single version of the manuscript and her insightful and constructive comments would almost qualify her as a co-author. This book is dedicated to her with much love.

To Judy, my one and only drug.

Preface

The 1990s will be one of the most exciting decades in the history of marketing practice in the pharmaceutical industry. The era also promises to be very challenging, and may even be frustrating for pharmaceutical companies. Increased regulation, generics' competition, movement towards harmonization of regulations around the globe, pressure on margins and proliferation of 'me-too' products are all factors that will severely constrain the strategic thinking of pharmaceutical companies. Biotechnology and a more rational drug development approach, mergers and acquisitions, new communications technologies and global economies of scale are all opportunities that will have to be integrated into practical strategic management in the drug industry.

The purpose of this book is to provide a comprehensive analysis of strategic marketing decisions in the pharmaceutical industry. The focus of the book is on the prescription drug industry, to the relative neglect of OTC business. The latter has much in common with consumer goods business and has been treated in detail in a number of other publications. The main features which characterize this book are the following.

1. The focus of the book is on strategic marketing. Allocating scarce resources across strategic business units, defining target markets, selecting product positioning and rigorous competitive analysis are the key ingredients of such an approach. The tactical marketing decision, i.e., the marketing mix including pricing, communication and distribution are discussed in the final chapter but these considerations are not the main aim of this book.
2. Marketing strategy in the pharmaceutical industry cannot be viewed in a vacuum. Its interaction with Research and Development and its political and legal environment (to a large extent controlled by

government regulations) are vital elements that cannot be over-looked. Separate chapters are devoted to 'Research and Development and marketing' and 'Government and marketing'.
3. The book is written for practitioners and not for academics. Therefore it tries to be pragmatic and managerially oriented rather than theoretical. The starting point of the book is managerial problems rather than academic theories. Theories and conceptual frameworks are integrated in the text to the extent that they can address and improve solutions to practical problems.

The book is divided into four parts and contains nine chapters. Part one is an introduction to marketing strategy in the drug industry. Chapter 1 clarifies the notion of a market driven pharmaceutical company. In the next chapter the context in which marketing strategies are developed is explained. Part two examines the major building blocks of a marketing strategy: market segmentation (Chapter 3), product positioning (Chapter 4) and competitive analysis (Chapter 5). The impact of Research and Development (Chapter 6) and government regulations (Chapter 7) on marketing strategies are investigated in the third part of the book. In the final part of the book, the implementation issues of marketing strategies are discussed: strategic marketing review (Chapter 8) and the marketing mix (Chapter 9).

ONE

The marketing concept

1.1 INTRODUCTION

> There is only one valid definition of business purpose: to create a satisfied customer. It is the customer who determines what the business is. Because it is its purpose to create a customer, any business enterprise has two – and only two – basic functions: marketing and innovation. Marketing is the whole business seen from the point of view of its final result, that is, from the customer's point of view (Drucker, 1954, p. 37).

This is the marketing orientation as summarized by one of its early pioneers, Peter Drucker. Marketing, and the way that marketing interrelates with innovation, is also the basic theme of this book. The long-run objective of a commercial enterprise is to maximize its shareholders' return on investment. There is a multitude of ways to achieve this objective, but many recent studies (e.g., Peters and Waterman, 1982) converge on the marketing orientation as the most effective one for achieving long-run profitability. The belief is simply that satisfying customers is an organizational goal that can be second to no other. Marketing, in this broad sense, means that the interests of the customer are considered to be the first and foremost responsibility of general management, in the priorities of the firm. This business philosophy implies that success comes through determining what customers really want, and focusing all the company resources on satisfying these wants at a profit.

In this introductory chapter, a number of misconceptions about marketing are laid to rest before the meaning of the modern marketing concept is explored in detail. The chapter goes on to explain the idiosyncrasies of pharmaceutical marketing and the reasons why the

marketing orientation is gaining in importance in modern pharmaceutical companies. The principal marketing tasks are overviewed in
the last section of the chapter.

1.1.1   Partial views of marketing

Asking a random sample of pharmaceutical executives to describe
marketing and their company's view of its use usually elicits a surprising
range of definitions and opinions. Most companies assume either that
they are already implementing marketing to the full, or, conversely, that
it is unnecessary. These attitudes usually spring from misunderstand-
ings of the role of marketing, or from a distorted and incomplete picture
of what marketing is all about. These incomplete pictures often take one
of the following forms:

1. Marketing is a delivery service: Research and Development develops
    the products; marketing then delivers them to the prescribers and
    consumers. This view identifies marketing closely with the sales arm
    of the company. The aim of marketing is seen as using advertising,
    promotion, the sales force, mailings and samples to deliver infor-
    mation about the product, and eventually the product itself, to the
    actual and potential prescribers who already recognize a specific
    clinical need for the product.
2. Marketing is information: In this view marketing is identified mainly
    with market research. Marketing provides pharmaceutical com-
    panies with information about their prescribers and consumers.
    Market research tells the company how it is doing compared to the
    competition, how demand is moving, what the competition is doing
    (e.g., prices, new products). Marketers receive and analyze IMS
    (International Medical Statistics), study doctors' prescribing habits
    and analyze the competition. As such marketing is seen as being
    rather passive, reporting rather than influencing, a cost rather than
    an investment which can itself lead to enhanced profits.
3. Marketing is tactics, 'the four Ps': Marketing is often identified with
    one of its most visible outputs: the company's tactical marketing
    approach. To maximize profits in a highly competitive market it is
    essential to manage the four Ps: product, place (distribution), pro-
    motion and pricing of the company's market offerings as effectively
    as possible. Optimizing the 'market-mix' is what marketing is all
    about.
4. Marketing is the creation of wants: Marketing is occasionally char-

acterized as an undesirable force that creates new needs in order to sell unnecessary products, usually to an increasingly superficial and materialistic society. Marketing is hucksterism, manipulation. At the extreme, this view identifies marketing with the use of high-pressure sales techniques such as gifts or extravagant hospitality to push the company's products.

The purpose of pharmaceutical products is basically to improve health. Since everyone needs good health, and knows they want good health, the industry has sometimes dismissed marketing as superfluous, or at best, a necessary evil. If one could do without marketing, the world would be a better place. Especially in the pharmaceutical industry, this distorted image of marketing can create a serious obstacle to the implementation of appropriate marketing concepts and strategies.

1.2 THE MARKETING CONCEPT

Fundamentally, the marketing concept is a philosophy about doing business. It describes the overall orientation of a company and not just the marketing function. This orientation argues that for a company to secure its objectives, it must satisfy customer needs better than the competition by means of an integrated company effort – and at a profit.

This approach to management has contributed to the great success of companies in a wide spectrum of industries. In the pioneering book, *In Search of Excellence*, Peters and Waterman (1982) make it abundantly obvious that the key to success is to put the customer at the centre of all company activities. From McDonalds to IBM, the marketing concept is the common factor that explains excellent performance. As opposed to both the traditional product (or Research and Development) and selling orientations (see below), which consider the product as a given quantity, with a marketing orientation the product becomes a variable. The product offering has to be tailored and modified, continually responding to changing customer needs (Webster, 1988, p. 4). *Fortune* magazine recently highlighted Merck's ability to manage its research and marketing synergistically, as one of the keys to the company's impressive success.

A marketing orientation in a company should not imply that the marketing function dominates the other functions in the company. In the pharmaceutical industry the successful Research and Development function will always be at least as important as marketing. What it does imply is that the key orientation of the Research and Development function should also be satisfying consumers' genuine needs, in close collaboration with the other functions in the company. It was its marketing orientation that inspired Swiss-based Serono to buy two of the world's leading fertility-treatment centres. Serono already dominates the world market in infertility drugs: these centres will help Serono learn more about the needs of physicians in fertility drugs and keep hold of their lead (Marsh, 1989).

A truly marketing-oriented company is one where not only the marketing, but also the Research and Development, registration, finance, planning and production people approach their task from the point of view of providing the best possible value for the customer. For this to happen, top management's role is crucial: they have to inject this attitude throughout the organization, and set objectives and incentives to facilitate and reinforce this orientation. This can, for example, mean being ruthless with research projects which show little market promise. It can mean improving communications between the departments, for example, by fixing procedures for early consultations between the functions on issues such as location of clinical trials or dosage levels. It can simply mean physically locating these business functions to facilitate interactions between them.

1.2.1 Alternatives to the marketing orientation

Although the marketing orientation may seem to be rather a common-sense approach, it has not been the dominant influence in the pharmaceutical industry to date.

Product orientation

This is the oldest concept, and one which still dominates the thinking of many pharmaceutical companies. The key assumption is that customers always behave rationally and are well-informed about all the competitive offerings. Such customers will buy 'good' products that are 'reasonably' priced. Let the product speak for itself is the motto of this approach. The key weaknesses with this orientation are, first, the definition of a 'good' product, and second, the narrowness of the competitive base.

One product orientated manufacturer complained bitterly about the poor success of his new range of filing cabinets. 'These remarkable crates are world beaters!' he argued, 'they can be dropped from a fourth-storey window without a dent.' The buyers of office files were apparently unimpressed. 'Nobody in this damn country cares about quality anymore,' said the manufacturer (Kotler, 1986).

In the pharmaceutical industry this attitude pervades a large number of companies. Research and Development provide new products that may represent genuine scientific progress, but that are not necessarily in line with what the market wants. Developing a new anti-rheumatics drug with 2% fewer side-effects or a 3% improved potency profile as compared with the existing anti-rheumatics drugs, might be considered a significant advantage by the developers of the drug. It comes as a surprise, and may seem unfair, when prescribers and users persist in choosing a drug which is, technically, inferior.

The marketing view differs from a product-orientation, in that it is the customer who defines what is and is not a good product, rather than the company's technical or Research and Development people. Marketing companies do not aim to 'sell what they can produce', but as Drucker says, they aim to 'produce what the customer wants' (Drucker, 1973).

The second problem is that a product-orientation depends entirely on product performance, and more specifically, patents to protect the company's profitability. Once patent protection expires the drug which competes purely on a product platform is vulnerable to generics. Companies in other (consumer and industrial) markets have long had to market physically similar brands, and pharmaceutical companies can learn from their experience.

Selling orientation

This management orientation is founded in the notion that pharmaceutical companies are often in the position of selling a product which is perceived to be more or less substitutable with that of one of its competitors.

Prescribers are assumed to be unable to differentiate clearly between the competitive options on offer. Therefore, strong sales efforts (advertising, sales forces, promotion) have to be directed to sway the potential prescribers towards the company's option. This aggressive sales approach to the assumed passive market has been typical of automobiles. Aggressive salesmen use all sorts of tricks ('another customer is already interested in the car,' etc.), or special promotions and deals ('the boss will probably not like it!'), to try to sell whatever is available. Unfortunately, this is an image sometimes attributed to the whole marketing profession, and members of the Research and Development department occasionally view the marketing function in this perspective. Current mergers and co-detailing* and co-marketing arrangements, as well as the fact that several companies continue to have or create several separate field forces don't dispel the image of the pharmaceutical industry as a proponent of the selling orientation.

The marketing concept is fundamentally different from the selling orientation in that it focuses on the needs of the buyer and not the needs of the seller. Theodore Levitt puts it as follows: 'The difference between marketing and selling is more than semantics. Selling is preoccupied with the seller's need to convert his product into cash, marketing with the idea of satisfying the needs of the customer by means of the product and the whole cluster of things associated with creating, delivering, and finally consuming it' (Levitt, 1960).

1.2.2   Evolution towards the marketing concept

The marketing-orientation started in the consumer goods industries and has trickled across to industrial goods and services.

Technical goods categories, such as industrial goods and pharmaceuticals, have a natural tendency to concentrate on the technical aspects of the business and the product, i.e., be inward looking as opposed to a marketing orientation which looks outward to the market. In the fifties, sixties, and even seventies, multiple discoveries of new effective drugs provided the motor for the impressive growth of the industry. Research and Development, as the source of such new products, overshadowed all other departments in the company. However, in more recent times, because of tougher competition, internationalization of markets and changes in the approach to Research and Development within the drug industry, there is a clear trend towards a more marketing-oriented point of view. Research and Development is still a *conditio sine qua non* in the industry, but a number of factors have contributed to the increasing importance of marketing.

First, fewer 'quantum-jump' new drugs are being developed by Research and Development departments. The rate of the new drugs being approved for human use is slowing down (only fifty-two new

---

* Co-detailing is an arrangement where a pharmaceutical company is allowed to use, temporarily, a number of sales representatives of another pharmaceutical company to detail a specific drug.

prescription drugs were approved in 1988, worldwide), but more importantly the cost of developing significantly improved and unique products is increasing more quickly than other costs. American drugs companies spent more than $5bn on Research and Development in 1988, a four-fold increase in ten years. In such a situation more 'niche-products'* come on to the market, competing for shares of existing markets and increasing the level of competitive pressure. For such 'niche' products, and for the products already on the market, fine-tuning to the exact needs of different market segments becom the key to profitability. Targeting and positioning the thirty-sixth entry in an established and well-served market such as anti-rheumatic drugs, is a much more subtle task than launching the first vaccine against AIDS.

Second, certain competitors (e.g., GLAXO, MSD and Ciba-Geigy (CG)) have become very proficient marketeers, which puts pressure on their competitors to become equally marketing-oriented. Just as Proctor and Gamble contributed significantly to making the consumer goods industry more marketing-oriented during the 1960s, the drug companies mentioned above are playing a similar role in the drug industry today.

Third, the professionalism and the competence of marketing executives has dramatically increased in the pharmaceutical industry in recent years. Traditionally, Research and Development executives, with strong academic backgrounds, tended to be sceptical about the contribution made by their marketing colleagues. The marketing people had often risen through the organization after starting as representatives and salesmen, and were not a strong match for Research and Development executives in decision-making at the top level of the company. Increasingly, the academic level and the professionalism of marketing executives have improved to a point where marketers are considered equals by their Research and Development colleagues.

Fourth, the competitive arena has become tougher in the pharmaceutical industry, creating a need for more marketing analysis. Maturing markets, generics, shorter life-cycles, and stronger internationalization of drug markets have all contributed to a demand in the industry for competent and sophisticated marketing executives. Marketing strategy and implementation have become ways of developing

---

*Niche products are products positioned for relatively small segments of the market where they can make fast inroads because they can address the idiosyncratic needs of that segment.

differential advantages in the industry, in the same way as new drug development.

Finally, consumers, prescribers, and those able to influence opinion have become more difficult to approach. The increasing specializations in the medical profession, and the increasing costs of field forces, mailings, journal advertising, and conferences, have increased the need for market segmentation and positioning. Since it is too expensive to reach every possible prescriber, the need for improved marketing approaches has become more important.

These trends provide the motivation for drug companies to become more consumer- and competitor-oriented. From a Research and Development credo (develop technically great products) the industry is moving towards a marketing credo where the consumer and the competition are the central issues of strategic management.

The key message of the marketing orientation is that marketing is not just a mission for the marketing managers while the rest of the organization goes about its business as before. It is the responsibility of the whole management of the company, where the goal is to see the business from the customer's viewpoint. As summarized by managers of General Electric: 'Marketing is too important to be left to marketing people' (Webster, 1988).

It is in this context that this book has been developed: to provide a tool for pharmaceutical companies to be and to become better marketers, and to help students of the pharmaceutical industry obtain a deeper understanding of the fundamental principles of pharmaceutical marketing.

1.2.3   The current status of marketing in the industry

The above remarks should not be taken to imply that all large pharmaceutical companies have become marketing-oriented. Reorienting a company's basic business philosophy takes time. Even in consumer goods companies the transition to a marketing orientation is still considered to be a major challenge.

Although in a number of drug companies marketing orientation still seems to be confined to the sales effort of the company, there are indications that some companies are genuinely moving towards a more marketing-oriented business philosophy. In a significant number of pharmaceutical companies, including Abbott, Beecham, Eli Lilly, Pfizer, Roche, Schering-Plough, Ciba-Geigy and Glaxo as well as the pharmaceutical divisions of more diversified companies, managers with a strong marketing background can be found at the very top (Fletcher and Hart, 1990).

Such an orientation of the heads of pharmaceutical companies (or divisions) towards marketing was unthinkable fifteen years ago. Even for pharmaceutical companies with non-marketing heads, marketing has become more important in recent years. In the late seventies and the eighties, most large pharmaceutical companies have invested heavily in the marketing education of both their marketing and non-marketing people to instill a marketing spirit in the company. Sandoz is another specific example of such a company, where in recent years marketing has transcended its traditional selling function to become a company philosophy.

1.3 THE SPECIFICITIES OF PHARMACEUTICAL MARKETING

The basic marketing concepts in the pharmaceutical industry are similar to those of other industries. The idiosyncrasies of the drug business, however, require a modified marketing approach. A systematic coverage of this approach is the major purpose of this book.

Traditionally, in marketing, a distinction is made between three types of industries: consumer goods, industrial goods, and services. Consumer goods marketing deals with products that move from the producer to the final consumer without any major transformations. The buyer of the product, unless there is a wholesaler or distributor, is also its consumer.

Industrial marketing focuses on products that are investment goods that yield services; the buyer doesn't consume the product. Instead the buyer uses the product as an imput in a production process. Service marketing is different again, because it involves intangible products for which production and consumption occur simultaneously.

The same marketing principles of segmentation, positioning, competitive analysis, and marketing-mix allocation apply for all three categories. The specific contexts of the production-consumption process for those three types of product category, however, require adjustments to the basic marketing principles that give rise to three unusual marketing disciplines.

Pharmaceutical products includes prescription and non-prescription ('over the counter', OTC) drugs. OTC products are somewhat similar to consumer goods and are therefore not explicitly treated in this book. The focus of this book is on prescription drugs, which share some characteristics in common with industrial goods and some other characteristics with consumer goods.

The similarities with industrial goods are due to the multi-party aspect of the buying process. In the industrial goods markets a distinction is usually made between the following parties in the buying process: the initiator, the influencer, the decider, the purchaser, and the user. For ethical drugs the following different buying parties can be identified:

1. Prescriber – Doctor.
2. Influencer – Hospitals, nurses, professors, reimbursement agencies (government).
3. Consumer – Patient.
4. Financer – Partly patient, partly government or third party (varies by country), managed health care organizations (hospitals, HMOs etc.).

The investment intensity in Research and Development, and the fact that products are patentable in most major Western countries, are also similar to industrial goods. Finally, the lengthy Research and Development process from chemical compound to finalized new product is also common to some industrial goods (e.g. aeroplanes).

Prescription drugs also have similarities with consumer goods – they are often aimed at relatively large populations of customers and consumers.

Table 1.1 summarizes the main difference between the marketing of pharmaceutical goods, consumer goods, and industrial goods. The main idiosyncrasies of the prescription drug industry are the Research and Development process, health dimension, and government and third party intervention.

1.3.1   The Research and Development process

Research and Development activity is very expensive in the drug industry – between ten and fifteen per cent of sales for the large research-intensive drug companies. The Research and Development process is usually very long, taking on average between ten and twelve years to discover, develop, and fully test a new drug. The process is also expensive: the cost of bringing a new drug through the necessary trials is currently estimated at $100m. The procedure is risky, with low probability of success for a new research project. The attrition rate of new substances is extremely high; most estimates suggest that only one

Table 1.1 Some differences between consumer goods, industrial goods and pharmaceutical products

	Consumer goods	Industrial goods	Pharmaceutical goods
Customers	– large population – relatively simple decision – consumer pays	– small population – complex buying organization within the company – buyer pays	– large population – complex process, prescribers and users do not belong to same economic unit – the consumer only pays a small part
Products	– usually small transactions at relatively low unit value – purchase is not a major one	– usually large unit value – purchase is a major one for the buyer	– small transactions for relatively high unit cost – high risk involved in products – health is concerned (ethical dimension)
Regulation	– relatively minor – patents not crucial	– relatively minor – patents can be important	– very important – patents crucial – government regulation touches on all elements of the marketing mix, pricing, advertising, distribution, new product development
Research and Development	– Research and Development is not as crucial for most consumer goods as for the industrial or pharmaceutical goods	– Research and Development can be crucial but 70% of all successful new industrial goods come from customer suggestions (Van Hippel)	– Research and Development is the complex, risky *sine qua non* for new products – biological knowledge gap and 'trial and error' research approach – development is complicated because new products have to be tested on human beings

compound out of every five to ten thousand examined reaches the market. The integration of this expensive, risky, and time-consuming Research and Development activity with the marketing dimension poses unique challenges to pharmaceutical marketing.

In many industrial and consumer markets products have long been designed to answer recognized needs of their markets. Until recently, the limited knowledge of drug action and of disease processes in humans meant that the development of new products targeted at specific unmet therapeutic needs was a difficult task. The majority of drug research projects were based on screening large numbers of active chemicals, to discover their therapeutic qualities (if any). However, as the biological knowledge gap decreases, a new 'tailored drug design' approach is becoming more feasible. This approach identifies the key steps in the development of an illness and then aims to develop drugs which can arrest their development at some specific point. The highly successful new drug, Mevacor, launched by Merck in 1987 and selling $200m in 1988, was the result of a very specific effort to produce an anti-cholesterol agent.

A trial-and-error Research and Development approach leads logically to a technological, rather than a market-driven new-product development process. Trial-and-error research confronts marketing management with new products with certain product characteristics for which a target market has to be selected, rather than the other way around. As the biological knowledge gap decreases, and more sophisticated methods of chemical synthesis, biotechnology, genetic engineering, computer modelling and other new technologies come into use, the implementation of a true marketing orientation by pharmaceutical companies will be significantly eased.

1.3.2   The ethical dimension

The ethical dimension of its products puts the drug industry in a special category. Health, and the products related to it, are in a very sensitive area for consumers, prescribers, influencers, and financers. The risk involved in the use of pharmaceutical products has important marketing implications. Relatively low price-sensitivity for the patient, exogenous restrictions on marketing activities, inertia in prescribers' behaviour to switch away from trusted brands, evidence of side-effects and litigation problems of drug companies and the impact of new drugs on the overall health of society, all lead to rather specific marketing problems in the pharmaceutical industry.

1.3.3 Government intervention

Government and third party influences are constraints that have to be integrated, and eventually turned into an opportunity, in the marketing of pharmaceutical products. These issues (product approval, patents, price controls in some countries and potential withdrawal of products) have to be addressed in any effective marketing approach in the pharmaceutical industry.

1.4 THE TASKS OF MARKETING

The marketing function in a drug company is responsible for two crucial tasks: to develop a marketing strategy and to implement the strategy via marketing tactics.

The development of a marketing strategy can be conceptualized at two levels. First, at the level of the product portfolio of the company, scarce resources have to be allocated to the different products. A company cannot simultaneously pursue heavy investments in all of its products, so inevitably, priorities have to be established for the different elements of the product portfolio. Subsequently, a marketing strategy has to be developed at the level of individual products in line with the objectives for those products as they were specified in the product portfolio decisions. To specify the marketing strategy for a particular product requires answers to two fundamental questions.

1. Who are the target customers?
2. What is the differential advantage of the product that is offered to these target customers?

The identification of target markets requires continuous market segmentation analyses and the matching of the Research and Development output (i.e., new products) with potentially viable market segments. The determination of the differential advantage is the outcome of positioning and competitive analyses. Once the strategy is determined, the marketing function is also responsible for the implementation of the strategy, i.e., the marketing tactics. Via a coherent marketing-mix, i.e., field force, journal advertising, mailings, samples, conferences and pricing, the marketing strategy is communicated to the target market. The marketing mix has to be streamlined in such a way that it is consistently directed at the selected target market, and that it supports and reinforces the differential advantage.

Three important principles about the marketing tasks should be stressed from the outset of the book.

1. Marketing strategy precedes marketing tactics. Prior to the mid seventies, the marketing approaches were basically centered around what was called 'the four Ps' (product, price, place, and promotion). Increased competition has made the strategic dimension of marketing more important. It is not reasonable to address, for example, the pricing problem before having decided on the target market and the differential advantage of the product. Once the latter are clearly specified, the pricing problem becomes much more transparent.
2. Target-market selections and the determination of the differential advantage are strongly interdependent decisions. A strong differential advantage for one target market might only be a weak differential advantage for another target market. The differential advantage (DA) of a contraceptive in an underdeveloped country has to be very different from its DA in a developed country like the USA. In the underdeveloped country the DA might be its simplicity of application. In the USA, the DA might be advantages in terms of, for example, less serious side-effects compared to other brands already on the market, without any reduction in reliability.
3. In theory, target-market selection precedes the specification of the DA. New products are developed for the specific needs of a certain target markets. In the pharmaceutical industry, this process is sometimes reversed. Research and Development innovations are often somewhat unpredictable. Discoveries can happen by chance or by serendipity. The strategic marketing task can then be reversed in the sense that, given the specific characteristics for the new product, a target market has to be identified for which these characteristics could be a strong key benefit.

1.5   THE STRUCTURE OF THE BOOK

The overall aim of the book is to give the reader sufficient background information, marketing theory, and practical guidance to understand and practise strategic decision-making within the pharmaceutical industry. With this overall aim in mind, the book is organized as shown in Figure 1.1.

The four following chapters (2 through 5) cover the basic elements of marketing strategy in the drug industry.

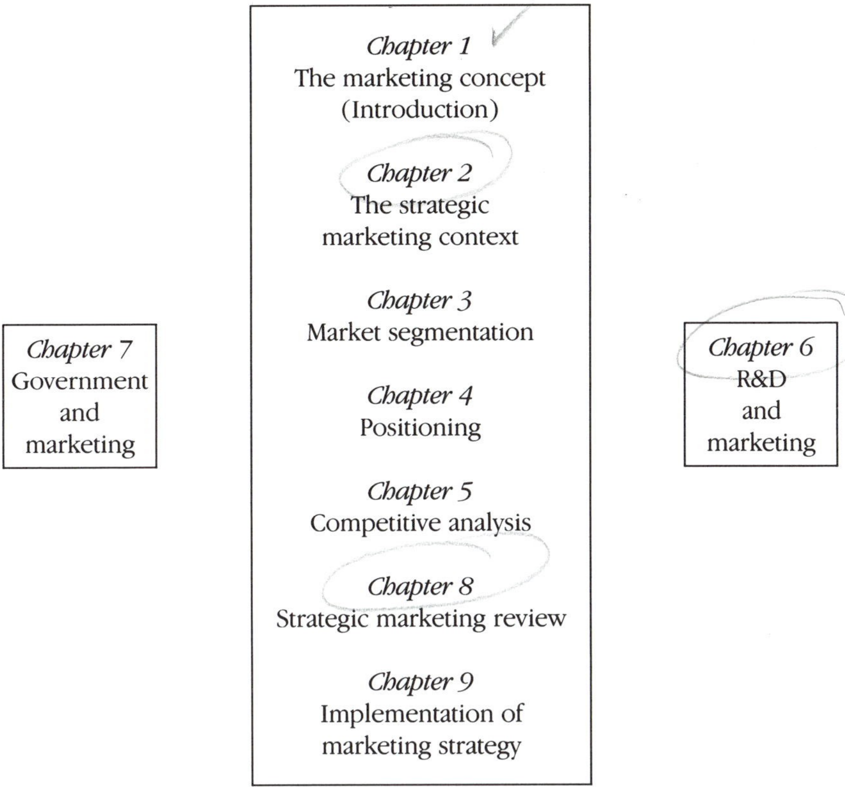

Chapter 1
The marketing concept
(Introduction)

Chapter 2
The strategic
marketing context

Chapter 3
Market segmentation

Chapter 4
Positioning

Chapter 5
Competitive analysis

Chapter 8
Strategic marketing review

Chapter 9
Implementation of
marketing strategy

Chapter 7
Government
and
marketing

Chapter 6
R&D
and
marketing

Figure 1.1   Book overview

'Strategy' is a term that is often used loosely and in many separate and distinct contexts. Chapter 2 sets out to clarify the meaning and levels of strategy, i.e., corporate (defining the company's overall scope and freedom to act), portfolio (setting investment priorities among alternative business units), and product (selection of target market and the definition of the product's differential advantage). Marketing strategy is positioned within its interrelations with these other levels, and with respect to the strategic territories of the different groups and functions within a pharmaceutical company.

Segmentation, positioning, and competitive analysis are the main components of marketing strategy, and the primary preoccupations of marketing managers on a day-to-day basis. Chapter 3 defines and explores the concept of segmentation as it applies to the pharmaceutical industry, aiming to create a framework that will aid managers to apply the ideas in practice. Chapter 4 continues in a similar vein, tackling the key strategic marketing issue of how to develop a sustainable differential advantage within the pharmaceutical industry, both at the product and corporate levels. Chapter 5 covers competitive analysis, starting with a review of the main forces influencing competitive structure now, and those expected to be major influences by the end of this century. The second half of the chapter is devoted to the development of a practical framework for organizing and implementing an effective competitive analysis.

Chapter 6 considers Research and Development as an influence on strategy, as well as from the point of view of its integration within the company, and particularly with marketing. The problem of integrating Research and Development and marketing is not unique to the pharmaceutical industry, but the difficulties in creating a productive dialogue between the two functions are as marked in that industry as anywhere. The chapter discusses the Research and Development process and the issue of project selection, but the main focus of the chapter is on the creation of a real benefit for a pharmaceutical company by integrating the marketing approach into Research and Development. Some tentative guidelines are proposed for strengthening this interface and improving the interaction.

Chapter 7 examines the influence of government intervention and legislation as a major external force to be considered in the context of the strategic decisions taken by pharmaceutical companies. Governmental controls via pricing, patents, and trademarks, new product licensing and *ad hoc* intervention, can be seen as acting upon all the issues discussed in Chapters 2 through 6, creating both barriers or limits, but also opportunities. These threats and opportunities, and their likely evolution, are discussed with respect to marketing strategy.

Chapter 8 (strategic marketing review), offers a framework for bringing together the ideas described in the previous chapters and a practical tool for assessing a company's current strategic position, and monitoring its success in the future. This chapter will be of particular interest to senior management as a practical approach to strategic planning and control.

The last chapter makes the link between marketing strategy and marketing tactics by discussing in detail the interactions between the different marketing mix elements: pricing, clinical trials (phase 4), sales force, advertising, promotion, samples, mailings, and symposia and conferences.

REFERENCES

Drucker, P. (1954) *The Practice of Management*, Harper, New York.

Drucker, P. (1973) *Management: Tasks, Responsibilities, Practices*, Harper and Row, New York.

Fletcher, K. and Hart, S. (1990) Marketing Strategy and Planning in the UK Pharmaceutical Industry: some preliminary findings. *Eur. J. Marketing*, **24** (2), 55–68.

Kotler, P. (1986) *Marketing Management*, Prentice-Hall, Englewood Cliffs, New Jersey.

Levitt, T. (1965) Marketing Myopia, *Harvard Business Review*, September–October, pp. 26–44.

Marsh, P. (1989) Medicine men differ over magic formula, *Financial Times*, November.

Peters, T. and Waterman, R. (1982) *In Search of Excellence*, Harper and Row, New York.

Webster, F. (1988) Rediscovering the Marketing Concept, *Business Horizons*, November–December, pp. 29–39.

TWO

The strategic marketing context

2.1 INTRODUCTION

Given the particularly long lead times in research and development in the pharmaceutical industry, building a market-driven organisation demands close integration of corporate and marketing strategy. Together these strategies should address two crucial issues: (1) which customer needs and markets to serve and (2) how to allocate the company's scarce resources to the selected target customer needs.

Corporate strategy sets out the way a company elects to relate to its environment and how it expects to excel in its selected product markets. Corporate strategy defines the company's action space and it guides the allocation of the company's resources and efforts. As Day puts it: 'It provides a logic that integrates the parochial perspectives of functional departments and operating units, and points them all in the same direction' (Day, 1986). Thus corporate strategy delineates the arena in which marketing strategies have to be developed. Marketing strategy is concerned with product-group (portfolio) and product decisions. Portfolio strategy prescribes the allocation of scarce resources across the independent strategic business units (SBUs) of the company. The selection of target markets and differential advantages of the products that comprise the SBUs is the concern of the product strategy.

2.2 OVERALL COMPANY STRATEGY

Companies operating in the healthcare business have a multitude of market opportunities: human health products (prescription and over-the-counter drugs), animal health products, diagnostics, healthcare services etc. Each of these market opportunities have specific requirements in terms of resources and capabilities. It is often possible to find good arguments for investing in each of these individual market

Table 2.1   The strategic planning process

Strategic hierarchy	Key decision	Unit analysis	Responsibility	Time horizon
Company strategy	Scope of the company	Customer needs and markets	Top management	Long term
Portfolio strategy	Priorities over SBUs	Product market combinations or SBUs	Top management and marketing management	Medium term
Product strategy	Target markets and differential advantages of products	Products or brands	Product management	Yearly

opportunities. Limited resources and competitive pressures usually preclude a company from having a presence in all of those potentially attractive health care markets. The first strategic decision the company must therefore take is to select those markets in which it wants to participate, i.e. it has to specify its scope and, as a company, to recognize its limitations. These scope decisions define the company's opportunity set. A small opportunity set limits the size and the growth potential of the company, but might be realistic given limited resources. A broadly defined opportunity set allows for growth and diversification, but requires extensive resources. This risks spreading the available resources too thinly.

Specifically, a pharmaceutical company has to define its scope in terms of the *set of product-market targets* in which it wishes to develop or maintain a presence and the *geographic spread* of its operations.

2.2.1   Range of product-market targets

Baxter Travenol derives 90% of its sales from health care markets, mostly from the sales of medical supplies and medical equipment. Health care sales, mainly pharmaceutical products, represent only 9% of ICI's sales. Merck Sharp and Dohme, Glaxo and Boehringer Ingelheim all depend on the health care business for over 80% of their income, while differing substantially in their areas of expertise and concentration. Companies such as Ciba-Geigy and Bayer depend less on the health care and pharmaceutical business. Health care companies can be more or less involved with and dependent on the pharmaceutical industry, and each has to define its objectives at this macro level before seeing clearly the challenges at the division or product level.

Recent years have seen some major companies in other fields make the decision to enter the health care market. They have done this either through investment in their own start-up operation or via acquisition. Kodak set up Eastman Pharmaceuticals initially, but then bought Sterling Drug to bolster their entry. Proctor and Gamble entered the OTC area with the acquisition of Richardson-Vicks. Volvo took a participation in Pharmacia, a Swedish pharmaceutical company. The targets and investments set in these entry decisions by the top level of the company's corporate strategy makers define the scope of the lower level strategy makers. This is no less the case in established pharmaceutical companies where the business targets of the company, its objectives and stance within the health care market provide the direction for all the strategy decisions which follow at lower levels.

The pharmaceutical market itself is very broad and covers a wide variety of markets and options. In general it can be divided along several criteria: type of disease (therapeutic groups), type of product (original/generic), type of distribution channel (wholesalers/hospital/drugstore, pharmacy), type of disease (acute/chronic) and type of prescription behaviour (prescription/over the counter (OTC)). Defining the company's scope implies that clear choices are made in view of all these possible options.

Different therapeutic areas represent different types of opportunities for a pharmaceutical company. Some areas are important current profit sources for the company. Some are attractive because the company has a strong, sustainable differential advantage there, some because of a relative weakness of the competition, some look set to provide long-run growth. A company needs to balance these different advantages. Diversification in itself offers a type of security plus greater opportunities for growth. Concentration implies certain economies of synergy and scale, and potentially a local dominance over competitors. Syntex and Searle each obtain more than 95% of their sales from only three therapeutic areas. In Europe, Boots, Fisons and UCB are all reputed to be highly skewed towards a narrow band of therapeutic areas. Conversely there are many companies, Abbott, American Home Products, Bristol-Myers, Ciba-Geigy, Merck, Sharpe and Dohme and Pfizer to cite a few, who through design or accident have significant interests in a vast range of therapeutic areas.

The relative importance of the directness of the distribution channel is clearly an important issue for a pharmaceutical company. Although the actual choice is often influenced by the existing distribution channel structure in a given country, companies can still exercise some choice. For example, in the US, some firms, like Eli Lilly and Smith Kline, were known for their intensive use of wholesalers; whereas others, like Merck and Upjohn, have a tendency to bypass the wholesaler.

The prescription/OTC dichotomy is another important variable. Most large pharmaceutical companies are present in both markets, but for some companies, for instance, Johnson & Johnson and Warner Lambert the OTC business is much more important than for others, say Eli Lilly or Merck (MSD).

Searle and Syntex seem to have chosen an orientation towards chronic treatments, while Squibb, Schering-Plough, Sterling Drug and Johnson & Johnson concentrate more on acute therapies.

The issue of generics is also a 'scope' issue. Some companies (Merck, Sharp and Dohme, Lilly and Upjohn fall in this category) believe that their profitability depends exclusively on innovation and totally shun generics, while some companies (e.g. Ratiopharm in Germany) tailor their cost structure and distribution methods to an exclusively generic orientation. Still other companies, actually more and more, are involved in both original and generic products. This allows them to capitalize on governments' push for generics and to some extent to control and manage the inevitable development of generics.

These scope decisions not only define the boundaries of the company's pharmaceutical business territory but they also dictate the resources necessary to achieve a position of sustainable competitive advantage over competitors. A pharmaceutical company aiming at a large number of therapeutic categories, with original, prescription drugs for acute therapies, distributed directly via drugstores and hospitals, will need very different capabilities (in terms of research and development, sales force, production, registration and logistics) as compared to a pharmaceutical company which focuses on a smaller number of therapeutic categories with an important generics component.

2.2.2 Geographic scope

Although their home markets tend to retain a particular importance, most large pharmaceutical companies are truly international with production, research and development and marketing activities spread throughout the world. Recent changes in Eastern Europe and the USSR are likely to open up further strategic windows for these internationally orientated companies, as could China in the longer run.

For large American drug companies, between 40 and 50% of total sales come from abroad. Some large pharmaceutical companies still face an important internationalization challenge. Eli Lilly, for example, generated in 1988 about three quarters (75%) of their total sales in their home market (North America) while this market only accounted for about 28% of the total world pharmaceutical market. In fact although Eli Lilly was one of the top three players in their home market, they only ranked twenty-fifth in the European market. In comparison, Merck (MSD) was first in the North American (with about 50% of their total sales), fifth in Europe and ninth in Asia, Africa and Australia combined (Yoshino, 1990). For large European drug companies the proportion of international sales is substantially higher because of the smaller potential of their home base. Co-marketing and co-detailing agreements which have become popular in recent years, have a tendency to reinforce the general trend towards internationalization. Firms which concentrate on generics tend to be smaller and less international.

Japan's pharmaceutical industry evolved in a rather different pattern until recently. International companies found it relatively difficult to penetrate the Japanese market, and the major Japanese pharmaceutical companies were not very active outside their home country. This is now changing, with Japanese companies expanding via joint ventures, licence agreements and wholly-owned subsidiaries in a number of major European countries and in the US.

An important strategic question for large pharmaceutical companies is the extent to which they want to maintain a direct presence in underdeveloped countries. Continuing poor patent protection, lack of hard currencies, and political instability have made some large drug companies reconsider their strategies in the Third World.

A very important strategic issue in the context of a company's geographic market is the nature of the relationship between headquarters and subsidiaries. Do headquarters control the strategy of local subsidiaries, or do they give local subsidiaries the power to have their own strategies? Given the high research and development investments necessary to develop new pharmaceutical products, headquarters in most companies will lean heavily on subsidiaries to have global strategies and introduce products in most parts of the world. The tendency towards harmonization of government regulations (especially in the EEC countries but also between the EEC countries and the US) will strengthen control by headquarters even further, or at least put more emphasis on coordination across companies borders. Local subsidiaries are often allowed to adjust the specific target markets and positionings of their products as well as the galenical forms and dosage forms. More specifically, different functions and activities within functions have to be managed in a flexible manner. As illustrated in Figure 2.1, basic research requires more global coordination and integration than marketing. Development and clinical trials will need coordination and integration as government regulations are harmonized, but room has to be left to optimize, for example, specific forms of the products to local habits and preferences. Within the marketing function communication media have to be adjusted locally. Increased harmonization of prices across countries (especially EEC countries) will force drug companies to manage the pricing decisions more centrally. Of all the marketing mix elements, product policy is the most open to globalization. As Bartlett and Goshal point out, the winners in the competitive market struggle will be transnational companies, acting in a global and coordinated fashion when possible, and making local adjustments when necessary (Bartlett and Goshal, 1989).

In the future more centralization can be expected, at least at the company strategic level. A significant source of competitive advantage will be sensitive implementation of the strategy to respect local idiosyncrasies of the market, the competition and the regulation.

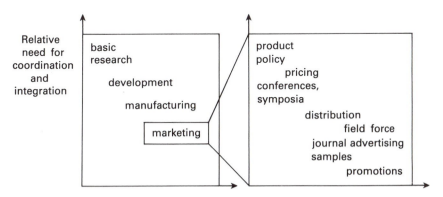

Figure 2.1   Relative need for local differentiation and responsiveness (adjusted from Bartlett and Goshal, 1989)

2.2.3 Evolution in scope

Currently, two scenarios exist concerning the evolution of the scope of pharmaceutical companies. The most popular suggests that the industry will 'shake out' into two tiers of companies: a restricted group of large companies with worldwide scope in a broad range of therapeutic areas and a second group of smaller, niche companies. The current spate of mergers and aquisitions (Merrill Dow and Marion, SmithKline Beckman and Beecham, Squibb and Bristol-Myers, Rorer and Rhone-Poulenc) is cited as evidence of a trend towards a small number of broad-scope companies. Further supporting evidence for this scenario are the increasing marketing costs, the pressure on margins, the generics threat, increased government intervention, globalization trends and product assortment synergies. This concentration tendency will simultaneously provide opportunities for smaller companies to concentrate on special markets. Since the remaining large companies cannot cover all therapeutic categories in all parts of the world, profitable market opportunities will continue to exist for smaller more focused companies.

An alternative scenario predicts a pharmaceutical industry where a number of functions traditionally carried out 'in-house' will be farmed out to specialist agencies (J. Zammit-Lucia, 1989). Because of the questionable link between research investments and research outputs (e.g. Comanor, 1965, Schwartzman, 1970, Angelley, 1973), the task of generating new products might indeed be carried out more efficiently by a number of university departments and small specialized research institutes or companies. In theory, specialized development companies could also carry out clinical trials and registration requirements more cost effectively than their pharmaceutical company clients through being the most efficient size for that function and through specialization. The marketing and sales tasks can be partly fulfilled by specialized sales and marketing organizations that operate as separate companies.

This scenario of functional fragmentation is based on the intrinsic difficulties of integrating Research and Development, registration and marketing and on the hypothesis that all of these functions can be carried out more efficiently at different optimal levels of company size. This argument goes back to the basic economic theory of the firm based on functional specialization which will determine the functional scope of an efficient company (Stigler, 1951). The success of MSD and Glaxo are exceptions rather than the rule according to the protagonists of the fragmentation hypothesis. The recent mergers in the drug industry would be explained by these protagonists as opportunistic financial manoeuvres where some companies, in shaky positions, prefer to merge with a white knight rather than their being gobbled up in a hostile takeover.

The actual configuration of the industry will probably be a mixture of the two scenarios. For some functions, specialization is already taking place, e.g., specialized development companies and companies which can hire out their sales forces to pharmaceutical companies to deal with short-run special needs (e.g., launching of new products). Specialization in research is perhaps more questionable because of the very high risk factor in generating marketable research leads, and because of secrecy in basic research. This form of specialized research company already exists in the biotechnology area, but is the exception, and is unlikely to become the rule.

2.3   MARKETING STRATEGY AT THE PORTFOLIO LEVEL

Once the overall scope of the company's activities is defined, the limited resources available to the company have to be allocated between each of these activities. The two most critical resources in the drug industry are Research and Development and marketing resources. Other resources, e.g., production and finance, are also limited but they are generally accepted to be less critical than Research and Development and marketing.

A workable conceptualization of activities has to be defined to enable the company to assign resources to well-defined units. These units are called strategic business units. Conceptually, strategic business units (SBUs) can be defined in terms of demand-related, cost-related and organization-related criteria. On the demand side, the elements (products) aggregated in an SBU should have homogeneous growth rates, similar customers and customer needs, similar competitors, and no demand interdependencies with other SBUs. On the cost side, the SBU should also be self contained, i.e., no shared costs with other SBUs. It is also important to delineate SBUs in such a way that within the organizational structure (existing or new) a distinct decision-maker exists for each SBU.

In the pharmaceutical industry, SBUs are usually defined as therapeutic groups. A frequently encountered typology distinguishes ten SBU types: cardiovascular, nutritional, pain control, internal medicine, mental health, topical, anti-infective, respiratory, cancer therapy and others.

The arguments in favour of this definition are that prescribers often think about companies as specialists in specific therapeutic areas, that salesmen usually are experts in certain therapeutic categories, that product and marketing management in pharmaceutical companies are often organized along the lines of therapeutic groups, that Research and Development is or can be departmentalized in therapeutic areas, and that most secondary data available in the pharmaceutical industry are categorized in therapeutic groups. There are, however, some drawbacks with such a delineation of an SBU. Production capacity is not always organized in therapeutic groups, and even in Research and Development certain projects can span several therapeutic groups. In addition, the products within a given therapeutic area may be very different in terms of their market potential and their resource absorption. For example, the cardiovascular area includes beta-blockers, hypertensives and other preparations, which all differ substantially in terms of their stage in the market life cycle. The use of this definition also throws up the problem of the 'other' (residual) therapeutic categories which for certain companies can include such divergent product categories as nasal decongestants and oral contraceptives. It is hard to imagine such a residual therapeutic group as a relevant unit for strategic analysis.

In practice any definition will show some deficiencies, and for most companies in the pharmaceutical industry the therapeutic area has become the basic unit for strategic portfolio planning.

Two alternative approaches exist to assist the manager in the definition of the missions for the different SBUs: the Boston Consulting Group (BCG) approach and the Composite Portfolio approach. Both approaches have their advocates in the pharmaceutical industry. Their logic, use, advantages and drawbacks are explained in detail below.

2.3.1 The Boston Consulting Group approach

The BCG approach to product portfolio analysis is based on satisfying two company objectives: growth and cash balance. The assumption that companies want to grow is generally reasonable. The assumption that every company wants to finance its growth completely internally, and therefore always seeks to balance its cash flow, is more difficult to accept. Although there are cash limits, many companies are able to generate external financing, e.g. via loans and equity increase, to fuel their growth. Be this as it may, the basic philosophy of the BCG portfolio

Table 2.2   Growth measures

	Market growth	Product growth
SBU A	5%	20%
SBU B	20%	5%

approach is that some SBUs will have to generate the cash necessary to support the growth of the other SBUs such that the overall company can grow without running out of cash.

To operationalize the 'growth potential' dimension of the portfolio, BCG proposes as a proxy the growth rate of the market in which the SBU is positioned. This is because the objective is to measure the future potential of the SBU, which is assumed to be controlled by the stage in the market life cycle of its relevant market. Suppose two SBUs, A and B, show the following characteristics (Table 2.2).

In the BCG framework, SBU B is much more attractive than SBU A, because its future, linked to its booming market, looks promising, whereas SBU A is in a mature market which will inevitably limit the future growth of SBU A.

Cash balance implies striking an equilibrium between cash inflows (revenues, contributions, profits) and cash outflows (investments). Cash inflows are operationalized via the concept of 'relative market share' (RMS). The RMS of an SBU is measured by its market share divided by the market share of the leader in the SBU's market; or if the company's SBU is the market leader, then RMS is calculated by dividing its market share by that of the second-largest brand. RMS is taken as a proxy for cash inflows because SBUs with larger RMSs are assumed to have lower average costs (experience curve*) and as such are expected to have higher margins and profits. Cash outflows are approximated by the growth rate of the market in which the SBU is positioned. The assumption here is that more investments will be needed to support SBUs that are in high-growth markets. The latter tend to be highly competitive because of their attractiveness to all competitors, as opposed to the less attractive low-growth markets.

BCG proposes the following 'portfolio matrix' to integrate all this

---

*The experience curve concept relates the average total costs (i.e., production, research, marketing, etc.) of a product to the cumulative output over time of that product. Empirical research (especially for industrial products) has shown in a large variety of industries that as the cumulative output increases the average total cost decreases.

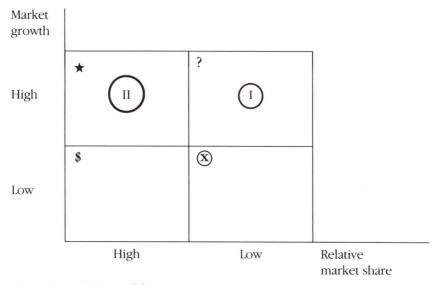

Figure 2.2   BCG portfolio matrix

information (Figure 2.2). The four quadrants of the BCG matrix are classified as follows. The low growth – low RMS box (also called the 'dog' box and marked Ⓧ in Figure 2.2) characterize SBUs that are not attractive to the company since they are in mature or declining markets and are dominated by their competitors. The high-growth – low RMS box (sometimes called 'problem children' or question mark products and marked with a ? in Figure 2.2) is the area in which new or young SBUs that are in attractive markets are placed. High relative market share SBUs in high-growth markets are quite naturally called 'stars' (★). SBUs with high relative market shares positioned in low-growth markets are identified as 'cash cows' ($). They generate a lot of cash since they have strong market positions and at the same time demand only modest resources because they are positioned in low-growth markets.

In applying the BCG analysis to a particular company, the market growth and the relative market share are measured for each SBU and, corresponding to the values of these two dimensions, they are placed in the matrix. Each SBU is then represented by a circle, the diameter of which is proportional to its sales level, e.g., in Figure 2.2 sales of SBU I are about half of the sales of SBU II. The position of each SBU within the matrix suggests a certain role for the SBU in the company's portfolio. 'Cash cows' provide cash in excess of their investment needs. 'Dogs' demand little investment (low market growth) but also generate little cash because of their low relative market share. 'Problem children' demand high investments for their struggle in a high-growth market, while their low relative market shares limit their ability to generate profit. Stars generate contribution (high relative market share) that is needed for investments to defend or improve their strong position in attractive markets.

Based on these roles specific strategies are recommended according to the SBU's position in the matrix.

1. The excess cash generated from the cash cows should be invested in some problem children and in the stars.
2. Dogs are to be avoided and should not receive any investments; if they take management time or other scarce resources they should be divested.
3. A selective investment policy is proposed for problem children. To ensure sufficient investments to turn problem children into stars, the company cannot invest in all their problem children – some will have to be divested to allow decisive investments in the remaining problem children.
4. Stars should be protected. Investments will be necessary to defend their leadership position and eventually improve it.

These typical strategies are summarized in Figure 2.3.

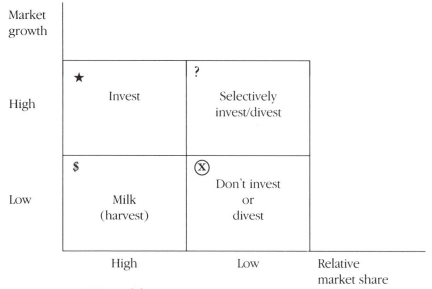

Figure 2.3   BCG portfolio strategies

Coming back to the original objectives of the BCG approach, growth and cash balance, a desirable portfolio is one in which a sufficient number (or proportion) of SBUs are positioned in high-growth markets and that a sufficient number (or proportion) of 'cash cows' exist to fuel the growth of the selected 'problem children' and to support all the star SBUs. Such a desirable, though realistic, portfolio is illustrated in Figure 2.4.

The broken line in Figure 2.4 illustrates the ideal path of an SBU through the BCG matrix over its effective life cycle. The SBU enters in what is hoped to be a rapidly growing market. Marketing investments and Research and Development improvements will push the SBU to gain RMS to become a 'star'. As the market matures, the SBU will drop to a 'cash cow' position, from where it might either leave the market directly, or pass through the 'dog' quadrant before being withdrawn.

If the SBU creates a new market, it might actually start in the 'cash cow' area, since the market might have low growth in the first stage of its life cycle and the SBU has the total market to itself. The growth of the market will push the SBU to the 'star' quadrant if it remains dominant or it will become a 'problem child' if the competition enters with stronger SBUs. From here on, it is likely to follow the classic path.

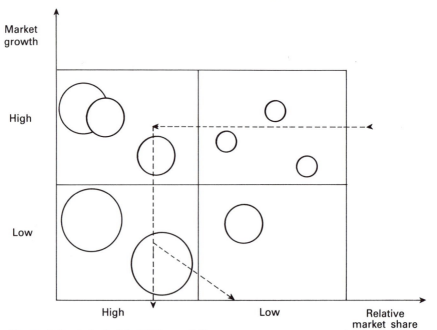

Figure 2.4   A desirable BCG portfolio

The BCG portfolio approach is an intuitively appealing strategic tool that is easy to implement. A few problems should be taken into account, however, when applying the BCG framework in the pharmaceutical industry. Firstly, recall the rather arbitrary definition of the SBU. Secondly, the division of the axes into high and low areas is conceptually not well defined. For the market-growth axis, the average growth of the pharmaceutical industry is usually taken as the separation point

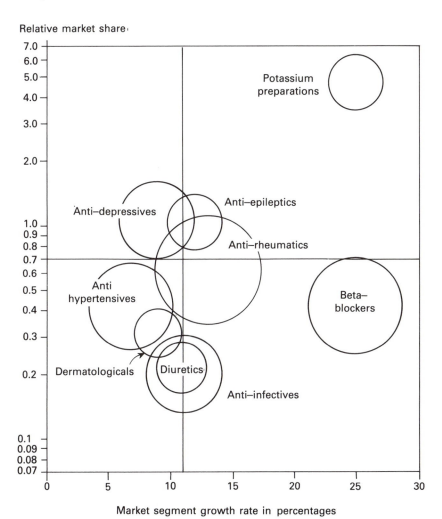

(Balloons size proportional to sale)

Figure 2.5 The BCG portfolio for a large pharmaceutical company (Buzzell, 1983)

between high and low-growth markets. This implies quite naturally that any SBU that is positioned in a market that grows faster than the overall pharmaceutical market is more attractive than the average and vice versa. Another option is to define the dividing point between high and low growth markets to be the company's target growth rate. No similar rule of thumb exists to define the dividing line between high and low relative market share. In line with the BCG's original concept, this separation should occur at a point where if the RMS is higher (lower) than the separation point it should generate more (less) cash than the average. Sometimes this separation point is put at 1.00, implying that only the market leader is a substantial cash-generator and that all other competitors have much less cash-generating power. In Figure 2.5 the dividing point is put at 0.8, implying that being a close second to the leader is still a guarantee for substantial revenue generation. In fact, in the pharmaceutical industry the crucial assumption that the RMS measure acts as a reliable proxy for cash generation is dubious. Indeed, a lot of old products in the pharmaceutical industry, even if they have small RMSs, are very profitable: very few resources have to be invested and some loyal (laggard) prescribers guarantee the continuation of substantial sales and profit levels. 'Dogs' can therefore be called 'cash dogs' in the pharmaceutical world. Divesting these 'cash dogs' would be a major mistake. Although they will not be a factor in the company's future growth, they are a secure cash base for which very few resources have to be invested.

Beyond these conceptual problems, there are some measurement problems involved with the BCG framework. How does one define a market? Are the market growth rates and the RMS measured in units, value, or in the number of prescriptions? These are all questions for which no definitive answers are available.

Another criticism levelled at the BCG framework is that it fails to integrate the full implications of the competitive situation. Consider the following situation of two competitors (us and them) that compete in four different markets. In each of these markets the SBUs have BCG matrix positions as illustrated in Table 2.3.

Following the BCG framework, we would be inclined to divest our 'dog' SBU in Market 3. The result of this decision would be that our competitor would gain market share and cash with the cash cow in that market. These additional resources could then be devoted to invest in their problem child in Market 4. This would jeopardize the situation of our star in Market 4 because it is directly attacked by their problem

Table 2.3 Competitive effects
and the BCG portfolio

Market	Us	Them
1	$	⊗
2	?	★
3	⊗	$
4	★	?

child. This implies that there might be strategic and competitive reasons
to defend our dogs, which are overlooked in the BCG framework.

Despite its shortcomings, the BCG approach to portfolio analysis can
still be a useful concept in the pharmaceutical industry. If one interprets
the RMS axis of the portfolio as an indicator of the competitive posture
of the SBUs rather than as a proxy for cash-generating power, the BCG
approach can give some fresh insights in the resource allocation
problem. Indeed, in this way it is clear that a company should have at
least a certain proportion of its SBUs in a strong position in the market to
foresee a bright future. Investments in SBUs need to be guided by this
need to obtain the dominant positions that ensure the future growth
and long-term cash balance of the firm.

2.3.2 Composite portfolio approach

Alternative portfolio frameworks have been proposed that claim to
redress some of the shortcomings of the BCG approach. McKinsey, A. D.
Little and Shell have all developed composite portfolio models.
Although they differ slightly from each other, overall they are very
similar in spirit. The basic impetus behind these composite models was
the feeling that the BCG approach oversimplifies the portfolio problem.
The 'composite modelers' propose replacing the market-growth criterion with a more comprehensive market-attractiveness dimension
(Market attractiveness in the McKinsey approach and Maturity of the
market in the Arthur D. Little approach). This market-attractiveness
dimension is composed of a number of factors, to be judged by the
specific company that uses the tool, that together reflect the attractiveness of the market in which they operate. The RMS dimension is
substituted by a competitive position criterion (in both the McKinsey
and the A. D. Little approach), which includes RMS but also takes into

account other factors, judged by management as important indicators of competitive position in the industry.

Table 2.4 is a list of factors that can be used to describe the market-attractiveness and competitive position dimensions. This list is not exhaustive and can be adjusted by managements according to their own understanding of their markets.

When applying one of the composite portfolio approaches, management has to do the following.

1. Assign relative importance weights to each factor according to its judgment.
2. Assign scores (usually on a 1 to 10 scale) to each factor for each SBU according to its judgement.

As illustrated in Table 2.5, for each SBU an index is then computed by means of a weighted average of the scores for each factor for that SBU and the respective importance weights for the corresponding factors. The next step is to draw the portfolio map as in Figure 2.7.

The interpretation of the matrix differs slightly from that of the BCG matrix. In general, the strategies implied by the composite model are very much along the lines of concentrating the company's resources on the areas where the company is strong.

Table 2.4   Indications of market attractiveness and competitive strength

Market attractiveness	Competitive strength
Size (Value, Units)	Market share
Growth (Value, Units)	Relative market share
Market fragmentation	Differential advantage
Price sensitivity	Company image
Therapeutic gap	Company expertise in marketing
Acute/Chronic	Research and Development
Cost of entry/exit	Patent situation
Marketing cost	Relationships with regulations
Number of competitors	
Type of competitors	
Liability/Risks	
Substitution threats	
Regulatory climate	
Importance of the managed health care business	

Table 2.5 An example of a composite portfolio model

Market attractiveness	Import-ance weight	SBU A	SBU B	SBU C
Market growth	.4	8	3	7
Size of market	.3	5	2	9
Margin	.3	3	2	9
Index		5.6	2.4	8.2
Competitive position				
RMS	.3	4	2	7
Marketing Experience	.3	6	3	8
Research and Development Expertise	.4	7	6	8
Index		5.8	3.9	7.7

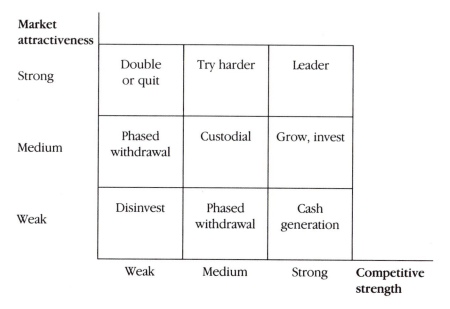

Figure 2.6 A composite portfolio model

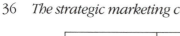

	Embryonic	Growth	Mature	Ageing
Dominant				
Strong				
Favourable				
Tenable				
Weak				

Figure 2.7   Composite portfolio for a major pharmaceutical company
(A. D. Little Inc., 1979)

Table 2.6   Comparison of portfolio approaches

	BCG	Composite approaches
Strengths	Simple Objective measures Readily available measures Theory-based (life cycle, experience curves)	Comprehensive Flexible
Weaknesses	Simplistic Rigid	Subjective

The major advantages of these composite approaches are that they are more comprehensive and more flexible and adjustable to the specific situations of the industries in which the company is involved. The major new drawback introduced by this method is the subjectivity in assigning weights to the factors and scores for each SBU on each factor. As a result, if a manager really wants to push a specific SBU he or she can 'adjust' its scores and the importance weights to make it fit in the desired area.

In Figure 2.7 the composite portfolio of another large pharmaceutical company (Company B), following the A. D. Little specification, is illustrated. The sizes of the circles represent relative sales levels of the SBUs.

When the two different portfolio models are applied to the same problem, the resulting strategies for the SBUs are not necessarily the same. Wind, Mahajan and Swire (1983), applied the BCG, the Shell and the McKinsey models to a company composed of fifteen SBUs. Their analysis showed that only three out of the fifteen businesses were classified in the same area of the three portfolios (6, 11 and 14).

In Table 2.6 the relative advantages and disadvantages of the two portfolio approaches are recapitulated.

2.4 TRANSLATING THE PORTFOLIO STRATEGY TO THE PRODUCT LEVEL

The outcome of the product portfolio strategy is a set of strategic objectives for each of the company's SBUs. These strategies, i.e., expansion, maintenance, milking or divesting, have to be refined at the product strategy level.

2.4.1 Expansion strategy

An expansion strategy for a product implies increasing its market share or its sales volume. To achieve this target four possible routes can be envisaged: attract new prescribers to the product category, expand the market to new segments, increase the usage rate among current prescribers, or attract prescribers from competing products. The attractiveness of these alternatives is usually linked to the stage of the life cycle of the product and its market. In the early stages of the market life cycle, an expansion strategy implies convincing prescribers of the validity of the new product category. This was the task for Tagamet when

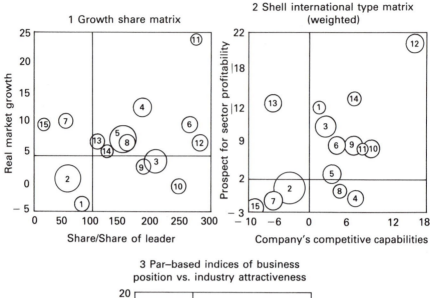

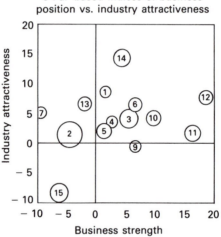

Figure 2.8   Comparison of three portfolio models (Wind *et al.*, 1983)

just introduced on the market. SKF had to convince prescribers of the therapeutic value of H_2 antagonists. Similar strategies had to be pursued by Capoten (first ACE-inhibitor), and Inderal (first Beta-blocker) when first introduced on the market. New early entrants into the market tend to develop the market by directing their positioning and marketing efforts to new market segments. Zantac's strategy when first introduced was aimed at expanding the market, initially created by Tagamet. Zantac focused its strategy on its better side-effects profile, thereby addressing less severe cases. Beyond this stage, sales and market share can be improved by increasing the number of patients on a specific drug with each prescriber, or perhaps by moving the product from a third- or second-line treatment to a first-line treatment. For example the CA-antagonist product Adalat (Bayer) has clearly moved from a second-line to a first-line antihypertensive to fuel its growth. At the maturity stage of the market, when the market becomes a zero-sum game, attracting prescribers of competing products to your product becomes a major target. At this stage of the life cycle it might also be viable to aim for expansion via the use of the drug for new conditions for which clinical and medical evidence should be developed early on. Simultaneously with this process it will be absolutely vital to aim for expansion (or defence) via new dosages and galenical forms and investigate new indications or combination therapies for which clinical trials and medical evidence should be accumulated from the time the new product is launched on the market. Beta-blockers, for example, are now moving from the area of cardiac problem indication to that of hyper-tension indication; Estraderm TTS (Ciba-Geigy) is moving from menopause indication to osteoporosis prevention.

In mature markets some pharmaceutical companies are pursuing a strategy of turning prescription into OTC product, thereby expanding their market without changing the product substantially. Boots was successful in turning their product BRUFEN (NSAID-prescriptions) into OTC (NUROFEN or NEROFEN) in some European countries. SKF is trying a similar strategy for Tagamet. Although this particular strategy is not viable in many therapeutic areas it seems like a promising direction for products in lower health-risk therapeutic areas.

2.4.2 Maintenance strategy

A maintenance strategy for a product is not necessarily a passive strategy. If a product is a market leader in an attractive market, mainten-ance implies the use of substantial resources simply to hold the current position (e.g. Tagamet's (SKF) defence against Zantac (Glaxo)). A maintenance strategy usually implies a rather defensive approach, whether the task is to consolidate market leadership, or to impose some 'status quo' position if one is not the market leader. The most critical example of this strategy is when a drug comes off patent and the key marketing objective becomes limiting the inroads that can be made by generics.

2.4.3 Milking strategy

'Milking' (or 'harvesting') refers to a strategy of holding back on resources and trying instead to generate as much cash revenue as possible within certain constraints. Milking usually implies cost-cutting in operations and capital expenditures, raising the price (if possible) and reducing (if any) field force and promotional support. The hoped-for result is a gentle loss of market share, which reflects the policy of capitalizing on the position achieved by past investment, restricting the resource input, and creaming off the generated revenue. Industry observers would argue that Merck, Sharp and Dohme is currently milking its diuretic and antirheumatic markets, partly because of competitive and market conditions, partly because of the abundance of strong new products which compete for Research and Development and marketing resources.

A danger to be avoided with more aggressive milking is the signalling to competitors and customers of such a strategy. This signalling might dramatically reinforce the loss of market share and hence jeopardize the cash generation. One should first cut back in less visible areas such as Research and Development rather than in promotional support. A 'thin' harvesting option may be more appropriate for leading products in mature or declining markets. Aggressive harvesting might not be appropriate for such products, because of the danger of starting a process of rapid decline, which would squander the rewards of past investments.

In some other cases, for example for older 'cash dog' products, the milking strategy is very passive. Since the product is still generating 'easy' revenue with no substantial investments, a maintenance strategy refers to the continuation of the existing low-key approach.

2.4.4 Divesting strategy

If the product has no future it is quite easy to reduce the investments to zero and to let the product die (a milking strategy). Because of strong generic competition Hoffmann-La Roche seems to be cutting off any marketing support to their 'ex-cash cows' Valium and Librium. An active decision to divest, however, is psychologically and politically more painful. This is particularly true if the product has, potentially, a bright future because it is positioned in an attractive market. Yet it is sometimes necessary to do so because spreading resources too thinly can mean failure in every action undertaken. Often one has to concentrate efforts in order to be successful with only a few products. Hence, the pressure of limited Research and Development resources and/or field force time and/or advertising or promotional funds can make it necessary to divest potentially interesting products and projects; especially where patent life is also ticking away. In the UK, for example, because of the cap imposed on marketing expenditure by government (Pharmaceutical Price Regulation Scheme), a number of companies have to withdraw all support for a number of products whenever they bring a new product on the market.

Whatever the strategic objective, developing successful product strategies will depend on two key issues: target market selection and differential advantage positioning. The answers to the questions 'Who are the target prescribers and/or users and/or influencers?' and 'What is the product's differential advantage?' fully specify any product strategy. Many marketing strategies fail because management has not successfully dealt with these two key issues. The marketing dictum that the customer is central and that products have to be developed to satisfy customers' needs, implies that to satisfy the customers, homogeneous target groups have to be identified and offered products to fit with their needs. The definition of the target market is important because of the heterogeneity in the customer population, the prohibitively high cost of reaching the total population and the impossibility of appealing to all of the population simultaneously. The key concept in this context is market segmentation: dividing up the market into homogeneous groups of customers to whom individual products can be offered. Developing a marketing strategy, then, implies selecting one or several segments, the target market(s). Market segmentation will be discussed at length in the next chapter.

To be successful in the target market, the product has to offer a plus, i.e., a differential advantage to the targeted customer. It is something perceived to be unique and important, and that cannot be copied immediately by the competition. All competitors in the market can segment the market and select target markets. Some products offer real, product-specific differential advantages to the customers. Unfortunately, this is only true for a minority of products. An important task of marketing management is to try to develop and defend differential advantages that are not so clear cut. As explained before, the fact that Research and Development cannot always provide the company with breakthrough, quantum-jump new products is the key reason why marketing has become so important to the pharmaceutical industry. The problem of developing differential advantages is fully discussed in Chapter 4 on positioning.

The key to success in marketing in the pharmaceutical industry is to integrate the target-market selection and the differential-advantage decisions. A strong interaction exists between the two dimensions of a product strategy. One approach is to select an attractive target market and guide the Research and Development department to develop products or to search for active substances that will generate a differential advantage for that target market. Unfortunately, in the pharmaceutical world there are substantial barriers to working that way. It can take ten to fifteen years to develop some new products. By the time a new product is developed, the needs of the target market might have changed. Furthermore, targeted Research and Development is difficult in the drug industry because the new product development process is often characterized by a trial-and-error process. In the past a large number of new products, successful and unsuccessful, were generated by accident or luck. Streamlining this process from the outset toward specific target-market needs is often unrealistic. Therefore, it is often equally important for marketing management to identify target markets for which the existing products or the projects in the Research and Development pipeline could provide a defensible differential advantage. In fact, it is this successful interaction of Research and Development with the marketing function that often forms the cornerstone of a company's success in the market place.

2.5   A CONCLUDING NOTE

A virtually unlimited set of market opportunities presents itself to any health care company. Selecting those market opportunities that fit best with the company's strengths is the art of strategic decision-making.

Accepting the fact that any pharmaceutical company has limited resources implies that a set of priorities has to be defined for the selected market opportunities. Different models to assist the manager in this task were presented in this chapter: BCG and composite portfolio models.

At the third level of strategic management (the product), the manager's job is to carefully choose the most attractive target markets for which the product can provide a sustainable competitive edge.

REFERENCES

Angilley, A. (1973) Returns to Scale in Research in the Ethical Pharmaceutical Industry, *Journal of Industrial Economics,* December, pp. 81–93.

Ansoff, I. (1979) *Strategic Management,* John Wiley, New York.

Bartlett, C. and Ghoshal, S. (1989) *Managing across Borders,* Century Hutchinson, London.

Buzzell, R. (1983) Ciba Geigy Pharmaceuticals Division, Case study 0–584–018, Harvard Business School, p. 17.

Comanor, W. (1965) Research and Technical Change in the Pharmaceutical Industry, *Review of Economics and Statistics,* May, **47**, 1982–90.

Cool, K. and Schendel, D. (1987) Strategic Group Formation and Performance. The case of the pharmaceutical industry, 1963–1982, *Management Science,* September, pp. 1102–24.

Day, G. (1986) *Analysis for Marketing Decisions,* West Publishing, St Paul, Minnesota.

Schwartzman, D. (1970) *Innovation in the Pharmaceutical Industry,* Johns Hopkins University Press, Baltimore and London.

Stigler, G. (1951) The Division of Labor is limited by the Extent of the Market, *Journal of Political Economy,* June, pp. 185–93.

Webster, F. (1988) Rediscovering the Marketing Concept, *Business Horizons,* November–December, pp. 29–39.

Wind, Y., Mahajan, V and Swire, D. (1983) An Empirical Comparison of Standardized Portfolio Models, *Journal of Marketing,* Spring, **47**, pp. 89–99.

FURTHER READING

Aaker, D. (1988) *Strategic Marketing Management,* John Wiley and Sons, New York.

Day, G. and Wensley, R. (1988) Assessing Advantage: A framework for diagnosing competitive superiority. *Journal of Marketing,* April, pp. 1–20.

Kerin, R., Mahajan, V., and Varadarajan, P. (1990) *Strategic Market Planning,* Allyn and Bacon, Boston.

THREE

Market segmentation

3.1 INTRODUCTION

Market segmentation starts from the premise that customers are not homogeneous. This postulate implies that the notion of an average customers is rather useless. Like the statistician who waded through a river with an average depth of one metre and drowned, the marketeer who develops a marketing strategy and tactics in terms of the average customer is on his way to disaster.

Market segmentation is the process of assessing how the total market is divided into customer groups that have similar product-needs or that react to a product offering in a similar way. The purpose of this subgrouping is to enable the manager to design a marketing mix that matches the needs of the individuals in a selected segment more precisely.

3.2 IDENTIFYING MARKET SEGMENTS

There is almost an infinite number of ways in which to segment a market. How can one differentiate between a 'good' segmentation scheme and one that is 'not so good'? Four fundamental criteria can be used to evaluate a segmentation scheme. First, a good segmentation scheme identifies segments that are (1) homogeneous within the segment and (2) heterogeneous across segments. Figure 3.1 illustrates an appropriate segmentation approach based on sensitivity to samples and the galenical form preference of prescribers in the market. Four distinct segments can be identified which are homogeneous within each segment and heterogeneous across them. Figure 3.2 indicates that a segmentation scheme based on medical rep. information and side-effects sensitivity does not satisfy this criterion, that is, prescribers do

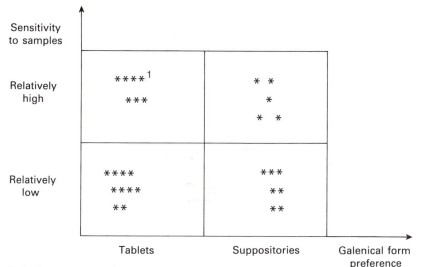

*: indicates a prescriber

[1] The seven stars represent seven prescribers that clearly prefer tablets over suppositories, and that are sensitive to mailing.

Figure 3.1   An appropriate segmentation

not differ significantly in their sensitivity to advertising and side-effects.

This homogeneity/heterogeneity criterion implies that if one identifies several segments within one market, these segments have to be significantly different from each other in terms of the needs of their members or their reactions to the product. Homogeneity within a segment implies that the members of a segment have similar needs and/or similar reactions to the product offerings (product features, price sensitivity, promotion and sample sensitivity, galenic form sensitivity, etc.). Of course, based on this criterion the best segmentation scheme is the one that identifies each individual prescriber as a separate segment. The fundamental problem with this microscopic segmentation approach is that it is not a viable approach in economic terms.

The potential profitability or the minimum size of a segment must be a second criterion that is satisfied by any segmentation scheme. In the long run, at least, a segment should satisfy a minimum size criterion. This threshold can of course differ from company to company and from market to market and, in fact, from segment to segment.

One could segment the market into introvert and extrovert doctors. Even assuming that these segments are homogeneous within and heterogeneous across, and that being introvert or extrovert is relevant to the product offering, and that they represent potential profitable markets, a crucial problem remains of how to identify the members of these segments. Since the objective of a segmentation strategy is to develop and communicate a product offering to a target segment, it is a *conditio sine que non* that these segments also be identifiable and reachable.

Take the following example as a corollary to this third criterion. Assume one has identified a target segment of doctors that is composed of innovator doctors, and that the product offering will be communicated via journal advertising. If the innovator, adopter and laggard doctors read the same journals, it is clear that part of the journal advertising investment would be wasted. Ideally, one would like to develop target segments that are selectively reachable. If, for example, innovator doctors read only journal A and laggard doctors read only journal B, then communicating with the younger doctor segment via journal A is much more efficient.

Conceptually, these four criteria are necessary for an appropriate target-market selection. In practice it will be difficult, if not impossible, to satisfy each of these criteria. The art of a good segmentation system, however, consists of minimizing the violations of each of them.

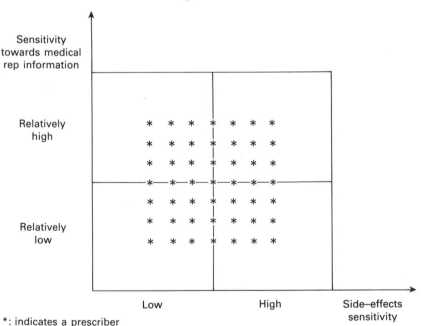

Figure 3.2   An inappropriate segmentation

3.3   THE ADVANTAGES OF SEGMENTATION

The fact that so many companies in the pharmaceutical industry have
come to accept and implement the notion of market segmentation bears
witness to the significant advantages to be gained from such an
approach.

By targeting specific customer groups the company will have better
information about the needs and the behaviour of these customers and
thus will be in a better position to offer products and marketing
strategies that are tailor-made to these customer needs.

Target-marketing is also a more efficient way of using scarce resources. For example, given the size of the physician population it is
impossible to reach all of these prescribers with the field force. Hence,
marketing efforts will inevitably have to be concentrated on those target
groups that are likely to yield higher profits or that play an important
role in the acceptance and growth of a product during the various
phases of its product life cycle.

Market segmentation can also allow a company with restricted
resources to compete with much larger organizations via a niching
strategy.

Target-marketing can also play a role in the competitive structure of
the market. In the case of an undifferentiated strategy everyone is in
competition with everyone else. By selecting specific target segments,
competitive pressure can be reduced or eventually avoided. A counter
argument, however, could be used by arguing that market segmentation
can also increase competition. Indeed, if everyone uses the same
segmentation scheme one is back to square one. For example, if all the
companies introduce their new products to innovator physicians (or
'neophils'), these neophil doctors will be bombarded with new products. If, in addition, as is the case in a lot of countries, several
companies use the same list of neophil doctors, provided by specialized
marketing research companies, the competitive nature of the market
will be even further reinforced.

Overall, market segmentation is a vital marketing tool which improves both the effectiveness and the efficiency of the marketing
programmes. It improves effectiveness ('doing the right things') by
enabling the company to develop products and marketing strategies
that have a better fit with the customer and by allowing for niching and
differentiated marketing approaches. It also reinforces efficiency
('doing things right') by reducing the competition in the market place

and by creating the opportunity for more focused and cost-efficient marketing-mix programmes.

3.4 THE POTENTIAL DRAWBACKS OF MARKET SEGMENTATION

It is important for managers to be aware of some potential problems with market segmentation. The fact that certain companies in the pharmaceutical industry have not yet adopted a market segmentation philosophy cannot be explained exclusively by an intrinsic aversion to new management tools on the part of management.

First, market segmentation as a 'rifle' approach, as opposed to an undifferentiated marketing 'shot-gun' approach, suffers from the idea that it 'puts all its eggs in one basket'. If one aims at a particular segment, that aim had better be right, because if the shot misses the target the result might be a complete failure. In the case of an undifferentiated approach this particular problem is reduced because the shot-gun approach is bound to hit some customers, if only by accident. Basically, managers may be averse to limiting their scope to a particular segment when an attractive overall market exists.

Secondly, market targeting may give rise to 'tunnel vision'. By focusing on innovative doctors for new product introductions, there is a danger of losing sight of certain developments with laggard-type doctors who may have experienced dramatic problems with existing products and could welcome a new drug. Since markets do not always develop smoothly, a 'strategic window' can open up outside the selected target market which might be overlooked. These strategic windows close quickly as soon as some competitors have spotted them and filled the gap. By zeroing in on particular target markets, there is a tendency to lose track of the overall evolution of the market. This can prove to be a costly mistake for the future. Tunnel vision is a very serious practical problem, because almost all pharmaceutical companies that adopt the segmentation approach, at some point in time, develop a specific segmentation scheme and select particular target segments and then keep working with the same segmentation scheme, in some cases, for a number of years. Carrying out a segmentation analysis is an extremely important investment and one is not usually ready to repeat the exercise a short while later. The market dynamics, however, may be such that the original target segment has, in fact, modified itself and the market developed in a totally different segmentation structure.

Thirdly, any market segmentation system is by definition arbitrary.

```
|------------------|--X----------------------------X|-X--------X|---
                   D                                C  B        A
      Laggards                    Adopters               Innovators
                   degree of innovativeness ----->
```

Figure 3.3   Segmentation and degree of innovativeness

Nobody can justifiably say that he or she has developed a perfect segmentation scheme. Segmentation implies allowing a certain level of heterogeneity within the segment, because perfect homogeneity does not exist. Within the segment of opinion leaders, some members have more opinion leader qualities than others. Where does one draw the line? Similarly, if a distinction is made between innovators, adopters and laggards, as illustrated in Figure 3.3, innovators A and B are clearly less similar in their degree of innovativeness than innovator B and adopter C.

By the same token, adopters C and D are less similar than innovator B and adopter C. Furthermore, this problem cannot be alleviated by using sophisticated market research tools. The best cluster analysis in the world applied to segmentation problems will still leave the manager to decide on the cut-off points between the clusters (segments). As illustrated in Figure 3.4, the two extremes of any segmentation system are on the one hand, the segment of one individual and on the other, the segment which includes all individuals. Neither extreme is very useful and the tough decision will be where to draw the limits of the segments. The closer the target market is to the one individual the more homogeneous but the less economically viable it will be. The closer the target market is to all individuals the less homogeneous the resulting segments will be.

Fourthly, any segmentation strategy is only *as good as its weakest link*. In general, several parties are involved in developing a segmentation system. The marketing manager and product line managers at head-quarters usually initiate the quest for a segmentation strategy. At the country level, this segmentation system is fine-tuned and adjusted to the

| |
| One | All
| individual | individuals

Figure 3.4   The extremes of segmentation

local situation by the marketing and product management assisted by the market research department from headquarters and/or the local country. This system is then communicated to sales management and executed by the sales force in the field and also by the product management for the other marketing mix elements (journal advertising, mailings, conferences, etc.). Frequently, the field force is not very enthusiastic about implementing such a system. The final result, even if the segmentation system and target-market selection are extremely well developed, can be very disappointing because of the lack of commitment of the field force. They often see the segmentation system as a nuisance interfering with the way they have been doing their job. Furthermore, they argue that they are in fact implementing a far superior segmentation strategy based on the individual physician. Indeed, they adjust their sales approach to each individual customer they call on. Perhaps the individual salesman knows the doctor's family situation, his extreme aversion to drugs with any side-effects or even his liking for football, and so on, and uses this information to tailor his message. Moreover, each salesman has his favourite doctors with whom he (or she) has a special empathy and some others whom he avoids because of personality problems.

If the sales people are already doing a perfect job at segmenting the market, why impose an additional segmentation layer? Several reasons can be put forward.

1. The objectives of the company might not coincide with the objectives of each of the members of the field force. The company may want to increase its market share in a certain segment to fit in with some long-term objectives. The company may want to prepare the territory for a new product introduction. The sales people, however, may want to improve the sales quota in a territory by working hard at some doctors whom they particularly like.
2. Each sales person has his (or her) own way of seeing the world and his (or her) own biases. When one aggregates all these biases over a field force, of, e.g., one thousand sales people the cost to the company can be phenomenal.
3. If the sales force's message varies between doctors, a serious problem can arise in terms of the effectiveness of journal advertising, mailings and conferences. The latter marketing-mix elements communicate a standardized message which has to be streamlined with the field force's personalized messages.

Overall, the key problem to the company is to motivate the field force to accept and execute a standardized segmentation approach and yet integrate in this standardized approach their knowledge of the idiosyncrasies of their individual customers. One way of achieving this objective is to get the field force involved in the early stages of the segmentation analysis. Do not dump the results of a finalized segmentation scheme on them. People always like the opportunity to make their own contribution. As a matter of fact, the field force, because of its customer contact, has probably very good segmentation information, so why not use it constructively?

Another way is to convince the field force of the fact that the segmentation approach to the market will help them to do a better job and will actually facilitate their task.

Fifth, some companies have been reticent in adopting a segmentation approach because it implies another way of managing the business and it requires new skills. One should not underestimate people's inertia when it comes to adopting a new idea. In the same way that a small proportion of physicians will adopt a new product early, a small percentage of pharmaceutical companies have initiated a segmentation philosophy early on. Some 'laggard' companies still have not really made the jump to a segmentation strategy and are still only paying lip-service to such systems. Such a transition also requires new skills in analyzing the market, in developing marketing strategies and in the organization of the sales department. Similarly, segmentation implies the availability of additional and costly data to provide insights into the market and feedback to check the appropriateness of segmentation approach and the performance within the chosen segments. Standardized syndicated data bases (e.g., IMS statistics) might not be the best basis for segmenting markets.

3.5 SEGMENTATION BASES

Three important types of customer intervene in the ethical pharmaceutical market: the user (patient), the prescriber (physician and hospital) and the influencers (nurses, hospitals, government). The segmentation bases presented in this section apply to all three types of customer.

There are five types of segmentation bases.

1. Demographics
2. Geographic

3. Socioeconomics
4. Behaviour and attitudes
5. Psychographics

These segmentation criteria differ in terms of the accessibility of the information and in terms of their usefulness in generating target-market segments. The first category is usually easy to implement because the necessary data are readily available. The buyer or prescriber behaviour data are somewhat more difficult to obtain but not as difficult as the psychographic type of data needed for the fifth type of segmentation base. As one moves from the demographic and geographic criteria towards behavioural, attitudinal and psychographic criteria the segmentation approach becomes more specific and subtle. By using the latter approaches, drug companies can turn segmentation into a differential advantage.

3.5.1 Demographic segmentation

Demographic segmentation implies that the market is divided into different groups of prescribers on the basis of age, sex, size of practice, specialization, race, nationality, etc. The size of practice and physician specialization can be especially useful segmentation variables. Large practices can be interesting targets because of the obvious economies of scale. Physician specialization is an obvious segmentation candidate for specialized drugs which are only prescribed by specialists. Often, however, it will be necessary to segment these demographic segments further with buyer behaviour or psychographic criteria.

3.5.2 Geographic segmentation

Geographic segmentation consists of subdividing the market into countries; urban, suburban and rural regions; north, south, east, west; cities; neighbourhoods, etc.

The urban–suburban–rural criteria can be useful in characterizing target markets since these three different territories can correlate with certain diseases and life styles which may influence the behaviour of prescribers.

3.5.3 Socioeconomic segmentation

Socioeconomic segmentation consists of clustering the market into mutually exclusive groups in terms of income, education, race, social class, etc. Race can be a relevant criterion in multi-racial societies where certain races have particular diseases which are more likely to be treated by physicians of the same race.

Education can also be important in the sense that prescription behaviour of young doctors may differ depending on the university at which they obtained their medical degree.

3.5.4 Buyer or prescriber behaviour and attitudes

Several behavioural or attitudinal criteria can be used to segment pharmaceutical markets.

One criterion which is often used is the key doctors approach. This consists of identifying doctors that are heavy prescribers in the product category. Similarly, one can also focus on light prescribers and try to convert them into heavy prescribers.

In a similar way, the market can be segmented into loyal versus non-loyal prescribers. By focusing on doctors that are loyal to the company's products an efficient, yet stagnant, segmentation system can be developed. The market can also be segmented in terms of other user-status criteria, for example ex-users, potential users, first-time users etc.

A third possibility might consist of segmenting the market in terms of the price sensitivity of the doctors. This can be especially appropriate in the context of off-patent and generic drugs. Along the same lines the market can be segmented in terms of the doctor's sensitivity to the company's other marketing-mix elements (mailings, samples, litera-ture, journal advertising, etc.).

A fourth approach might consist of segmenting the market in terms of the *benefits* sought by the doctor population. For example, the analgesic Tylenol was introduced into the market aimed at those consumers who were concerned about the sensitivity of the stomach to aspirin. Most benefits can be categorized in terms of fewer side-effects and/or more potency. Other benefits have been developed and have become very successful, for example, transdermal forms of administration using a patch, etc. The benefit segmentation approach is also the most appropri-ate segmentation basis for brand positioning strategies (Wilkie and Cohen, 1987). This approach, however, becomes difficult to implement for 'me-too' products.

A fifth axis for behavioural segmentation is based on *use occasions or situations*. For example, a product may be used as a second or third-line therapy with certain doctors. Targeting these doctors to try to bring the product into first position might be a viable segmentation approach.

A sixth axis consists of focusing on the *stages of readiness of a prescriber*. These stages might include awareness, liking and intentions. For example, one could segment the market in terms of those doctors who are aware of a particular drug and those who are not. The target segment could be those prescribers who are not aware of the product offering in order to try to make them aware. Alternatively, one might choose as a target segment those doctors that have a relatively positive attitude towards the product but do not prescribe it, in the hope of turning them into prescribers.

3.5.5 Psychographics

Psychographics are a way of describing (graphics) the psychological (psycho) make-up of a customer or segment of customers. Psychographic segmentation refers to an approach based on individual psychology. Three major types of psychographic segmentation schemes can be identified in the ethical pharmaceutical market.

Life-style segmentation is based on the overall manner in which people live and spend their money and time. Usually these segmentation analyses are based on a battery of life-style characteristics spanning the activities, interests, opinions and values of the target population. This approach is very popular in consumer goods marketing and is moving into the pharmaceutical industry.

A UK market research company (Taylor-Nelson) provides a doctor typology based on life-style criteria. They distinguish between six types of doctors:

1. Disillusioned:
   (12% of doctor population)

   Doctors that chose to become medical doctors for idealistic reasons but have become disillusioned by the profession. They look for new drugs as a means of contributing to the patients' health. They tend to be disappointed by existing drugs.

2. Overstretched:
   (12% of doctor population)

   Doctors that are more demotivated than disillusioned doctors; they feel overworked. They have little time for immersing themselves in scientific information about drugs. They tend to appreciate concise, sharp presentations of new drugs. They tend to be above average prescribers of established drugs.

3. Postgraduates (19%): They are keen on formal methods of education (symposia, medical journals, postgraduate courses). They want to develop themselves. They have a pronounced orientation towards generics. They include an above average percentage of female doctors. They are not spontaneously driven to new drugs.

4. Experimentalists (19%): Confident to try new drugs, they look at the pharmaceutical industry as a source of information.

5. Progressive (19%): Broad-minded doctors, keen to develop themselves as doctors. They tend to be positively disposed to clinical trials.

6. Self-satisfied (19%): More complacent type of doctors. Successful, they don't see a need to be involved in further formal education. Feel good about themselves and aren't keen to see medical reps.

The Taylor-Nelson service provides subscribing companies with a list of doctors (by name) for each of the six categories. Their life-style types tend to be general and not therapeutic category specific.

Segmentation based on *opinion leaders* is frequently used in the pharmaceutical industry. Especially for new products or for new indications of existing products it is quite natural to focus on the opinion leaders in the market, in this way hoping to convert the followers at a later stage. These opinion leaders are usually well known and include university professors, researchers and famous physicians. This identifiability makes the opinion leadership segmentation very attractive in the pharmaceutical industry.

A third approach to psychographic segmentation is based on the notion of the *diffusion of innovation*. As far back as 1958, in a study on the acceptance of new technologies among American farmers, E. Rogers, a behavioural scientist, tested the hypothesis that new technologies and new products are invariably accepted first by a small group of 'progressive', 'dynamic' farmers and eventually spread via this group to others (Rogers, 1962). Subsequently Rogers devised a typology of consumers in terms of how they behave towards an innovation (Fig. 3.5).

A few years later a group of scientists (Coleman, Katz and Menzel, 1966) published a study on the introduction of a new antibiotic. In this study they found confirmation for Rogers's theory in the pharmaceutical industry. Since then, the adopter sequence has been successfully applied by pharmaceutical companies all over the world. It has become such a useful technique that some research companies have developed nominal lists categorizing doctors within a country in one of the five categories hypothesized by Rogers, Coleman, Katz and Menzel.

The actual segmentation criteria used in pharmaceutical companies depend to a large extent on the data available in the company. Pharmaceutical companies can be classified into three categories in terms of their segmentation approach.

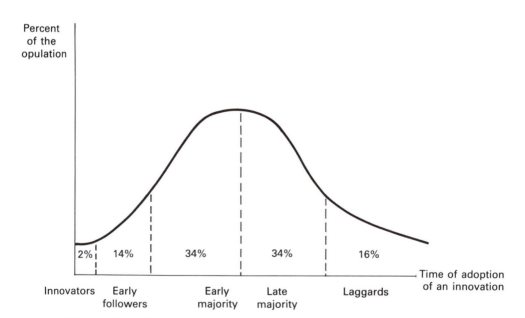

Figure 3.5   Adopter categorization

1. *Demographic, socioeconomic and geographical approach.* This approach is most frequently used by traditional companies that lack advanced information systems to go beyond the traditional segmentation approaches of geographical segmentation, prescriber specialization, size of practice and age of the prescriber.
2. *Segmentation based on syndicated segmentation studies.* A large number of pharmaceutical companies that lack the necessary segmentation data in-house can buy syndicated segmentation studies from market research companies. For example, IMS provides such a segmentation system, STAR, and in Germany a system called MEDI-LOG is available for pharmaceutical companies. These types of studies tend to focus on identifying high volume prescribers. Similarly, in different European countries syndicated studies are available that classify doctors in the innovator–adopter–laggard typology. The problem with using this type of study is that all companies that subscribe to them get the same information. It is therefore not surprising that 'high volume prescribers' are 'bombarded' with medical rep visits, samples, mailings, etc.
3. *Home made segmentation approach.* Several more advanced pharmaceutical companies have over time developed their own segmentation system via a purpose-designed information system. These systems are usually based on 'call sheets' from their medical reps and include information about individual doctors' prescribing behaviour, their price sensitivity, their attitude towards the efficacy and side-effect of drugs, their sensitivity to scientific information, their loyalty to the pharmaceutical company and their attitude towards new drugs. This wealth of information is subsequently analyzed and via more or less advanced statistical methods (e.g., factors and cluster analysis) used to segment the market.

Most of the actual segmentation efforts in the drug industry have focused on the individual prescribers to the relative neglect of the segmentation of the hospital and managed health care (HMOs, etc.) markets. The location, specialization and loyalty to the company are used frequently in these institutional markets.

Finally, not all segmentation criteria are equally appropriate to define a segmentation strategy. It is important to make a distinction between real segmentation variables and profiling variables. The real segmentation variables relate to the customers' (or prescribers') needs with respect to the product or to the sensitivity of the customers (or prescribers) to the company's marketing actions. Profiling variables are secondary variables in segmentation approaches. Their role is to describe the segments in such a way that members of these segments can be identified and reached via the company's marketing actions. The example in Table 3.1 illustrates this distinction between segmentation and profiling criteria. This real world example is drawn from the JIGSAW service provided by Isis Research Ltd, in the UK. The segmentation study is based on 250 general practitioners' (GP) prescribing behaviour over a fifty-two week period in the treatment of arthritis with NSAI drugs during 1986 in the UK (Western, 1987).

The price–sensitivity of the GPs is the real segmentation variable. The other variables (profiling variables) are equally important and serve as indicators to identify and reach the different segment. This segmentation approach seems to indicate that for this product category 'cheapskates' and 'spendthrifts' are below average prescribers. The 'cheapskates' tend to be younger, more inclined to prescribe generic and somewhat less accessible for the medical rep. The 'spendthrifts' are a bit older, less interested in generics and more oriented towards new drugs and also more favourable to medical reps.

3.6 TARGET-MARKET SELECTION

After having segmented the market, the choice of the actual target market will depend on three key issues.

1. *The economic attractiveness of the target segment.* The size, growth, price sensitivity and entry and exit costs are important indicators for the appeal of alternative target markets.
2. *The competitive activity in the proposed target-markets.* How tough is the competition? How strongly will the competitors react to a new entrant? Will it be feasible to carve out a market position without strong retaliation from the existing competitors?
3. *The strength of the differential advantage for the target customers.* In the drug industry one often starts out with a product with given strengths and weaknesses. The task of target-market selection will then consist of searching for groups of customers for whom these product strengths can form the basis for a competitive edge.

In general three possible market approaches follow from the target market selection process.

Table 3.1 Segmentation and profiling criteria

	Cheapskates	Economical	Dr Average	Unconcerned	Spendthrifts	All GPs
Cost per prescription £	5.27–9.21	9.22–10.28	10.29–10.86	10.87–12.03	12.04–15.25	
Annual scripts per GP	50	74	58	61	47	57
% of scripts written by generic name	28	11	6	7	4	11
Single-handed GPs	12	8	14	16	18	14
Attitude						
Encourage generic prescribing	66	59	57	56	45	57
Reluctant to try new drugs	52	43	35	40	28	40
Trying to reduce prescribing	80	69	69	74	63	71
Limit the list of drugs	42	33	33	30	28	33
I see all reps who wish to see me (%)	30	25	39	64	47	41
I do not see any reps (%)	10	4	2	2	0	4
Reps are 'useful'	68	69	82	80	88	77
Reps are 'waste of time'	14	10	4	2	4	7

Source: Western, 1987.

1. *A single niche strategy* implies the selection of a particular segment of the total market and focuses all the marketing efforts on that particular niche. This idea is usually associated with smaller market segments that might offer special quasi-monopolistic opportunities for the company that decided to focus its efforts on this segment.
2. *A differentiated or multiple niche strategy* identifies several segments in the market and develops unique strategies for each of these segments separately.
3. *An undifferentiated strategy* emphasizes common features across existing segments and focuses the marketing effort on the total market.

The choice between these three strategies depends on the company's resources, the differential advantage of the product offering and the heterogeneity of the customer population.

When the company's resources are limited and when the needs of the market differ greatly between different market segments, a single niche strategy is recommended. It allows companies to build strong differential advantages targeted at the selected niche. This is usually a clever way of dealing with the 'majority fallacy', which implies that everyone in the market is attracted to the larger segments in the market, which as a result become crowded, difficult to enter and less attractive.

When the company resources are less limiting and the heterogeneity of the customer population is still important *a differentiated strategy* is to be preferred. Different differential advantages (for example, dosage levels, galenical forms, communication media, etc.) are needed to satisfy the distinct market segments.

Undifferentiated strategies emphasize common features across existing segments and focus marketing efforts on large subsets of the total market. The current emphasis on globalization of markets and its focus on economies of scale and standardization of customers' needs and wants seem to advocate this direction. The trade-off between these economies of scale in production, marketing and Research and Development and the differentiation of consumer needs is the key parameter in deciding on niche (single or multiple) or undifferentiated target market decisions. For real breakthrough products undifferentiated strategies might be a viable option. 'Me-too' products on the other hand can only be successful in differentiated or niche strategies. The fundamental difference between niche, differentiated and undifferentiated strategies is usually more a question of degree rather than a black and white situation. In undifferentiated approaches one looks for common features whereas on the other hand in niche approaches one tends to push the search for differences in customers' needs to extremes. The choice between the three approaches is often a question of the extent of the benefits of the product in question.

The forecast increased harmonization of government regulation, escalating Research and Development costs, increasing marketing costs and falling margins, will all put pressure on pharmaceutical marketing specialists to move away from oversegmentation and look for larger segments and common features in customers' and prescribers' needs.

3.7   CONCLUSION

By now almost all pharmaceutical companies have taken market segmentation on board in some way as an important strategic tool. Some companies are better at doing it than others, but over time, the successful segmentation schemes used by one company will be copied by its competitors. Improving a company's segmentation approach, moving towards the behavioural and especially the attitudinal and psychographic segmentation approaches, will be a prerequisite to building competitive advantages in the pharmaceutical industry. In the foreseeable future, major strategic windows will be opened to improve segmentation tools using improved information technology. Indeed, the future sales rep, equipped with a lap-top personal computer, will be able to come out of a doctor's surgery, key in the relevant information and call up a special software programme to find out which doctor to visit next. This is not science fiction. Some pharmaceutical companies are becoming hot prospects for lap-top personal computer manufacturers! Wow

The single most important message here, however, is that the effectiveness of any segmentation scheme is limited by the level of integration, the acceptance and the execution of the segmentation guidelines by all the members of the marketing team, including the sales force.

REFERENCES

Coleman, J., Katz, E. and Menzel, H. (1966) *Medical Innovation: A Diffusion Study*, Bobbs–Merrill, Indianapolis.
Rogers, E. (1962) *Diffusion of Innovations*, Free Press, New York.

Western, R. (1987) Doctors and Prescribing: Cheapskates or spendthrifts? *Pricing and Forecasting in the Pharmaceutical Industry*, Esomar, Copenhagen, March pp. 211–30.

Wilkie, W. and Cohen, J. (1987) *An Overview of Market Segmentation*, Marketing Science Institute.

FURTHER READING

Bonona, T. and Shapiro, B. (1983) *Segmenting in the Industrial Market*, Lexington Books, Lexington, Mass.

Lidstone, J. (1987) *Marketing Planning for the Pharmaceutical Industry*, Gower, Aldershot.

Mitchell, A. (1983) *The Nine American Life-Styles*, Macmillan, New York.

O'Shaughnessy, J. (1984) *Competitive Marketing*, George Allen and Unwin, Boston, Chapter 5.

FOUR
Positioning

4.1 INTRODUCTION

Positioning is the process of establishing an object in the minds of the members of a target-market in such a way that it is perceived to answer the needs of that market. Invariably, positioning refers to the identification and the communication of a differential advantage.

The positioning of the product will determine the following.

1. The type of condition for which the product will be prescribed.
2. The type of patient for whom the product will be considered suitable.
3. The products with which it will compete most closely.

Together with the selection of target-market, the positioning decision is of crucial importance to the success of a new product launch or the revitalization of an existing product. The key aim in positioning is to offer a benefit to the target-customer that competing products cannot offer or are not offering.

The interaction of target-market selection and positioning strategy should be emphasized. Since positioning refers to the perceptions of the customers and their needs, different target groups need to be approached with different positioning strategies. In some cases, the target-market is identified first and an appropriate differential advantage is then sought for it. In other cases the reverse happens, i.e., the starting point is a differential advantage associated with the product, and a target-market is selected for which the differential advantage provides a motivating benefit. The trial and error nature of pharmaceutical Research and Development means that it is, in fact, more common to discover the differential advantage first, and chose the target audience subsequently. Sandimuun from Sandoz was originally developed in response to the market's need for alternative antibiotics, i.e., a target audience was chosen. In fact the product was shown to have significant immuno-supressant qualities, which led to the choice of a new target audience: organ-transplant patients.

4.2   DIFFERENTIAL ADVANTAGE

A differential advantage is one or more features of the product offering* which satisfies three fundamental criteria.

1. It differentiates the product from all others, creating a perception of uniqueness.
2. It is important, or can be made to seem important, to the target audience.
3. It is sustainable, over time, against the competition.

Each of the three criteria used above to define a differential advantage, is vital in establishing a viable positioning for the product.

Uniqueness, or rather perceived uniqueness, is a product's only protection against commodity status, i.e., of being bought solely on the criterion of price. Often, in the pharmaceutical industry, uniqueness is related to the intrinsic qualities of the product itself. Such uniqueness is made particularly powerful when covered by patent. It is also understandably tempting, after a lengthy Research and Development exercise, to overestimate the rationality of the prescribers and users, though it is debatable whether a drug that is 1% more potent or 2% less toxic can offer a discernable benefit. However, focusing on these intrinsic qualities can lead to undervaluing and therefore under-exploiting the product's name, colour, form, size or shape, its packaging, taste and/or consistency, etc. as potential features with which to generate a unique position. There are already examples of products, such as Migraleve, a migraine product in the UK, which are popular for reasons other than therapeutic effect. Migraleve has developed the appeal of its tablet colours and packaging to patients, as a viable differential advantage.

In other industries, examples of uniqueness not based on the product are abundant. For example, IBM's uniqueness is its size and (related) after-sales service. Heineken Beer's uniqueness is its advertising image,

---

*The term 'product offering' is used in the definition, rather than the term 'product', to include not only the physical product but also the marketing programme (price, advertising and communication message, distribution, packaging, etc.) which presents the product to the customers.

especially in the USA and the UK. Coca-Cola's uniqueness on a world-wide basis is its distribution system and American origins. These non-product uniqueness opportunities are not yet fully exploited in the prescription drug industry.

Of course, government regulation is a limiting factor on claims and positionings in the drug industry. The drug industry, far more than other industries, has to conform to strict guidelines laid down by government. This, however, still leaves sufficient room for a variety of effective positioning strategies.

The search for product uniqueness is often a primary task of the Research and Development department; uniqueness can also stem from the creativity of the marketing department. More and more of this burden is now being passed to the marketing department as it becomes increasingly difficult for the Research and Development group to create significant, unique product features.

Clearly a positioning which is perceived as unique is only of value if that unique quality is also perceived to be important. A car with five wheels may be perceived as unique, but is there a target market which values five wheels on a car? In some cases the key task for the marketing function is to increase the importance of the feature(s) for which the product offering is perceived as unique. Alternatively, the marketing task may consist of reducing the importance of those features for which competitive offerings are perceived to be unique.

The uniqueness and the importance criteria distinguish product features from product benefits. A listing of all the features of a product offering is not the product's positioning. A feature becomes a benefit only if it is perceived to be both unique and important. Such benefits create the value for the customer or prescriber, and it is the creation of this value that is the final objective of positioning.

The distinction between product features and benefits is not always well understood or applied in the pharmaceutical industry. The mis-understanding manifests itself in two common types of error. Firstly, the use of claims, well supported by clinical trials, which are not in fact perceived as important by prescribers. This is often because the amount of effort invested in developing product features or collecting evidence of the product's effects make it difficult to reassess the value of the features with respect to the target audience. Secondly, a series of claims, for which evidence is provided in the clinical trial process, are used to position the product, the implicit assumption being that the more claims a product can make the better. This is not necessarily true as prescribers, despite being educated and intelligent people, suffer, as do all of us, from limitations in the capacity to process information. A clear positioning, i.e., association of a distinct differential advantage with the product, is often more easily achieved with a limited number, for example two or three, well considered product benefits, and not an exhaustive list of product features.

Sustainability. There is little point in investing in a differential advantage that cannot be protected from copying by the competition. If the unique and important feature of the product offering is easily imitated by competitors, the differential advantage will simply evaporate. The art of developing a 'differential advantage' involves identifying features that can be protected and defended. Patent laws exist in most countries which provide the pharmaceutical industry with effective protection for some differential advantages. Unfortunately, this patent protection is temporary and is not available for all differential advantages (e.g., price, packaging, etc.). In other cases patents may be difficult to define and enforce. This, for example, is one of the key problems with the new products coming from biotechnology techniques. There is currently considerable dispute as to whether companies can enforce patents on products which are the result of genetic manipulation of natural molecules. This problem was recently highlighted in London by the court case between Genentech and Wellcome, in which Genentech's patent on the genetically engineered tissue plasminogen activator (TPA) for heart disease was ruled as invalid. Wellcome were thus not required to pay Genetech any royalties if they wanted to make TPA by similar methods.

Positioning dynamics are such that if a product has a strong differential advantage which is not protected by patent, competitors will try to copy the differential advantage or make it less important. Hence the task of marketing management is often to defend, reinforce or renew the existing differential advantages of established products and to try and preempt counter-attacks by the competition.

Whether a differential advantage will endure depends firstly on the resources, commitments, and strategies of competitors, and secondly on the ease with which they can copy and nullify that advantage. As pointed out before, the safest situations are patent-protected drugs. At the other extreme, price advantages are short-lived in mature product categories in which prescription patterns are stable and the product specifications are standardized.

The basis for defensible differential advantages result from the company's unique skills and resources, distinctive capabilities that set the company apart from its competitors. These skills may include special Research and Development capabilities, specialized knowledge of doctors' needs, or privileged relationships with the trade or prescribers, any of which can form the basis of a sustainable differential advantage. Superior resources include financial structure, production capacity, ownership of raw material sources or long-term supply contracts and corporate image. The art of formulating sustainable differential advantages lies in taking advantage of the opportunities provided by the unique skills and resources of the company.

The following story illustrates a sustainable differential advantage (Cool and Dierkx, 1989). An American visitor asked a British lord what he should do to make his lawn as beautiful as the lord's. The lord explained that the quality of the soil, the seed and fertilizers were crucial. The American felt he could copy these adequately and probed further. The lord went on to emphasize the importance of regular watering, mowing and rolling. The American confidently anticipated being able to imitate this type of care and persisted further. The lord replied that that was the whole secret – that and applying it diligently over five hundred years!

The qualities which make for a sustainable differential advantage, whether they are intrinsic to the product (Research and Development)

		No	Yes
Perceived	Yes	Relevance Problem Marketing task to increase importance	Excellent Defend to sustain the differential advantage
as unique?	No	Potential Disaster Perfect me–too Price available as a potential DA (but sustainable?)	Uniqueness or perceptual problem Marketing task to increase or create perception of uniqueness
		No	Yes

Important?

Figure 4.1   The differential advantage

or to the company that markets it (reputation, sales force) by definition take a long time to develop. Were this not so, another company could soon catch up, and the differential advantage would not be sustainable.

Figure 4.1 summarizes the previous discussion on the development of differential advantages.

4.3   TYPES OF POSITIONINGS

Traditionally, positioning strategies in the pharmaceutical industry have tended to concentrate almost exclusively on technical aspects of the product. Nowadays, it is fair to say that a large number of new pharmaceutical products do not have a real differential advantage based on the product itself and it is becoming vitally important to broaden the concept of the product in order to create greater scope for alternative differential advantages. A breakthrough new product (e.g., a cure for lung cancer) will usually have a strong and clear-cut differential advantage; the thirty-fifth anti-rheumatic drug which from a technical point of view is not a breakthrough, poses a much greater challenge to the marketing specialist. Six main approaches used to position pharmaceutical products can currently be identified (based on Aaker, 1988).

4.3.1   Positioning based on a specific attribute(s)

This is by far the most frequently encountered approach in the pharmaceutical industry. Potency, side-effects and tolerance are the most obvious attributes on which to focus. The majority of pharmaceutical products are positioned in this way: one example would be Ultradol from American Home, an arthritis therapy positioned on two attributes: lower gastrointestinal side effects and convenient dosing regime.

4.3.2   Positioning with respect to use or application

'Once-a-day' is a favourite positioning approach: Felden was positioned as the first once-a-day non-steroidal anti-inflammatory drug for arthritis. Tenormin entered the US market as the fourth beta-blocker, the second to offer cardioselectivity (after Zopress OR) and the second once-a-day agent (after Corgard). However its differential advantage was combining the two: cardioselectivity and once-a-day convenience. Drugs may also be positioned as first line, second line or third line therapies. A broad range of galenical forms can also be classed in this type of positioning strategy. Voltaren was first introduced in 25 mg and 50 mg tablets, as an acute anti-inflammatory. An injectable form followed for very acute inflammation, then a suppository for night-time relief and once-a-day tablets for chronic anti-inflammatory treatment. Finally a topical form was developed for localized pains.

4.3.3 Positioning with respect to the end user (type of patient)

Drugs can be positioned as most appropriate for minor or major degrees of a disease, acute or chronic sufferers, adults or children, old or young, by ethnic group or attitude to treatment. Although it is often tempting to aim for all possible cases, a more disciplined focusing often helps to establish a particular drug in the mind of a prescriber, even if it is eventually used in a wider range of cases. On the other hand a broad spectrum of applications is another viable positioning gambit and is another form of this type of positioning. When Glaxo launched Zantac, the second H_2 antagonist, rather than attack Smith Kline's Tagamat head on, they defined a broader target. To carry out this strategy a larger sales force was required, which was provided through an agreement with Roche for the US market. In effect, Glaxo managed to flank rather than attack Tagamat, and succeeded in significantly increasing the market. Similarly, the ACE-inhibitor Capoten (Squibb) had developed only the market segment of severe hypertensive cases, when MSD was planning the launch of their ACE-inhibitor, Vasotec. Merck introduced a lower dosage and expanded the market to less severe cases, also taking advantage of the greater reach of their sales force.

4.3.4 Positioning with respect to a competitor

The differential advantage can sometimes best be established by explicitly or implicitly taking the competition as a reference point. This is a useful way to piggy-back on the good image of a competitive product and add a plus. Ciba-Geigy (France) launched Rengasil into the same market as their product Voltaren. Originally Rengasil was positioned as being the more potent, but after a while it was repositioned with an emphasis on its analgesic properties, which distinguished it more clearly from Voltaren the anti-inflammatory.

4.3.5 Positioning with respect to a product class

Inderal, Tagamet and Capoten were positioned as the first drugs in a new product class, beta-blockers, H_2 antagonists and ACE-inhibitors respectively. This was also the fortunate position for Upjohn's Minoxidil (Regain), the first and only FDA-approved treatment for baldness, or retardation of hair loss.

4.3.6   Positioning with respect to marketing-mix variables

Price is of course the key positioning device for generics, though some branded products also use this frame of reference. As mentioned before, other parts of the mix of elements created by marketing, such as packaging, can be used to give a product a distinct place in the mind of its target audience. Size and quality of field force can give an important and sustainable edge to a product. Merck, Sharp and Dome demonstrated this with Vasotec (see above), while Glaxo achieved the same ends by effective co-marketing with Roche in the US for Zantac. Marion (US) capitalize on a talented sales force, by licensing-in good products from other companies. In the hospital and managed health care markets pharmaceutical products (and their companies) pursue positioning strategies based on custom labelling, instant delivery, frequent-buyer clubs and custom packaging.

4.4   CORPORATE POSITIONING

Although the main emphasis in the pharmaceutical industry is on product positioning, corporate positioning also plays an important role (Kotler, 1986). Creating and reinforcing a favourable overall position for a pharmaceutical company is important for five different target groups:

4.4.1   Prescribers and users

To the extent that the prescription and usage of medicines involves some risk on the part of both the prescriber and the user, a favourable company image can develop credibility and trust and serve as an important risk-reduction mechanism. Developing a company's relationship with doctors, in contrast to a reputation for hard-selling and promotion, is recognized by many companies as a worthwhile longer-term investment. In Italy, where the perceived trend has been towards the unethical 'buying' of doctors, Glaxo has launched a programme involving 30 000 key physicians, designed to strengthen Glaxo's ties in Italy with doctors on a 'correct and ethical, scientific basis' (*Marketletter*, 1987).

4.4.2 Stockmarket

The global company image is an important factor by which players in the stockmarket assess the value of a company's stock. This is important to the company's shareholders, and can be crucial in the case of potential mergers, capital expansion and takeovers.

4.4.3 Government and regulatory agencies

Obtaining a favourable overall image in the mind of the relevant government bodies is of crucial importance to pharmaceutical companies in getting speedy regulatory approval (or at least avoiding some negative 'halo').

4.4.4 Special interest groups

Unions and consumer organizations are two examples of special interest groups that should be addressed by corporate positioning to avoid or preempt actions on their part that might hinder the company's operations.

4.4.5 Employees

Corporate positioning is an important vehicle for improving the loyalty of current employees and attracting the best new employees from a competitive labour market.

The substance of corporate positioning depends on the target market and includes information on the company's experience, safety record, its image as an innovator, its specialization and leadership position in specific therapeutic areas and its commitment to basic research and development. Corporate position-building is often most visible in paid-for journal advertising, but to be effective it is important to promote a coherent image through all press coverage and behaviour, for example, in reactions to adverse publicity, such as accidents which result in pollution.

4.5   MEASURING PRODUCT POSITIONING

The starting point for developing a positioning strategy is the measurement of the current positionings of the products in the market to be entered by a new product or where an existing product is to be repositioned. The process of measuring product position involves three steps.

1. Identifying the competitive product offerings.
2. Determining how these competitive product offerings are perceived (perceived uniqueness).
3. Determining how the target market evaluates these product offerings (importance).

Each of these steps is discussed in turn:

4.5.1   Identifying the competitive product offerings

Listing the product offerings that compete with each other is often more difficult than it appears (Day, Shocker and Srivastava, 1979). For example, aspirin is prescribed for headaches, migraine, premenstrual pain, as a preventative after heart attacks and for several other common conditions. Does one include aspirin (and other aspirin-like drugs) in the definition of the markets for each of these conditions?

In most cases, there will be a primary group of competitors and one or more secondary groups. Thus, Felden competes primarily with other specific anti-rheumatic drugs (e.g. Opren, Fobren, Haprogyn, Brufen, Voltaren, etc.), with aspirin-type drugs possibly being important as secondary competitors.

A first approach to this definition of market boundary is to rely on the IMS statistics, which list the appropriate drugs for each condition. Managers do not always find this a satisfactory solution since certain drugs are prescribed for several conditions and the IMS data may not list these drugs for all conditions for which they are prescribed. IMS data are also not very useful when a brand is being positioned for a new therapeutic condition. Of course, deviating from the IMS market definitions can create practical difficulties when monitoring brand share and prescription behaviour.

A second approach is the development of product/condition associations (Aaker, 1988). A sample of prescribers might be asked to recall the condition for which a certain brand was last prescribed. This can be repeated for the major brands in the IMS category. For each condition prescribers are then asked to identify all the brands they consider appropriate.

These two approaches suggest a conceptual basis for identifying the competitive environment of products.

4.5.2   Capturing product offering perceptions

The objective characteristics of the competing brands can be determined from objective product information. The perception of these brands by the target market is much more difficult to measure.

Doctors are bombarded with stimuli in the form of competing products, advertising, visits by reps, etc. and given their own background and experiences they all perceive the various product offerings in their own way. Limited exposure, selective and distorted perceptions, limited memory and limited information-processing capacity mean that important gaps develop between the objective facts and the subjective perceptions of the product offerings (Bettman, 1979). Furthermore, 'halo' effects can severely bias product perceptions. For example, the perception of a Pfizer drug is strongly influenced by the overall image of Pfizer in addition to the technical profile of the product itself.

The perceptual nature of positioning complicates the positioning exercise, because subjective, cognitive constructs are more difficult to measure and compare than are the objective physical characteristics of a product. This is for two main reasons. Firstly, objective features can be measured unambiguously, while perceptions are, by definition, subjective, complex and therefore more difficult to measure. Secondly, the objective facts are invariant, while perceptions differ from one prescriber or user to the next, because of personal idiosyncrasies and experience, and change over time as the result of many influences, including the actions of the competition (e.g., the launch of a competing product).

A number of methods have been developed to help capture the perceptions of products. Broadly defined they fall in one of two categories: compositional and decomposition methods (Green *et al.*, 1988).

Compositional methods are based on the belief that prescribers can decompose their perceptions of brands into separate attributes and can evaluate each of the brands on this set of attributes. This leads to

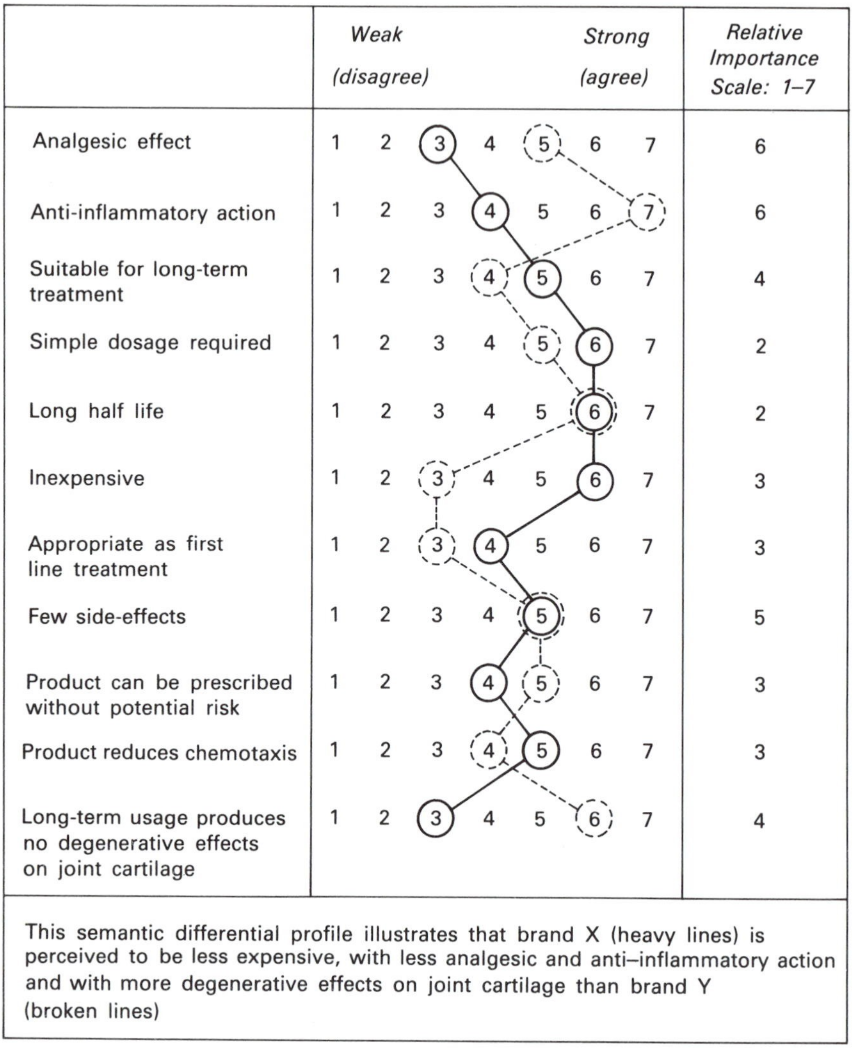

	Weak (disagree)	Strong (agree)	Relative Importance Scale: 1–7
Analgesic effect	1 2 ③ 4 (5) 6 7		6
Anti-inflammatory action	1 2 3 ④ 5 6 (7)		6
Suitable for long-term treatment	1 2 3 (4) ⑤ 6 7		4
Simple dosage required	1 2 3 4 (5) ⑥ 7		2
Long half life	1 2 3 4 5 (⑥) 7		2
Inexpensive	1 2 (3) 4 5 ⑥ 7		3
Appropriate as first line treatment	1 2 (3) ④ 5 6 7		3
Few side-effects	1 2 3 4 (⑤) 6 7		5
Product can be prescribed without potential risk	1 2 3 ④ (5) 6 7		3
Product reduces chemotaxis	1 2 3 (4) ⑤ 6 7		3
Long-term usage produces no degenerative effects on joint cartilage	1 2 ③ 4 5 (6) 7		4

This semantic differential profile illustrates that brand X (heavy lines) is perceived to be less expensive, with less analgesic and anti–inflammatory action and with more degenerative effects on joint cartilage than brand Y (broken lines)

Figure 4.2   Semantic differential profile of Brands X and Y

methods such as semantic scales (Wilkie and Pessemier, 1973). Figure 4.2 provides an example of this approach in the case of anti-arthritic products, where the perceived profiles of two brands are compared.

In addition, one can ask the target-market of prescribers to assess the relative importance of these attributes, as illustrated in the right hand column of Figure 4.2. It follows from the example that brand Y has some differential advantages: analgesic and anti-inflammatory action, and fewer side-effects.

Although this method is used frequently in the pharmaceutical industry, it has significant weaknesses. Firstly, the risk of omitting important attributes from the analysis. In the anti-arthritic example, 'gastric tolerance' and 'overcoming early morning stiffness', might be important attributes that were not included in the analysis. Although one can never exclude this problem, methods exist to reduce this type of error. One approach for creating an exhaustive list of attributes is to ask prescribers to identify the two most similar brands from a set of three competing brands and to describe why those two brands are similar and different from the third. This is repeated with all combinations of brands so that it becomes likely that all significant differentiating attributes are revealed. An alternative approach consists of asking prescribers which of two brands is preferred and why. As this is done repeatedly for all combinations of brands, it becomes unlikely that important criteria are missing (Green *et al.*, 1988).

The second problem is in a sense a result of the first: the methods cited for generating an exhaustive list of attributes usually produce lists of such length as to be impractical, and which include many overlapping attributes that really refer to the same underlying concept. Logic and judgement or statistical methods (e.g. factor analysis) can subsequently be used to reduce these redundancies (Hauser and Koppelman, 1979). In general, doctors use few characteristics (between two and five) to discriminate between competing brands. It is often difficult to identify these crucial dimensions directly from the doctor.

Thirdly, the semantic differential method assumes that the doctor can decompose the brands into a set of attributes and that when evaluating a brand he (or she) integrates all that information. Psychological research, however, tends to show that such a model is often unrealistic and thus that the semantic differential approach might not be an appropriate method for capturing doctors' perceptions of competing brands (Shephard, 1962).

Decomposition methods are generally better adapted to deal with the perceptual measurement problem. These methods are based on the idea that people have global perceptions of objects, which they are not necessarily able to decompose.

The first step in such an analysis is to identify the positions of the products relative to each other and then, in a second step, the underlying dimensions which span the global perceptions are subjectively

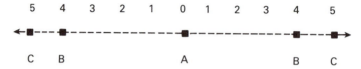

Figure 4.3   One-dimensional perceptual map

inferred. Perceptual maps, as a typical decomposition method, use as their input the doctors' global comparisons between competing brands. Subsequently, they try to represent these global perceptions graphically, via a perceptual map (Green *et al.*, 1988).

An example will illustrate this concept. Suppose one wants to understand the relative positionings of three brands – A, B and C. The starting point of the analysis is to ask the prescribers how they perceive the similarities between these three brands. The question is posed in terms of overall similarities and not in terms of similarities on specific attributes. Three comparisons have to be made: AB, AC and BC. Suppose a scale of 1 to 9 scale is used, where 1 implies very similar and 9 implies very dissimilar perceptions and suppose the following similarity judgements were given:

$$AB : 4 \qquad AC : 5 \qquad BC : 4$$

The simplest graphical representation of these similarities would be in a one-dimensional space, i.e., on a line. If A is arbitrarily located in the middle of the line, B should be at a distance of 4 (either to the right or the left of A). Now C has to be located at a distance of 5 from A and also 4 units from B. It is clear (consider Figure 4.3) that these two constraints cannot be satisfied if C is placed on the line. This implies that the given similarities cannot be represented in one dimension. Therefore, at least two attributes (dimensions) must be important to the prescribers to differentiate between A, B and C. If BC were 1, then one dimension (attitude) would have been sufficient (Figure 4.3).

A solution is, however, possible in two-dimensional space (see Figure 4.4a). B must lie on a circle around A with a radius of 4. Similarly, C must lie on a circle of radius 5, around A. These two circles are shown in Figure 4.4a.

If a point B is chosen on B's circle, C must lie on a circle of radius 4 centred at this point. Satisfactory locations for C can be located by choosing the two points of intersection of appropriate circles (cf. Figure 4.4b). Of course, these points are not unique. One could rotate the

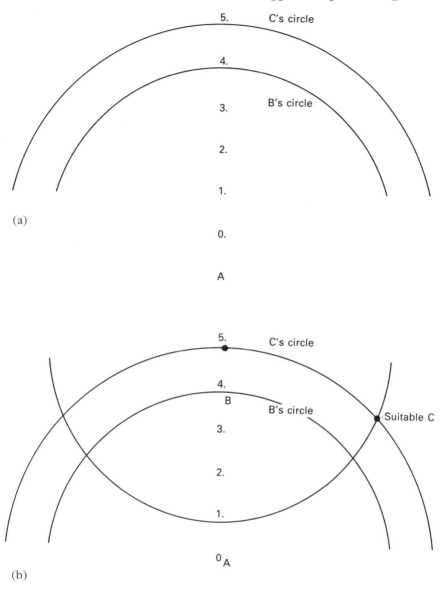

Figure 4.4a and b   Constructing a two-dimensional perceptual map

positions of B and C in an infinite number of ways (e.g., by turning the sheet of paper).

If more than three brands have to be positioned, the task becomes progressively more complicated and special computer programmes

Figure 4.5   Using nonmetric multidimensional scaling to reproduce a map of the UK

are necessary to deal with the complexity (e.g., MARKPACK, 1990). The principle, however, is exactly the same as with three brands. Figure 4.5 shows a map of the UK derived by such techniques, from the straight line distances between UK cities. The derived map, of course, doesn't determine the contours of the United Kingdom, but based on simple distance measures, a very accurate two-dimensional map of the location of UK cities is obtained (Doyle, 1973). In a similar way, one derives the perceptual map of competing brands that is in the head of prescribers based on the perceived distances (similarities) between competing brands.

A variety of mapping techniques have been developed ('multi-dimensional scaling' techniques) to deal with the complications which arrive with higher dimensionality, and the interested reader will find a detailed discussion of the methods in marketing research literature (Green *et al.* 1988).

Figure 4.6 is an illustration of a perceptual map of a pharmaceutical market segment.

Such a competitive map is extremely useful for understanding market dynamics. These maps can also help in deriving the underlying dimensions (attributes) that differentiate the prescribers' product perceptions. This identification is subjective and is done as follows. On the horizontal dimension the order of the brands as one goes from left to right is C, A, B, E, G, D and F. In the vertical dimension, from top to bottom, the order is A, E, B, C, D, F and G. What are the attributes that might classify the brands in those orderings? Maybe the horizontal dimension can be called 'potency' and the vertical, 'side-effects'.

This interpretation is necessarily subjective, which introduces some bias. This is inherent in the method because the starting idea was that

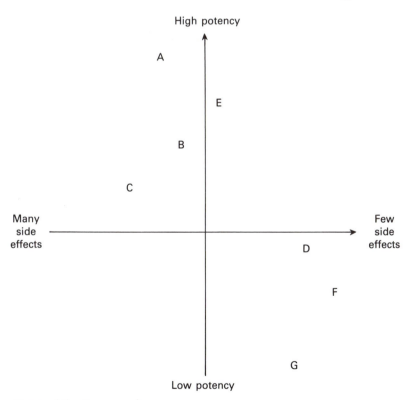

Figure 4.6 Perceptual map

doctors have global views of the product offerings and these global views have to be reconstructed and decomposed to derive the implicit salient attributes. Once the important discriminating attributes are identified, perceptual maps can be a useful vehicle for the positioning and repositioning of product offerings.

If one wants to develop a product that can compete with the successful product E, one can see from the perceptual map in Figure 4.6 that the new product has to be positioned as a high potency, with average-to-low side-effects drug product. Physicians' perceptions of varying positioning statements concerning a proposed new product can be plotted on such a map, to guide the future communication strategy.

Furthermore, perceptual maps can be used to identify gaps in the market that can be potentially useful for the positioning of a new product or for the repositioning of existing products. For example, Figure 4.6, suggests that a gap exists for a drug with just moderate potency but few side-effects. Maybe prescribers are not interested in this area of the perceptual map, but maybe they are interested in such drugs and an opportunity exists. In this manner, perceptual maps can be useful for uncovering strategic windows in the market.

Finally, perceptual maps can be a useful instrument for monitoring the evolution of the positioning of competing brands over time. By deriving perceptual maps at different points in time, one can trace how the prescribers' perceptions change over time. One can also check the success of repositioning exercises for existing brands by analyzing perceptual maps before and after the repositioning.

4.5.3   Target-market evaluation of product positions

The next step in a positioning study consists of finding out how the target-market evaluates the positions of the different product offerings. The crucial question here is: how important are the perceptual dimensions and what is the ideal product for the target-market? The way to discover the answers to these questions depends on how one has measured the prescribers' perceptions.

Using the semantic differential approach the relative importance of the salient characteristics can be obtained by direct questioning, as was illustrated in the right-hand column of Figure 4.2. The ideal product is, however, difficult to determine by direct questioning. Asked what this ideal product would be, a prescriber will probably answer with a set of

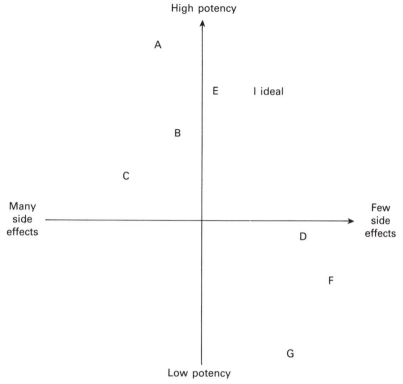

Figure 4.7   Perceptual map with ideal point

extreme statements: maximum effect, total safety, convenient dosage form and low cost. Such information is not very useful.

Perceptual maps can provide some insight into the question of the ideal product. The concept of an 'ideal product' can be introduced into the data collection for perceptual maps in the same way as any other existing brand. Based on the similarity rating of each existing brand with the prescribers' ideal product, the ideal product can be located on the perceptual map in the same way as an existing brand. This is illustrated in Figure 4.7.

The ideal brand derived via perceptual maps refers to a 'realistic ideal'. The prescriber is not asked to describe his ideal product, but to compare all existing brands to his ideal brand. Some of the existing brands will be located closer to the ideal than others. This is a realistic approach, which has considerable intuitive appeal.

Perceptual maps can also be used to derive the relative importance of the salient perceptual attributes, i.e. in the case used for illustration, potency and side-effects. Special techniques (e.g. PREFMAP, Green *et al.* 1988) exist to superimpose isopreference curves on top of perceptual maps. These isopreference curves encircle the ideal point (or points) and indicate that all brands located on the curve have the same level of appeal to the prescriber. Figures 4.8a, b and c illustrate this concept.

In Figure 4.8a, the isopreference curves are concentric around the ideal product. This implies that both dimensions are equally important to the prescriber. The most preferred brands are those that are on the closest isopreference curve to the ideal. More specifically, brands B and D are equally preferred and they are both preferred to A, which is, in turn, preferred to C.

Brand B is less attractive to prescribers than A because it deviates more than A from the ideal on the most important attribute, dimension 1. In Figure 4.8c, the isopreference curves are vertically elliptical around the ideal brand. This signifies that dimension 2 is more important than dimension 1, and as a result brand B is now preferred to brand A.

A word of caution about perceptual maps and isopreference curves. In Figure 4.9 one would be led to predict that brand A has a higher market share for this segment than brand B. One might actually observe the reverse in the real world, although brand A is preferred to brand B. This seeming contradiction could be due to the fact that brand A is new and not all doctors are aware of it, or because the doctor is a prescriber of brand B and doesn't want to change to the new brand A immediately.

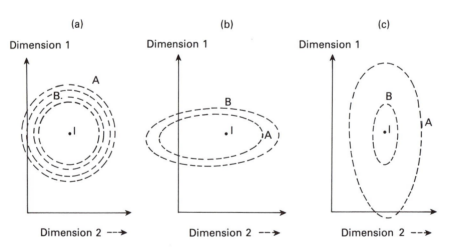

Figure 4.8   Perceptual maps with isopreference curves

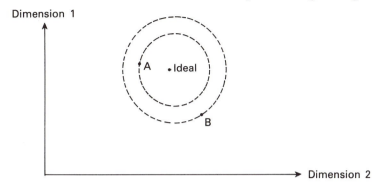

Figure 4.9   Perceptual map for two brands

It might also be that brand A has had some distribution and availability problems, etc.

Finally, the user of this technique should be careful about the problem of aggregating the perceptions collected from a number of doctors. Not all doctors in the target segment have the same perceptions of the competing brands or of the ideal product and averaging out this heterogeneity, as is sometimes done, destroys much of the information available from such a map. This lumping together of heterogeneous views should generally be avoided by using techniques (such as that provided by, e.g., MARKPACK) to integrate this perceptual heterogeneity in the perceptual maps. Different ideal products are thus generated for different segments of the target audience and these can provide very useful information for segmenting the market further.

Ideal products for a given target market can also differ, depending on the conditions the prescriber has to treat. For example, in a specific national market the perceptual map for anti-rheumatic drugs used three ideal products, one for 'soft tissue injuries', one for 'moderate rheumatic arthritis' and one for 'moderate osteoarthritis' as illustrated in Figure. 4.10.

4.6 ALTERNATIVE POSITIONING STRATEGIES

The most common and widely used type of positioning strategy is that implied by the description above, i.e., the target audience's perceptual map is identified, the positions of the competing brands are plotted and

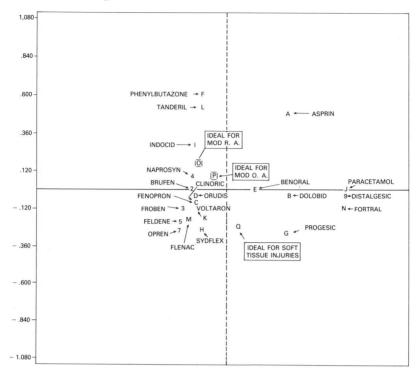

Figure 4.10   The perceptual map for anti-rheumatic drugs

the positioning strategy which results is a matter of deciding where one's own brand should be and repositioning it, or launching it, into that position. Although this is the most direct and usual procedure there are at least five alternative types of positioning strategy which are based on the same concepts but lead to somewhat different marketing approaches.

4.6.1   Changing the frame of reference

Even if no gaps exist in the market as it is currently defined and perceived, it may be possible to alter the map and thus create new opportunities. This may be done by introducing a new attribute and making it salient for the target market (or at least a segment of the target market). Buspar, from Bristol-Myers, may have succeeded in doing this in the anti-anxiety drug market. Buspar does not interact with alcohol, and is not a controlled substance, so it aims to create a new segment by converting some anxiety patients from reliance on acute therapy to chronic therapy. Tenormin, from ICI France, introduced the advantage of hydro-solubility in Beta-blockers, and succeeded in making this attribute important in that market.

Alternatively, it is sometimes possible to change the relative importance of existing attributes for the existing segments. Clinoril (MSD), a non-steroidal anti-inflammatory, successor to Indocid, was not a big success until it was repositioned on renal toleration. MSD succeeded in sensitizing prescribers to this aspect, and thus increased the appeal of their brand. If the brand already has an established positioning, increasing the perceived importance of its key strengths can be an opportunity for creating a sustainable differential advantage. These approaches, in fact, imply changing the ideal products in the view of all or some of the prescribers.

4.6.2 Multiple segment positioning

The first stage in new market development usually implies the existence of a single segment in the market. The product is new, and prescribers' preferences are not differentiated yet for lack of knowledge and experience with the new product and the new market. The new product is then positioned as close as possible to the overall ideal point of the market. As the market develops, prescribers' preferences start to fragment and, based on the increasing knowledge and experience of the products and the market, multiple segments start to develop. The question for marketing strategists then is whether it is possible to position the product in such a way that it can simultaneously retain its appeal to the multiple segments, against competition targeted at a single segment.

Trying to hold on to several segments with one product against more specialized competition involves the risk of losing out in all segments, while concentrating effort means, in effect, throwing away a certain proportion of sales. In such a situation it is possible to embrace a multiple segment strategy by, for example, using different forms of the product to cater to the different segments simultaneously (see the example of Voltaren cited above).

4.6.3 Moving the competition

Another alternative to trying to change the perception of the brand in the direction of the ideal product is to try to redirect the competitive brands away from the ideal position. Of course, openly denigrating the competition will generally be ill-advised in view of the risk of vigorous reaction, but within limits the opposition may have weaknesses which can be brought to the target's notice and used to ease the competition away from the ideal point. Similarly, competitive products can be contrasted to one's own product to establish the distinct cases in which the various products should be considered ideal.

4.6.4 'Me-too' positioning

If a very successful product exists in the market, an efficient positioning strategy may consist simply of copying the star product as closely as possible, and hoping to share some of the sales that would normally go to that brand. This is slightly contradictory to the classic positioning exercise which seeks to find an unoccupied niche and create a difference for its brand, and the strategy is likely to be limited in that the original brand can be expected to dominate. On the other hand, risks are lowered by the proven existence of a target market. Patent protection often limits or precludes such an initiative approach, but it is often feasible to position a new product (or existing product) as close as possible to the top product(s) in the market. If profitable sales can be made from this limited position, the strategy is perfectly valid.

4.6.5 Defensive positioning of a second ('fighter') brand

The classic positioning strategy, in response to a threat from a new or repositioning competitor, is to move towards that competitor, i.e., to try to meet or better the benefits offered by the competitor. However, this risks reducing the appeal of the original brand for some of its users, or in the case of price, forgoing considerable revenue. Brands without patent protection faced with generic competition always face this dilemma: should they reduce their price (i.e., reposition towards the competition on the dimension of price) and if so by how much?

An alternative is to launch or reposition a second brand (possibly another generic). When Ciba-Geigy's Voltaren patent ran out in France, Zyma (a company controlled by Ciba-Geigy) launched a branded generic ('Voldar') to protect Voltaren. Similarly, Smith Kline launched a branded generic to protect 'Tagamet'. The 'fighter' brand then competes with the new entry (or entries), while the original brand can maintain its successful position (or its profitable pricing position),

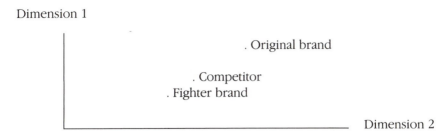

Figure 4.11   Positioning a fighter brand as a defence

perhaps with some sacrifice of volume. If the second brand can be positioned near to the competitor, but further away than the competitor from the main brand (Figure 4.11), it stops the competitor from moving up too closely to the original brand, while reducing as far as possible the additional competitive effect of the second brand on the first.

4.7   A CONCLUDING NOTE

A successful positioning strategy fulfils two key criteria. The product should be perceived by the customer as intended by the strategy, and it should result in a sustainable position. The effectiveness with which the intended position can be communicated to the target audience will determine the first criteron. The actual perceived position of a product in the minds of the target market is the result of the complex interaction of a large number of factors as illustrated in Figure 4.12. The manager responsible for positioning has to understand clearly that a positioning strategy can only be successful if its concept is sound and, equally important, if the concept can be implemented via all the elements of the marketing mix. All the tactical marketing weapons that the manager can use have to be channelled in a consistent way to obtain the desired positioning.

No positioning strategy can guarantee complete sustainability, but a good positioning strategy will be one that is sustainable for a longer period of time than other positioning strategies. Price is usually a weak differential advantage, unless it is based on substantial cost advantages. Marketing and positioning are all about making price less important to the customer, and some of the other benefits of the product more important.

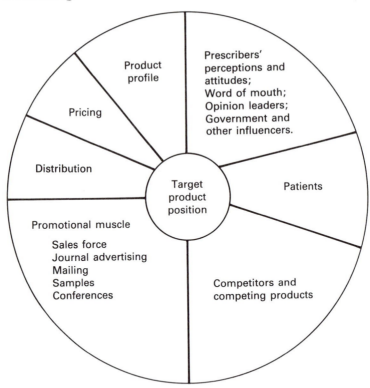

Figure 4.12 Product positioning factors

REFERENCES

Aaker, D. (1988) *Strategic Market Management*, John Wiley and Sons, New York.

Aaker, D. and Shansby (1982) Positioning your Product, *Business Horizons*, May–June, pp. 56–62.

Bettman, J. (1979) *An Information Processing Theory of Consumer Choice*, Addison-Wesley Publishing Co., Reading, Mass.

Cool, K. and Dierkx, I. (1989) Sustainable Differential Advantage, *Management Science*, December 1988.

Day, G., Shocker, A. and Srivastava, R. (1979) Consumer Oriented Approaches to Identifying Product Markets, *Journal of Marketing*, 43 (4), 8–19.

Doyle, P. (1973) Nonmetric Multidimensional Scaling: A User's Guide, *European Journal of Marketing*, Summer, pp. 82–86.

Green, P., Tull, D. and Albaum, G. (1988) *Research for Marketing Decisions*, Prentice Hall, Englewood Cliffs, NJ.

Hauser, J. and Koppelman, F. (1979) Alternative Perceptual Mapping Techniques, *Journal of Marketing Research*, November, pp. 495–506.

Kotler, P. (1986) *Marketing Management*, Prentice-Hall, Englewood Cliffs, NJ.

Marketletter, April 25 1988.

Shepard, R. (1962) The Analysis of Proximities: Multidimensional Scaling with Unknown distance function, *Psychometrika*, pp. 125–39.

Wilkie, W. and Pessemier, E. (1973) Issues in Marketing's Use of Multi-Attribute Models, *Journal of Marketing Research*, **10**, pp. 428–41.

FURTHER READING

Corstjens, M., Gautschi, D. and Naert, P. (1990) *Markpack: a decision support system*, Prism, Fontainebleau.

McKenna, R. (1985) *The Regis Touch*, Addison-Wesley Publishing Co., Reading, Mass.

Ries, A. and Trout, J. (1982) *Positioning: The Battles for your Mind*, Warner Books, New York.

Urban, G. and Hauser, J. (1981) Chapter 9, Perceptual Mapping, *Design and Marketing of New Products*, Prentice Hall, Englewood Cliffs, NJ.

FIVE

Competitive analysis

5.1 INTRODUCTION

In the seventies, marketing was essentially concerned with customers and products. Segmentation and positioning were the key concepts in the development of a marketing strategy. In the eighties, competitive analysis has been added as a key dimension of strategic thinking in marketing. More mature markets, slower economic growth, fewer quantum-jump new products, increasing transfer of technology, more sophisticated management, and the further internationalization of markets have all contributed to the increased importance of competitive analysis in marketing. Zero-sum market games should make managers more aware that the success of one product must be at the expense of a competing product. The small growth of most markets precludes 'everyone to be a winner'. In such a context, marketing strategies have to include the anticipation of the competitors' strategies. Competitive analysis leads managers to make better predictions of future competitive moves, to identify areas of competitive vulnerability and to predict competitive reactions to the company's future moves. The importance of competitive analysis is best illustrated by large Japanese companies that have a large staff whose only task is to analyze their competitors. In the current era one has first to analyze the competitor's strategies before one can decide on one's own strategic options.

This chapter focuses on competitive analysis in the pharmaceutical industry at the macro and at the micro level. First, at the macro level, the overall competitive structure of the industry and its evolution will be discussed. Second, at the micro level, a set of tools will be proposed which are appropriate to assist marketing managements in their assessment of competitors' current and future strategies.

5.2 COMPETITIVE STRUCTURE OF THE PHARMACEUTICAL INDUSTRY

To analyze the current structure of the competitive forces in the pharmaceutical industry, Porter's framework of industry structure will be used (Porter, 1980). According to this conceptualization the structure of an industry is determined by five basic forces which are illustrated in Figure 5.1. The collective strength of these forces determines the structure and profitability of an industry in the long run. It is therefore important to understand 'where the industry is going' by carefully analyzing the five forces and to identify future opportunities and threats to the industry. It is in this perspective of industry structure that the company's own strategy has to be developed.

Suppose one were to ask a marketing executive in the pharmaceutical industry to enumerate a list of their competitors. The executive would, most likely, come up with an elaborate list of other drug companies including Merck, Sharp and Dohme, Roche, Takeda, etc. This is, of

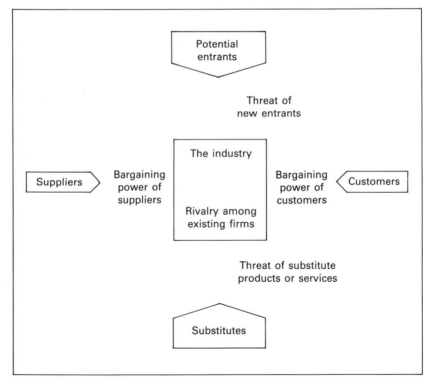

Figure 5.1 Industry structure forces (Porter, 1980)

course, correct. However, the true competition in the pharmaceutical industry is much broader. From a longer-term perspective one should also include potential newcomers, suppliers, buyers and substitute products or services.

Competition is fundamentally rooted in the underlying economic structure of the industry and its relation to suppliers and customers.

Suppose an industry is very profitable, i.e., its Return On Investment (ROI) is significantly above that of other industries. What would happen? Since this information is available to other industries, the latter would be attracted to the profitable industry. What factors would discourage companies from other, lower ROI, industries from moving into the high ROI industry? Such factors might include: the necessity of very high investments in equipment, marketing and Research and Development; the scarcity of raw materials or government protection of the high ROI industry for strategic reasons. All these factors are entry barriers. If there were no entry barriers, new competitors would enter, increase the competitive activity and drive the ROI down.

In some industries there might be high barriers to entry, but the ROI is still not very high. This might be due to the existence of substitute products or services. If prices are raised too much to increase the margin and the ROI, consumers would switch to substitute products. A second reason for the existence of low ROI industries might be that the raw materials are owned by a powerful supplier with very strong bargaining power. A third reason might be that the output of the industry is sold to only a few large buyers with very strong bargaining power.

All these factors, entry barriers, suppliers' power, buyers' power and substitute products, although not direct competitors in the industry, have a strong impact on the competitive posture and profitability of the industry, especially in the longer run. These four external competitive forces will now be discussed in the context of the drug industry, before looking at the problem of internal rivalry.

5.2.1 Suppliers

Of all five forces, suppliers play a rather marginal role in the pharmaceutical industry. The large pharmaceutical companies are usually vertically integrated and as such do not face strong threats from suppliers. For the majority of pharmaceutical products, raw materials supply is not a bottleneck. The exception is in biotechnology, where supply is often a problem because of the highly specialized nature of the inputs. Another area where the supply might be an important constraint is, for example, the scarcity of donor organs which severely limits the growth of immunity drugs.

If one includes labour as a supply source, significant bargaining power might exist for specialized Research and Development personnel in attractive research areas. For example, in order to recruit a British biochemist who is one of the world's leading authorities on Alzheimer's and other neurological diseases, Merck & Co built a brand-new 122 person neuroscience research centre in Harlow (UK) a short distance from the man's home. Merck's Chairman, Dr P. Roy Vagelos was quoted as saying 'We don't always get our man, but we have never missed hiring someone we wanted because of money' (Quickel, 1987).

Unions might also play a role as bargainers in the pharmaceutical industry, not only to protect the salaries and working conditions of staff, but also to enforce strong, and expensive, precautionary regulations to protect the work environment.

5.2.2 Potential entry

The pharmaceutical industry is a highly attractive industry for potential newcomers. At $80 billion, the total drug industry's sales revenues in 1985 were about the same as those of one giant oil company, Exxon. The oil company's profits, however, were exceeded by the combined profits of the top twenty drug companies in the USA alone. As a further indication of their profitability, twelve US pharmaceutical companies feature among the top fifty Fortune 500 companies by return on sales (net profit as percentage of sales). Finally, in any ranking of industries by profitability in terms of return on investment (or equity) or profit margin on sales, the pharmaceutical industry comes out very near the top. The comparison of the Return on Investment (ROI) of drug companies with All Industry median values from 1982 to 1987 in the USA shows that the ROI of the drug industry is consistently and significantly above the industry average (Table 5.1).

There is substantial evidence for the existence of barriers to entry into the pharmaceutical industry. Four potential barriers to entry can be identified in the pharmaceutical industry: patents, Research and Development (R&D) investments, marketing investments and company reputation.

Patents are a major hurdle precluding free entry into the market. Drugs are expensive to develop but once invented are inexpensive to

Table 5.1 Comparison of ROIs of drugs with all-industry median values in the USA, 1982–87

		Five year ROI	Twelve months ROI	Net profit margin
1982	Drugs	20.2	16.8	9.6
	All industries	15.9	12.7	3.4
1983	Drugs	18.5	19.0	10.6
	All industries	15.1	12.6	3.5
1984	Drugs	19.7	15.5	8.6
	All industries	15.1	13.4	3.7
1985	Drugs	18.9	17.0	9.6
	All industries	13.7	12.7	3.8
1986	Drugs	17.9	17.8	10.9
	All industries	12.6	13.0	3.9
1987	Drugs	17.5	23.4	9.2
	All industries	12.8	13.6	4.3

Source: Forbes Magazine Annual Reviews of Industry, 1983–1988.

copy. Without artificial barriers to entry such as patents, competitors could easily copy drugs, driving down prices and eliminating the return on Research and Development investments that produced the original innovation. However, while patents are a vital incentive for companies to engage in long and expensive research, they can also create artificial differentiation between drug which are 'me-toos'.

The arguments for and against patents have raged long and hard and continue to do so. It is generally agreed that patents are a prerequisite to making the market both product- and price-competitive. Abolishing them would probably mean less innovation and, in the long term, less competition. The opposing view is that some action could be taken to reduce the extent of patent protection in order to reduce prices. The key question for society as a whole, however, is whether lower prices now are worthwhile if they mean fewer new drugs in the future.

The second barrier to new entry is the very high cost of engaging in pharmaceutical Research and Development. The average cost of Research and Development to an average drug company in 1985 on a worldwide average basis was nearly 8% of sales, reaching 15% for some large pharmaceutical companies (Erickson, 1987). Potential new entrants, it is argued, are discouraged from entering the pharmaceutical market because of the huge capital outlays required in setting up research facilities that would allow them to compete with existing companies, as well as the time it takes to build up the Research and Development personnel and expertise. The very long lead times taken to develop new products, and the low success rate of Research and Development in the pharmaceutical industry, imply that companies have to invest very heavily now in order to get a return in ten to fifteen years' time.

The high cost of marketing new drugs, in particular the requirement of a large, globally distributed and highly-trained sales force who can promote the products directly to the prescribers, is an additional potent barrier discouraging new firms from entering the industry (Table 5.2).

A fourth barrier to entry, intrinsic to the pharmaceutical industry, is the credibility of a drug company in the professional health market. Since there is always some risk involved in the prescription and use of drugs, the name of the producer and inventor of the drug is an important risk-reduction mechanism for the prescriber. Of course, a reputation takes time to build and this time requirement acts as an important deterrent for potential newcomers to the pharmaceutical industry.

The relative ROI surplus of the pharmaceutical industry, however, is in the process of attracting some new players to the game. These new players, of course, need deep pockets to make the necessary huge investments in Research and Development in the pharmaceutical industry. These new entrants also need a strong and long-term commitment to the drug industry to build up the image and credibility with the prescribers necessary for success unless they choose to buy out existing companies that already have the necessary reputation.

In 1985 Monsanto bought G. D. Searle. Eastman-Kodak has made the decision to enter the pharmaceutical business with the objective of becoming a major player by the turn of the century. Synergy with their chemical research, projected high profitability in the pharmaceutical industry and slower expected growth rates and profitability in their own traditional markets have induced this large corporation to take this big step and buy out Sterling Drug in 1988 for about six billion US dollars. Volvo's recent involvement with Pharmacia, the Swedish drug company, is also an indicator of the drive for diversification of large non-pharmaceutical companies into the drug industry. By acquiring first

Table 5.2   Selling costs as a percentage of sales by industries, 1983 (US)

Industry	Percentage
Consumer goods	
Durable goods	9.0
Ethical pharmaceuticals, surgical supplies and equipment	16.9
Food	3.5
Major household items	4.4
Proprietary drugs and toiletries	7.9
Industrial goods	
Automotive parts and accessories	5.4
Building materials	5.4
Chemicals and petroleum	1.4
Computers, office and educational supplies and equipment	10.7
Containers, packaging materials and paper	1.6
Electrical materials	4.8
Electronics and instruments	5.2
Fabricated metals (heavy)	3.8
Fabricated metals (light)	4.9
Fabrics and apparel	4.2
Iron and steel	2.4
Machinery (heavy)	0.7
Machinery (light)	9.2
Printing and publishing	9.7
Rubber, plastics and leather	4.4

Note: Selling expenses cover costs of median compensation of sales people and sales management, travel, lodging, meals and entertainment, advertising and promotion. One of the major difficulties encountered in gathering such information is that wide differences exist between companies in the costs included in selling expenses.
Source: *Executive Compensation Service*, 1984.

Morton-Norwich and then Richardson-Vicks, Procter and Gamble is also trying to ease its way into the pharmaceutical world, predominantly via the OTC markets. Nestlé is following a similar path. These large consumer goods companies will probably attract some followers because their traditional markets are becoming mature, more competitive and burdened by lower margins. It is often argued that these fast-moving consumer goods companies will have a hard time moving into the prescription drug business because of their lack of personal selling expertise. In this context it is sometimes argued that insurance companies might be credible potential entrants into the prescription drug industry.

For a long time attempts by companies in technologically unrelated industries, such as fast-moving consumer goods industries and car manufacturers, to diversify into pharmaceuticals have met with little success. The pressures from their own environments might now be such that the future attempts will be more serious and sustained. Mergers with existing pharmaceutical companies might be a possible way into the pharmaceutical industry for those companies that currently have no pharmaceutical synergy.

For the marketing of generics the barriers to entry are substantially lower because virtually no Research and Development is necessary. For this reason profitable generics manufacturers will tend to attract profit-hungry competitors. Two possible barriers to entry, however, still remain for potential entrants in the generics business: economies of scale and marketing expenditures. To keep the prices low and generate volume business, efficient production and marketing will be necessary. Furthermore, price sensitive generics markets may not be all that attractive in the long run because of the threat of price wars resulting in a shake-out in the generics market (Codling, 1987).

With these potential new entrants, however, two major aspects of the pharmaceutical industry may drastically change. First, if Procter and Gamble and their followers were to enter the prescription drug market (probably via acquisition), the battle for market share will become more vigorous. Being the marketing specialists they are, they will force the existing leaders in the pharmaceutical industry to shift gears and become even more aggressive in their marketing approach. Secondly, and as a result of a more turbulent market, profitability will suffer, making the pharmaceutical industry a less comfortable industry for the less efficient and less effective traditional drug companies. The key to dealing successfully with these threats is to be prepared, to anticipate these entries and, if possible, to deter them.

5.2.3 Substitute products or services

Two major types of substitutes influence the ethical pharmaceutical industry: alternative therapies and the health-consciousness of the customers. Alternative therapies, such as joint replacements for arthritis or organ transplants for organ failures cut directly into the potential growth of the pharmaceutical industry. Replacing bad kidneys with healthy kidneys inevitably reduces the market for drugs dealing with kidney problems. The extent of this phenomenon is limited by the restricted supply of healthy replacement organs and by the immunity problems inherent in the transplants. These immunity problems in turn can create new opportunities for drug development as in the case of the anti-rejection product Sandimuun developed by Sandoz.

Preventive health care, acupuncture, herbal medication, phyto-pharmaceuticals, increased health consciousness, physical fitness, re-duced tobacco and alcohol consumption and similar developments might also act as substitutes for ethical drug products. In the same way as organ transplants, these health care developments act not only as a limiting factor on the drug industry, but can of course also create new strategic windows for marketing-oriented pharmaceutical companies. For example, within the foreseeable future, the jogging craze might create a whole new area of medical problems associated with joints, which can be captured by proactive drug companies. Furthermore, drug companies, as companies dealing with health care, could also move into the health consciousness market themselves. Increased health consciousness of the final consumer and general medical prog-ress will also lead to increased life expectancies which will create new therapeutic needs especially for the elderly.

An area of potential substitutes, as yet in its embryonic stage, is the use of various electromagnetic fields and/or light frequencies. The former have already been used experimentally in healing difficult fractures or suppurating leg ulcers; the latter include laser and X-ray technologies. Direct and controlled electric current procedures have been used clinically in experiments aimed at controlling carcinoma in breast and lung tissues or in stimulating nerve growth/maintenance and avoiding muscle atrophy.

Overall, it is likely that the threat of substitute products or services will be relatively mild and will indeed create opportunities for proactive pharmaceutical companies.

5.2.4 Customers

Broadly defined, several customer groups have a decisive impact on the current and future structure of the pharmaceutical industry. *Prescribers, health maintenance organizations, hospitals and patient pressure groups* form a category of customers that will progressively put more pressure on drug companies to develop genuinely 'new, effective and efficient' drugs, and to inform the customer better about the value of the available drugs. Furthermore, concentration in the prescriber population (e.g. from prescribers in solo practice to group practices, HMOs and hospitals in the US) will have very serious implications for the marketing of pharmaceutical products. More specifically, pharmaceutical companies will be competing for fewer direct clients. Pharmaceutical companies will also have to rethink the size and the role of their exorbitantly expensive sales forces in the light of a more concentrated prescribers' market (Table 5.3).

The role of *wholesalers* is dramatically different from country to country. In West Germany, for example, a highly concentrated wholesale sector has strong bargaining power both with drug manufacturers and pharmacists. In Belgium, a fragmented wholesaling industry used to have no power whatsoever in the market. In the USA, the growth and greater efficiency of retail chains and wholesalers through mergers and the formation of buying co-ops has increased the distributors' leverage with manufacturers. In Japan, most of the major pharmaceutical companies have direct interests (and investments) in the wholesale distribution sector. This may also be a barrier to entry by outsiders.

Protected by the government in almost all countries and in some countries highly concentrated, *drug retailers* can certainly curtail some of the power of drug manufacturers. In some countries, they can also put some pressure on drug companies through their ability to encourage generic substitution.

Institutional customers, e.g., hospitals, constitute another force in the market with strong bargaining power with the drug manufacturers. Since they can place large orders and are regarded as opinion leaders by some prescribers, hospitals are powerful negotiators in the drug industry.

Table 5.3   Concentration of prescribers in the US

	1980	1985	1990	1995
Physicians in solo practice	285 250	225 700	155 300	0
Group practices and hospitals	10 760	21 900	30 700	33 400
HMOs	235	400	900	2 100
	296 245	248 000	186 900	35 500

Source: E. Strosberg (Arthur D. Little), *The Changing Basis of Competition: A Long Term View*, presentation at Management Center Europe, 28–29 November 1988.

The *government* plays a crucial role in the industry through the exercise of its regulatory powers. Their interventions in the drug industry vary from country to country. On a worldwide basis, however, it is fair to say that they are intervening more and more. For governments, confronted with almost insurmountable health bills, are getting tougher with the drug industry all over the world. They have a dual role to play: to provide the incentives to encourage Research and Development activity in order to discover quantum-jump drugs, and at the same time to reduce the cost of drugs to health authorities, and control the level of profitability (i.e., monopoly power) in the industry. Reducing effective patent life, extending the administrative procedures for new product approval, actively supporting the generics business and holding back on price increases, are some of the effective tools the government has at its disposal to affect the structure of the pharmaceutical industry. In some countries, e.g., COMECOM, the government used to be itself the only drug manufacturer or importer, thus controlling the industry completely. The role of the government in the pharmaceutical industry is discussed in detail in Chapter 7.

Overall, several major external forces shape the structure of the pharmaceutical industry. Focusing the competitive analysis exclusively on the internal rivalry between the existing pharmaceutical companies, would be a serious mistake. Long-term strategic analysis in the pharmaceutical industry is deeply rooted in the effect suppliers, customers, potential entrants and substitute products or services can have on the global industry. In the next section the internal rivalry or the short-term competitive threats will be discussed.

5.2.5 Internal rivalry

At the industry-level

An often-cited summary measure of the market power of firms in an industry is the concentration ratio. The usual way of constructing this measure is to compare the sales of the top four or eight manufacturers with the overall market volume. These ratios are referred to as the C4 and C8 indices respectively. These concentration ratios can be computed at a number of different levels. For the drug industry these levels could be the total market, the therapeutic class, and the product level.

Table 5.4   Concentration in the
US prescription drug industry

Year	C4	C8
1963	24.1	42.6
1964	23.6	41.9
1965	23.4	42.3
1966	24.4	42.7
1967	25.2	42.8
1968	25.4	42.2
1969	25.9	43.1
1970	26.3	45.1
1971	26.6	45.6
1972	27.5	44.7
1973	27.4	44.5
1974	27.5	44.3
1975	26.7	42.4
1976	27.6	44.1
1977	27.0	43.4
1978	25.7	42.1
1979	25.6	42.6
1980	26.5	43.7
1981	26.3	43.3
1982	26.8	44.3

Source: Cool, 1985

Table 5.4 shows the C4 and C8 indices for the US prescription drug industry over a twenty year period.

The average concentration ratios have remained stable over the entire period and indicate that, overall, the industry remains relatively fragmented. On a worldwide scale the concentration ratios are even smaller. For example, in 1986–7, the top two manufacturers, Merck Sharp and Dohme and Hoechst, together controlled only about 6% of the total market. The characterization of the industry as relatively unconcentrated, however, is somewhat deceptive when one turns to the second level, that of therapeutic class. Table 5.5 shows the results of the C4 and C8 concentration ratios for the nine major therapeutic classes in the US market.

From this it can be seen that both the four firm (C4) and eight firm (C8) concentration ratios are significantly higher than those of the global company sales.

Table 5.5   Concentration in therapeutic classes in the US drug industry, 1963–82

Therapeutic	Class	1963	1967	1971	1975	1979	1982
Cardiovascular	C4	59.2	49.6	47.0	46.9	48.3	43.0
	C8	70.9	64.3	65.9	65.8	65.1	60.6
Nutritional	C4	29.2	33.2	47.1	48.7	47.5	48.5
	C8	42.9	46.2	64.2	62.1	58.9	57.6
Pain control	C4	46.0	53.2	48.0	44.1	52.7	51.4
	C8	64.4	70.0	72.4	68.6	74.1	70.5
Internal medicine	C4	36.0	31.2	29.1	28.2	31.1	38.4
	C8	50.7	47.1	46.6	44.8	50.8	57.3
Mental health	C4	58.6	60.1	61.6	65.9	60.3	51.1
	C8	75.3	78.5	79.5	82.0	80.2	75.4
Topical	C4	28.6	35.5	36.8	36.2	31.6	38.8
	C8	43.9	52.7	52.5	52.6	44.6	52.4
Anti-infective	C4	39.3	41.7	46.5	46.4	46.6	48.6
	C8	60.2	66.6	68.7	66.0	63.7	65.6
Respiratory	C4	35.4	41.9	45.8	43.4	38.2	35.2
	C8	51.9	57.9	65.8	65.6	58.2	53.5
Cancer therapy	C4	65.7	68.0	76.3	66.8	58.9	61.6
	C8	n.a.	n.a.	95.8	78.0	66.7	67.5
Average	C4	44.1	46.0	48.7	47.4	46.1	46.3
	C8	57.4	60.4	67.9	65.0	62.5	62.3

Source: Cool, 1985.

Finally, if one looks at the level of individual products, the concentration ratio tends to be relatively high in most countries. In 1984, the top hundred pharmaceutical products accounted for 36.5% of total sales (Scrip, 1985, Oct. 2, p. 4).

In many countries, the concentration of the top products is even higher, as demonstrated in a survey of a number of EEC countries in Table 5.6.

If one also looks at the relative market shares held by some products within a therapeutic class or sub-class, the concentration can be extremely high. For example, in the anti-peptic ulcer market, 70% of the world market in 1987 was held by only two brands, Tagamet (Smith, Kline, Beckman (SKB)) and Zantac (Glaxo) (Glaxo, 1988). This can lead to very skewed sales concentration within companies, with large percentages of their total sales resulting from only one or a few brands. On average, it has been estimated that a company's top product accounts for 15–30% of total pharmaceutical sales (Burstall and Senior, 1985). In some cases, this figure can be even higher, for example, 53% of SKB's world sales of ethical pharmaceuticals in 1986 resulted from the sales of just one brand; Tagamet (SKB Annual Report, 1986).

A number of mergers and acquisitions are currently reshaping the internal rivalry among pharmaceutical companies. In 1986, Schering-Plough acquired Key Pharmaceutical. In 1989, the merger trend was accelerated by the mergers of SmithKline Beckman and Beecham, Squibb and Bristol–Myers, Merril Dow and Marion Laboratories, and Rhone-Poulenc and Rorer. The acquisition raid is still not finished as illustrated in Table 5.7. This table deals with the battle of the Titans, so to speak, and is by no means exhaustive. There are, in addition, medium-sized and even still family-owned companies such as Boehringer Fry (German) or Sevicol (France) which may be unable to sustain their independence in a maturing industry where, as in other industries, maturity usually results in concentration, shake-outs and the 'dominant survivors'.

The two major reasons for this merger and acquisitions drive seem to be astute opportunistic financial operations and the creation of synergy and critical mass. It could be argued that some drug companies preferred to merge to preempt foreseeable hostile takeovers. Research and Development and marketing synergies leading to the critical mass economies might be the second explanation of this recent merger mania in the drug industry.

Another potential force that might jeopardize the current competitive structure of the industry is the expansion of Japanese pharmaceutical companies into the US and Europe. The modern international pharmaceutical industry is dominated by American and European multi-

Table 5.6 Concentration of market share by number of drugs in 1982

Country	Top 10	Top 50	Top 100	Top 250
Belgium	15.4	37.1	50.1	69.3
France	9.4	27.1	38.9	59.1
West Germany	8.3	21.9	31.6	49.6
Italy	12.0	27.9	39.2	58.2
Netherlands	14.3	37.0	51.2	73.1
UK	17.9	43.0	57.5	77.5

Source: Burstall and Senior, 1985.

Table 5.7   Potential drug company acquisitions

Target	Suitors	Strategic need	Probability
Warner-Lambert	Roche, Ciba-Geigy Dow, P&G, Bayer	OTC healthcare products; Rx drugs and marketing resources	High/ Medium
Schering-Plough	Ciba-Geigy, Sandoz, P&G, Dow Bayer, BASF	Niche Rx drugs and Research and Development pipeline; consumer products	Medium OTC
Pfizer	Hoechst, BASF	Major Rx drugs; large Research and Development pipeline and global marketing resources	Low

Source: Adapted and updated from *Market Letter*, April 25 1988, p. 25.

nationals that discovered the medicines in the first place. In 1987 only one Japanese company, Takeda, with annual sales of $1.7 billion and two Japanese research-derived drugs feature among the top twenty companies or top twenty drugs worldwide, respectively (Marsh, 1987). Japanese drug companies tend to be small and fragmented and have, until recently, relied on the West to provide the drugs for them to sell. However, a number of signs exist which indicate the intention of Japan to become a major force in the drug industry worldwide. In 1965 the average Japanese drug company spent 1% of sales on research; in the early eighties this figure had gone up to 7.5%. Japanese companies are also very active in the licensing-in market. In addition, the Japanese government – no slouch at encouraging exports and growth – is actively assisting the Japanese drug companies by changing the licensing policy and extending the patent system to encourage innovation. It seems likely that after television sets, cameras, steel, motorcycles, hi-fi, cars and computers, those tough competitors from the land of the Rising Sun are aiming at the international drug industry. Prime targets for the Japanese seem to be the antibiotics, anti-cancer and central nervous system drugs. It would be in the interest of the current leaders in the drug industry to take them more seriously than, for example, the European motorcycle industry did. Norton-Villiers Triumph used to be a major European motorcycle manufacturer. They underestimated and neglected the Japanese entrants in the motorcycle market. They used to have a work force of around 2000. Today they are out of business.

In spite of this, many industry experts argue that it will still take until the turn of the century before the Japanese become a strong force internationally in the pharmaceutical industry. The reasons cited for this are: their lack of experience in distribution and marketing in the Western pharmaceutical world, the long lead times for Research and Development, and the fact that for many of the most successful products in Japan, there is limited demand outside Japan because their diseases have a lower incidence in the Western World (personal communication and Marsh, 1987).

At the product market level

At the level of specific product markets the pharmaceutical industry has a two-tier structure with original brands and generics. The former compete mostly on non-price benefits and the latter are generally driven by price competition.

Original brands. The original (innovative and 'me-too') brands, which account for the lion's share of most product markets compete in different ways depending on the customer type. In the *traditional prescribers' markets* competitive warfare focuses on the therapeutic value (e.g. efficacy, side-effect, galenical form and dosage level) and the sales force effort; and to a lesser degree on journal advertising, samples, mailings and conferences. In their struggle for market share personal selling via a highly trained sales force has always been an important marketing tool for pharmaceutical companies, but obtaining an audience with key physicians is becoming more difficult and expensive. In order to justify the high cost of personal selling, most pharmaceutical companies now try to focus their efforts on 'high prescribers'. This means that the sales force effort from all companies tends to concentrate on the same group of physicians. This target audience is then forced to react either by rationing the time they are willing to spend with them or simply by refusing to see medical reps. As the number of physician practice sites concentrates, doctors are more able to delegate or share the task of seeing reps, again reducing the number of opportunities available to pharmaceutical companies to communicate directly with prescribers. One tactic some companies have adopted to gain more time with prescribers is running *multiple sales forces*. Prescribers who ration the time they spend with representatives are particularly inclined to avoid a second visit from the same company, within a short space of time. If the representatives are clearly differentiated, representing different groups of drugs or therapeutic areas, the physician is more likely to grant a second audience. So, for example, American Home Products runs two separate field forces, Ayerst and Wyeth. Similarly, McNeil, Ortho and Jansen are all field forces of Johnson & Johnson. There has also been a marked increase in the popularity of *co-marketing* (and co-detailing) arrangements among drug companies in recent years. This may be one more indication of the increased competitive pressure in the pharmaceutical industry. Maintaining a large field force represents a major fixed cost, but increasing or decreasing the size of a sales force is also expensive. Co-marketing grew out of the fact that there are times, particularly during a major new launch, but also for a special promotional effort on an existing product, when a pharmaceutical company would like a much stronger sales force than at other times. In a co-marketing (or co-detailing) arrangement, two or more companies join their field force for specific products for a specific period of time. An early example of a highly successful co-marketing effort was that of Glaxo and Hoffmann-La Roche in the US for Zantac in 1983, but there have been many since (see Table 5.8). Such

Table 5.8   Competition through cooperation

Company	Partner	Product	Combined US sales force
Glaxo	Hoffmann-La Roche	Zantac Azoril	1790
	Schering	Vanceril Beclovent	1790
SmithKline	Du Pont	Tagamet	1430
	Bristol-Myers	OTC Tagamet*	2800
Squibb	McNeil	Capoten	1144
Abbott	Burroughs Wellcome	Hytrin	1200
Merck	ICI	Zestril	2204
Du Pont	Hoffmann-La Roche	Versed	1230
Knoll	Searle	Verapamil	881
Schering	Sandoz	ACE Inhibitor*	1700
Beecham	Upjohn	Eminase	1800

*These products are not yet approved for marketing.
Source: Kaplan, 1988, p. 58.

arrangements provide much-needed flexibility in the field force size, while avoiding the costs of recruitment, training, organization and, eventually, disinvestment once the need for field force effort has passed (Kaplan, 1988).

In the *institutional market* (hospitals, HMOs, etc.), especially in those product categories with a plethora of 'me-too' products, value-added services (e.g., customer hotlines, custom labelling, low-cost voucher-ing, instant delivery, frequent buyer clubs and patient education) have become crucial elements in the struggle for sales and market share.

Generics can afford to compete mainly on price because of their low Research and Development costs and their younger and more flexible organizational structure. However, because of the profit implications of price wars among generics, 'value-added' generics are becoming increasingly important. These value-added services add benefits to the generic copies through custom packaging, custom labelling, etc. (Zimmerman, 1989).

In their competition with original products generics are gaining share for two principal reasons: the slow rate of development of new innovative products and government (and third party) actions to reduce the costs of pharmaceutical products. The first reason is primarily the result of the fact that the industry is now undoubtedly being affected by

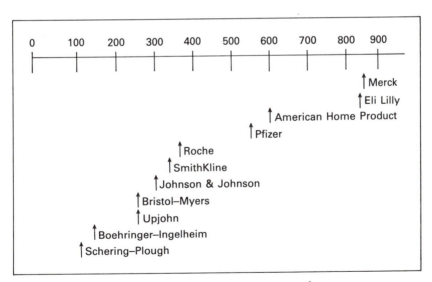

Figure 5.2   Drugs off patent, 1981–91, revenues (in 10^6\$) in 1985 (Wyke, 1987)

the legacy of the innovation boom of the 60s and 70s. By the end of 1986, 120 of the two hundred top-selling products of 1983 were out of patent and by 1990, the patents on nearly all of the 1987 top two hundred prescription drugs in the USA alone had expired (Wyke, 1987). Figure 5.2 represents the opportunities for generic firms to sell cheap generics for the period 1981–91.

Another important factor, certainly in the USA, has been the introduction of Abbreviated New Drug Applications (ANDAs) by the FDA in 1984. The purpose of this new procedure for accelerated passage of a drug through regulation is to encourage price competition by simplifying the approval process for duplicate drugs already shown to be safe and effective (FDA, 1987). In 1986, the FDA had 734 ANDAs under review, an increase of 27% on 1985. This single change in the USA has reduced the cost of preparing a generic product for launch from several million dollars to less than $150,000 and the length of approval to as little as a year (Wyke, 1987).

In Europe, favourable government treatment of generics is under way. The Federal Health Office in West Germany is currently changing its approval system to speed the passage of generic drugs as well as actively encouraging their use. As a result the sale of generics (by value) rose to 15% of the market in 1986, an increase of 10% over 1984. Similar trends could be expected if other European countries were to follow suit.

In the USA, where a pharmacist is permitted to substitute a generic form of a product prescribed by a doctor by its brand name ('generic substitution'), the role of the pharmacist is increasingly important. This is not only due to the shift of responsibility that substitution represents but also because generic companies can offer greater profit margins to the pharmacist to improve their attractiveness.

US government agencies handling reimbursement schemes such as Medicare (for the aged) and Medicaid (for the poor) are strongly in favour of generics. In some states, with the former two systems, the government already pays only for the cheapest available substitute on a doctor's prescription, termed the 'maximum allowable cost' or MAC scheme (Chew *et al.*, 1985). Hospitals, HMOs and large employers who strongly support the generic substitution process. General Motors, for example, pays more for employees' health insurance than it does for the steel in its cars. It is therefore not surprising that such employers and their lobby support the generics' grip on the market.

In Europe, where health schemes cover virtually the whole population and are generally publicly funded, there is growing concern by governments to reduce expenditure on health bills in general and pharmaceuticals in particular. In 1982 the UK came close to introducing generic substitution (Chew *et al.*, 1985) and their final decision not to go ahead with it was based on their belief in the importance of the brand-name system to the research-based pharmaceutical industry, as well as the role of the original manufacturer in providing services in addition to the bare product such as information to prescribers. The arguments against generic substitution in Europe have generally centred on concerns for the safety and potency of generic drugs, and it is clear that changes in the approval system, such as those being made in Germany, could change the current situation quite rapidly.

A factor likely to affect the nature of the generic drug industry is the threat of substitutes. Research-based companies are continually developing and launching new products that eclipse older therapies and create new markets. Generic drugs are especially vulnerable to this as they represent technology which is off-patent and therefore likely to be over twenty years old. Major advances through techniques such as biotechnology could lead to whole new approaches to therapy in the 1990s making the older generic substitutes out of date.

In the face of increasing competition from the generic industry, the manufacturers of original branded products have a number of defence options available to them and these also are likely to dampen the success of the generics companies. The main options are as follows.

1. Companies can encourage loyalty to the original drug brand-name and capitalize on the inertia of prescribers.
2. Companies can increase their marketing efforts to support their own branded products, and transfer the differential advantage from the patent to the brand-name, since trade marks have a longer life than patents.
3. Companies can develop new products or product forms (for example slow release), reducing the advantage of generic copies of older therapies.
4. The original manufacturer can preempt a generic manufacturer by launching its own generic version of a product before the patent is expired or by coming to an arrangement of this kind with a licensee.
5. Companies can reinforce the existing ambiguity, on the quality of generics thereby reducing the confidence of the prescribers in these products.

6. Companies can lower the price of the original drug to reduce the price advantage offered by a generic copy.

Through analyzing the competitive forces that will shape the pharmaceutical industry in the future it becomes apparent that the industry will change drastically. The competition will get stronger and the profitability of pharmaceutical companies will deteriorate. Especially because of the new entrants, the government's and other customers' actions, the pharmaceutical industry will have to face some very important challenges in the years to come. The concentration within the industry, through intensive merger and co-marketing activities, will heighten these trends even more strongly.

In these circumstances it will become more and more important to analyze the competition. Careful analysis of the competitive action space will have to precede any company's definition of its own strategic terrain and objectives. The process of competitive analysis is discussed in the next section.

5.3   THE PROCESS OF COMPETITIVE ANALYSIS

To understand the competitive threats and opportunities four crucial issues have to be addressed.

1. Identification of competitors.
2. Their competitive behaviour.
3. Competitors' performance.
4. Competitors' motivation.

As illustrated in Table 5.9, for each of these four issues appropriate managerial tools are available. Each of these will now be discussed.

5.3.1   Identification of competitors

Depending on the purpose of the analysis, different sets of competitors are relevant. At the level of company strategy, the Porter framework discussed earlier can be a useful vehicle to identify the relevant competitors. The competition at this level goes far beyond the pharmaceutical companies and might include the global health care sector, potential new entrants, the government, organ transplantation centers, etc. The set of competitors at the level of a therapeutic group is more restricted, including those pharmaceutical companies present and/or those that might enter the therapeutic area. For a specific brand the set

Table 5.9   Competitive analysis process

Step 1:	*Identification of Competitors* Competitive forces analysis Strategic groups
Step 2:	*Competitive behavior* Value chain analysis Portfolio analysis
Step 3:	*Competitors' performance* Market share analysis Hierarchy of effects
Step 4:	*Competitors' Motivation*

of relevant competitors is probably even smaller depending on the segment in which the brand is positioned.

A key problem in the identification of competitors is the prevailing feeling among marketing executives that they basically know who their competitors are, their strengths and weaknesses, their people, their strategies and so forth. The fact is, however, that they rely on rather partial (IMS) statistics or biased (their own experience) information. Often, management's understanding of competition continues to be casual, clumsy, and frequently inaccurate. Systematic, appropriately organized and objective information is the key to rigorous competition analysis.

Common sense and experience can be supplemented by two tools to identify competition: competitive forces analysis and strategic groups. The former is more useful at the level of the brand and the therapeutic group, whereas the latter is more appropriate at the aggregate level of company strategy.

Competitive forces analysis is based on market segmentation, product positioning and analyses of Research and Development capabilities. Target-market and positioning analyses are useful approaches to identify the key players in the market place. By studying the target segments of the competitors and their perceived position by those target-market customers one can conveniently pinpoint direct competitors. Alternatively, one could go immediately to the prescribers and ask them which drugs they would consider prescribing for a specific disease. The available research capabilities of the existing and potential competitors can further expand the previously identified competitors.

Healthcare
sales contribution, percent

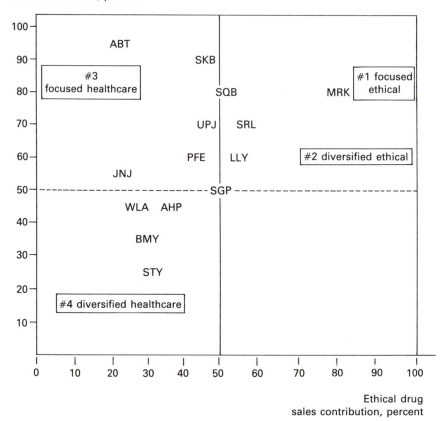

Figure 5.3   Strategic groups (Sammon, 1985)

Strategic groups are basically groups of competitors in an industry pursuing similar strategies and having certain characteristics in common (e.g., size, commitment to the ethical drug business, Research and Development intensity, etc.) (McGee and Thomas, 1986). These strategic groups are useful tools for identifying barriers protecting each group, to spot marginal groups, and to predict possible competitive actions and reactions.

The notion of a strategic group is similar to the concept of a segment. Ideally, a strategic group contains companies that have similar buyers and sellers, have similar cost structures, have similar product and business mixes, target the same markets, and share common strategic assumptions and goals. Companies belonging to different strategic groups are heterogeneous in terms of the strategies they pursue.

Sammon (1985) grouped a set of large US pharmaceutical manufacturers together in four strategic groups as a function of their dependence on health care sales in their total sales (healthcare sales % of total sales) and the importance of the ethical drug sales in their total sales. The four resulting strategic groups might be useful indicators of the current and future strategies pursued by the members of these groups.

The companies indicated by the initials in Figure 5.3 are as follows. ABT: Abbott Laboratories, AHP: American Home Products, BMY: Bristol-Myers, JNJ: Johnson and Johnson, LLY: Eli Lilly, MRK: Merck & Co, PFE:

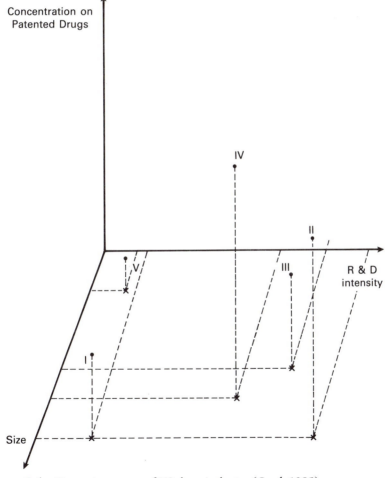

Figure 5.4   Strategic groups of US drug industry (Cool, 1985)

Pfizer, SGP: Schering-Plough, SKB: SmithKline Beckman, SQB: Squibb, SRL: Searle, STY: Sterling Drug, UPJ: Upjohn, WLA: Warner Lambert.

Cool (1985) identified five strategic groups among the top twenty US pharmaceutical companies. As illustrated in Figure 5.4, these five groups differ in terms of their size, their Research and Development intensity and their concentration on patented drugs.

The composition of the groups is as follows.

Group I   Abbott, American Home, Warner-Lambert, Bristol-Myers, Pfizer, SmithKline. These companies are large, present in a large variety of therapeutic areas, with below average Research and Development investments but advertising intensive, with a mixed RX-OTC product line.

Group II   Merck Sharpe and Dohme, Lilly and Upjohn. These are large companies, Research and Development intensive, differentiated, ethical drug companies with a wide range of scope commitments.

Group III Johnson & Johnson, Schering-Plough and Sterling Drug. Medium-sized pharmaceutical companies, with average Research and Development investments, strong advertising intensity, differentiated drug firms with a wide range of scope commitments.

Group IV   Syntex and Searle. Medium-sized, Research and Development (non-NCE) intensive, focused, ethical drug companies with a narrow scope.

Group V   Morton-Norwich, Carter Wallace, Richardson-Vicks, Robins, Marton and Roher. Smaller pharmaceutical companies, not Research and Development intensive drug companies

The result of this first step in the competitive analysis process should be a list of competitors. These competitors usually fall into three categories: prime (or close) competitors, more distant existing competitors and potentially new competitors. The longer the strategic planning horizon the more relevant the second and the third categories of competitors become.

5.3.2 Competitive behavior

It is a difficult task to anticipate what the competiton will do next. Nevertheless, it is crucial to try to figure out explicitly what strategies the competition might pursue in the future. To improve the understanding of what competition will or could do, two tools can be used: value chain analysis (Porter, 1985) and portfolio analysis.

Value chain analysis decomposes the total activity of a pharmaceutical company in a chain of its underlying functions that build up the value added by the company. This type of analysis focuses on the activities that intervene in the input/output transformation of a pharmaceutical company. As illustrated in Figure 5.5, the value chain in the drug company is composed of five major functions: Research and Development, registration, manufacturing, marketing and distribution. Analysis of how each of these five functions is performed by the competitors could provide a deeper understanding of the competitive advantage and the likely future moves of the competitors. This business system analysis identifies the strengths and weaknesses of the competition and therefore indicates where the competition will be aggressive and where it is vulnerable. Value chain analysis is a useful tool to get a better understanding of the sources of the competitors' strengths and weaknesses.

The *research function* is complex and can be broken down in several sub-functions: raw materials, basic research, clinical trials, product formulations and galenical forms. In the context of competitive analysis the key Research and Development questions are: what are the new products, galenical forms and new indications in the pipeline? In what stage of development are these projects, what priorities have been set, which projects are at which stage of the clinical trial process? What is the Research and Development expertise of the competitor? What are the bottlenecks in bringing these projects to fruition? Closely linked to these questions is the issue of the likelihood of *government acceptance* of these projects. How many products are under investigation and what is the likelihood of them successfully passing this hurdle? What is the registration track record of the competitor?

Investigation of the competitor's *manufacturing function* could reveal important information on his capacity utilization. Similarly, the

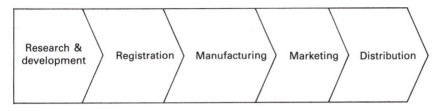

Figure 5.5   The value chain in the pharmaceutical industry

aspect of efficiency in manufacturing could be useful in determining the profitability of competing products. In the context of generic competition information about the extent of economies of scale in production (or procurement systems) could give clues about the potential price and cost levels of the generics manufacturers.

The *marketing function* analysis should provide insights on competitor's strengths and weaknesses in their ability to market new products and their deployment of the field force, journal advertising, mailings and samples. Can they expand their field force? Will they shift some resources from one marketing mix element to another? Is their field force strong in both the private and the institutional market? Given the new products that they will bring out, do they have the resources to fully support these new products or will they have to reduce the efforts for the existing products? What is their attitude towards co-marketing and/or co-detailing? What are their value-added services policies towards institutional buyers? Answers to these questions should provide useful information for understanding the future moves of the competition.

Finally, logistical strengths and weaknesses in the *distribution* network, the bargaining power of drug companies with their distributors and their overall relationships with wholesalers and drug stores or pharmacists should also be analyzed.

Most of these questions surface regularly in any pharmaceutical company. Answers are not always easy to come by. Even rough and partial answers don't reduce the relevance of the questions. What is important is that companies should move towards a *systematic gathering and organization of this type of information about their competitors*. A crucial aspect in the development of such a competitive analysis information system is that all information sources (secondary data, product management, field force, etc.) are tapped. In the majority of companies that have gone beyond paying lip service to the notion of competitive analysis, this function is still fulfilled in an ivory tower environment where crucial pieces of the competitive puzzle are neglected because not everyone in the organization is involved in providing the information. For example, often the market intelligence of the field force is not integrated in the competitive analysis. Similarly, information must be accessible and available (returnable) to users, and preferably circulated to designated managers on a proactive basis.

A second tool to improve the understanding of the future behaviour and attitudes of the competition is *portfolio analysis* (discussed in

Chapter 3). By categorizing the Strategic Business Units (SBUs) of the competition in portfolio grids, strengths and weaknesses of the competition can be classified. It can help to predict their future investment and harvesting priorities, and indicate competitors' vulnerability and the intensity of their reactions if they are being attacked. By studying the overall portfolio of a competitor the relative importance of the SBUs to the competitor can be assessed. For example, 'Company A' will probably respond vigorously to an attack on their cardiovascular market (Figure 5.6). By the same token, their defence in the topical and internal medicine markets will be much more passive. Similarly, a company that has a rich new product arsenal will probably be constrained to reduce its competitive efforts on their older products.

Competitive position	Embryonic	Growth	Mature	Ageing
Dominant		Cardio-vascular		
Strong				
Favourable			Pain control	Mental health Respiratory
Tenable			Topical Internal medicine	
Weak				

Market development stage

Figure 5.6 Company A's US portfolio

5.3.3 Competitor's performance

Past performance is an important indicator of future strategy. If a competitor has performed very well (relative to its objectives) in one year, it is more likely that it will continue the past strategy in the same direction than if this performance was below target.

Indicators of performance are usually market share, sales growth, profitability and the change of these indicators over time. Pharmaceutical companies have sufficient information (IMS etc.) to assess the performance of their competitors.

Market share information is crucial to assess competitors' performance. Traditional market share information, however, might not be sufficient to understand market dynamics. An increase in market share might be due to a number of factors, not all equally desirable. Suppose a product is positioned in a particular market segment. The first piece of information necessary is the total evolution of the segment, say in number of prescriptions and in value terms. Market sales might increase because of a general increase in the price level, or because of an increase in the number of prescriptions, or both. Next, it is interesting to know how loyal prescribers from the previous period have evolved, and what happened to the previous period prescriptions for each brand, i.e., a distinction has to be made between the existing pool of prescribers and the new prescribers. The market shares in each of these three categories might reveal important information about the performance

Table 5.10 Market performance evaluation

Market segment: Adopter generalist doctors				
Size of Market				
	Year t		Year t + 1	
Number of prescriptions	1 000 000		1 200 000	
Value	10 000 000		14 000 000	
Market share				
	Number of prescriptions		Value	
Brands	t	t + 1	t	t + 1
A	50%	55%	40%	42%
B	20%	25%	35%	40%
C	30%	20%	25%	18%

of individual drugs. The following hypothetical example illustrates these issues (Table 5.10).

According to these figures the market segment is becoming more attractive both in value and in number of prescriptions. Brand A is reinforcing its market leadership, brand B is improving its position, whereas brand C is losing market share. More detailed analysis might indicate rather different conclusions as illustrated in Tables 5.11a, b, and c.

This analysis shows that brand C is actually doing rather well with new prescribers. Their poor performance is due to the fact that their past prescribers are massively moving to brands A and B. The brand switching matrix between year t and year t + 1 shows that of the 100%

Table 5.11   Detailed market performance evaluation

(a)

Brands	Prescriptions in year t	Prescriptions in year t + 1 for year t prescribers	Prescriptions in year t + 1 for new prescribers
A	500 000	580 000	80 000
B	200 000	260 000	40 000
C	300 000	160 000	80 000

(b)

		Year t + 1		
Year t prescribers' habits in year t + 1 (brand switching)				
Brands		A	B	C
	A	90%	9%	1%
Year t	B	20%	75%	5%
	C	30%	22%	48%

(c)

Brands	New Prescribers
A	40%
B	20%
C	40%

prescribers of brand C last year only 48% are continuing to prescribe brand C. Thirty percent have switched to brand A and 22% have moved to brand B. The market leader has a solid position (90% loyalty) in the existing market and is getting a good share of the new prescribers. Actually, brand A is slipping in the subsegment of new prescribers. Brand B has a satisfactory position, mainly due to the high price per average daily dosage of its brand.

In terms of competitive analysis, the following inferences can be hypothesized.

1. Brand A has to improve and modify its approach to new prescribers and consolidate its leader position with existing prescribers.
2. Brand B must stop its loss of prescribers to brand A and make an effort to improve its position with new prescribers.
3. Brand C has to stop the deterioration of its share with the existing prescribers and continue with the same approach to new prescribers. Maybe this brand has some serious problems (for continued use) given the severe deterioration of its share with existing prescribers (especially towards brand A).

This example illustrates that more in-depth analysis of the market performance of the competition clarifies the understanding of their potential future moves. Unfortunately, all the necessary data are not always available to make such a detailed analysis. An effort should be made, however imperfect the data, to come to grips with the market dynamics underlying the overall market performance indicators.

In addition to market share analysis, competitive analysis requires more in-depth analysis of what precedes actual market share movements. In this context, the 'hierarchy of effects' (HE) approach might prove to be a very valuable tool. The HE model shows a chain of events that have to happen before a prescription is made (Vaughan, 1980). As illustrated in Figure 5.7, prescribers first have to be aware of the brand, subsequently they must show a positive interest in the brand before they intend to prescribe it. The actual prescription and the purchase of the drug is still contingent on the availability of the drug in the retail outlets, and the pharmacist should not substitute the drug by its generic equivalent. Once the first prescription and purchase (trial) is made, the prescriber will on the next occasion either repeat the same prescription or not. The outcome of this process is a specific market share for the brand under consideration.

This HE model contains three important messages. First, the final

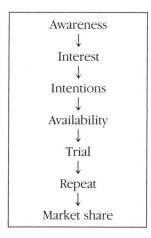

Figure 5.7   The hierarchy of effects

result, i.e., market share and sales, will only be as good as the weakest link in the chain. A specific brand might be exceptionally good, but if the prescribers are not aware of it, the market share will be rather poor.

Second, the HE approach provides a simple, yet intuitively appealing and systematic method to analyze the performance of products in the market.

Third, market share, often the only criterion considered in evaluating the performance of competing brands, is only the tip of the iceberg. To fully understand how competing brands are performing, perceptual and attitudinal measures have to be integrated in the analysis.

As illustrated in Table 5.12, Brands 1 and 2 have the same market

Table 5.12   An application of the HE models

	Brand 1 (1000*)	Brand 2 (1000)
Awareness	300*	700
Interest	250	600
Intentions	200	300
Availability	180	300
Trial	180	300
Repeat	160	160
Market Share	16%	16%

*These are 1000 prescribers in the target market for Brand 1, 300 of these 1000 prescribers are aware of Brand 1.

share, however the HE model indicates rather different potentials for them. Brand 1 could drastically improve its market share in the next period by improving its awareness level via sales force and advertising efforts. Brand 2 has a less rosy future, the brand's current market share is carried by its high level of awareness. The dramatic drop from trial to repeat is indicative of the fact that the product does not live up to its expectations. These insights are crucial for predicting future competitive moves and to understand the threats and opportunities created by competing products.

HE type data are usually only available on an *ad hoc* basis, although some market research companies, e.g. PERCQ in the US are providing such data on a syndicated basis for the major brands in a substantial number of product categories (Status, 1990).

5.3.4   Competitors' motivation

It is important to grasp the competitors' philosophy and the way they perceive themselves and their competitors to anticipate their future moves. Do they perceive themselves as the clear leaders in the market or simply as followers? How are they and how do they want to be perceived: aggressive, defensive or conservative? Does their organization allow them to act and react quickly to their opponents' moves? Do they provide substantial autonomy to their subsidiaries? For example, everything else being the same, Swiss companies have the reputation of being slower and more conservative than their American and Japanese counterparts. Japanese companies are perceived as centralized and managed from the company's headquarters in Japan (Bartlett and Goshal, 1989).

The point is that when one predicts a competitor's strategy one should try to think as they would, and not to think in terms of what your company would do in the given circumstances. Another danger in this context is to become deceived by some existing 'halo' effects in the market about certain competitors. These company stigmas could be rather inappropriate generalizations, and not hold in particular market situations.

Finally, one should build up some expertise in deciphering the market signals that are abundant in practically all pharmaceutical markets. These signalling sources are summarized in Table 5.13 below.

Table 5.13 Sources of information

	Public	Trade/ professionals	Government	Investors
What competitors say about themselves	Advertising	Technical papers	Lawsuits	Annual meetings
	Promotional materials	Licences	Antitrust	Annual reports
	Sales force	Patents	Patents	Speeches to security analysis
	Press releases Articles Personnel changes Want ads.	Courses Clinical trials	Investigations	
What others say	Books, articles	Suppliers/ distributors	Lawsuits	Reports
	Case studies	Industry study	Antitrust	Industry studies
	Consultants	Customers	Patent commission	Credit reports
	Newspaper reporters Environmental groups Unions 'Who's who' Recruiting			

5.4 A CONCLUDING NOTE

Overall, systematic analysis of the competition is a *conditio sine qua non* in today's pharmaceutical markets. Before developing one's own strategy, one should first try to understand the strategies (or possible strategies) of the competitors. It is only after studying the competitors' strategies that the company's own strategic opportunities and threats become clear. Figure 5.8 summarizes the objectives of any competitive analysis exercise. As proposed by Porter (1980), this framework clearly indicates the key questions that have to be addressed by a serious competitive analysis effort.

It will always be difficult to answer these questions accurately. Some

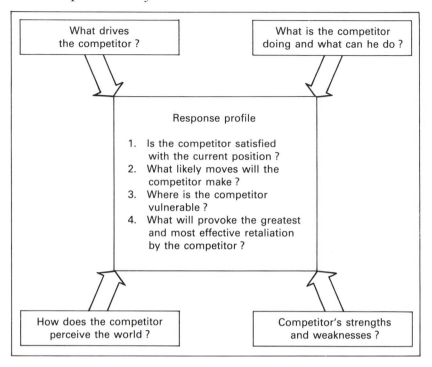

Figure 5.8   Porter's competitive response framework (Porter, 1980)

pharmaceutical companies, to deal with this problem, get involved in role-playing exercises where their own managers get assigned to different teams and are asked to put themselves in the shoes of their competitors and develop their respective marketing strategies. Such sessions are usually run before or during the strategic planning exercise of the company and provide very useful insights into the behaviour and strategies of the various competitors.

REFERENCES

Bartlett, C. and Goshal, S. (1989) *Managing Across Borders*, Century Hutchinson, London.

Burstall, M. and Senior, I. (European Advisory Group) (1985) *The Community's Pharmaceutical Industry*, Office for Official Publications of the European Community, Luxembourg.

Chew, R., Smith, G. and Wells, N. (1985) *Pharmaceuticals in Seven Nations*, Office of Health Economics, London.

Codling, M. (1987) The Over-the-Counter Drug Industry: A Quiet Revolution, *Spectrum*, A. D. Little, January.

Cool, K. (1985) *Strategic Group Formation and Strategic Group Shifts*, Unpublished Doctoral Dissertation, Purdue University.

Erikson, S. (1987) Pharmaceuticals, *Spectrum*, A. D. Little, February.

Forbes Magazine Annual Reviews of Industry, 1983–88.

Kaplan, S. (1988) Co-marketing Drug Companies Double Team the Competition, *Pharmaceutical Executive*, September, pp. 52–5.

Marsh, P. (1987) Breakthroughs and Red Tape, *Financial Times*, October 1.

McGee, J. and Thomas, H. (1986) Strategic Groups: Theory, Research and Taxonomy, *Strategic Management Journal*, March–April, pp. 141–60.

Porter, M. (1980) *Competitive Strategy*, The Free Press, New York.

Porter, M. (1985) *Competitive Advantage*, The Free Press, New York.

Quickel, (1987) *Market letter*.

Sammon, W. (1985) *Assessing the Competition: Business Intelligence for Strategic Management*, Esomar Seminar, Lisbon, pp. 105–64.

Status (1990) *Status Report*, PERCQ Corporation.

Vaughn, R. (1980) How Advertising Works: A Planning Model, *Journal of Advertising Research*, 20(5), pp. 27–33.

Vaughn, R. (1986) How Advertising Works: A Planning Model Revisited, *Journal of Advertising Research*, 26(1), pp. 57–66.

Wyke, A. (1987) Pharmaceuticals, *The Economist*, February 7.

Zimmerman, J. (1989) Simple no Longer: Generics in Tomorrow's Marketplace, *Pharmaceutical Executive*, April, pp. 52–9.

FURTHER READING

Cool, K. and Schendel, D. (1987) Strategic Group Formation and Performance: The case of the US pharmaceutical industry, 1963–1982, *Management Science*, September, pp. 1102–24.

Day, G. and Wensley, R. (1988) Assessing Advantage: A framework for diagnosing competitive superiority, *Journal of Marketing*, April, pp. 1–20.

Kevin, R., Mahajan, V. and Varadarajan, P. (1990) *Strategic Market Planning*, Allyn and Bacon, Boston.

Vaughn, R. (1986) How Advertising Works: A Planning Model Revisited, *Journal of Advertising Research*, 26(1).

Wyke, A. (1988) Biotechnology, *The Economist*, April 30.

Zimmerman, J. (1987) Rewriting the Script for a New Stage in Marketing, *Pharmaceutical Executive*, September, pp. 80–4.

SIX

Research and Development and marketing

1 INTRODUCTION

The major form of competition among ethical pharmaceutical companies is the introduction of new products for the prevention, diagnosis and treatment of diseases. The Research and Development department in any pharmaceutical company is the crucial element in this new-product race. This drug research as we know it in the late twentieth century is a fairly recent phenomenon. According to Tischler and Denkenoter (1966), 95% of all pharmaceutical research, measured in man-years, carried out since the dawn of history has occurred since 1935.

The success of a pharmaceutical company depends fundamentally on the quality of its Research and Development and marketing activities. At least as important as the separate performances of these two pillars of any drug company is the interaction and synergy between them.

For many years the output of every drug company was driven by its Research and Development department. Marketing was simply the selling annex. Selling the marvellous products generated by the geniuses in the Research and Development department was the simple task of any marketing man in a pharmaceutical company. The marketing input into Research and Development was negligible and vice versa. As the research productivity of drug companies declined, marketing became more important in the company, but the interaction between marketing and Research and Development is still a weak link in most pharmaceutical companies. In some drug companies, for example, the divergences between Research and Development and marketing sometimes contribute to an antagonistic and mutually suspicious relationship, leading to a situation where they blame each other for the lack of new products in the pipeline or the market failure of a newly introduced product. The main reasons for this misfit between the marketing and Research and Development departments seem to be due to two phenomena: firstly, they involve different disciplines with different orientations; and secondly, the people, culture, or the organization differ enormously. The Research and Development function is usually portrayed as scientific, pure, abstract and noble with a very long-term view. The goal of the Research and Development department is to invent new substances and to make scientific breakthroughs following the scientific method, which adhers to notions of freedom of scientific inquiry and independence. The marketing function is perceived as being more applied, concrete, and down to earth: notably, selling and stimulating sales. Marketing's goal is to generate profits in the short, medium, and long term, within the bounds of the limited resources at its disposal.

Research and Development people are primarily scientists who often consider the scientific community to be the ultimate judge of their performance. The majority of marketing people in the pharmaceutical industry, however, have come up in the organization via the sales organization (field force) to become product managers and eventually marketing managers. Their background is rooted in their market intuition. Integrating these two types of people is extremely difficult. It would seem that a first step in the process should be a better understanding of the complexity and the intricacies of the Research and Development process for marketing people, and vice versa.

6.2 THE RESEARCH AND DEVELOPMENT PROCESS

It is often difficult to partition precisely the activities covered by the term Research and Development. In the context of the pharmaceutical industry research can be considered to be the knowledge (chemistry, physiology, biochemistry) and the skills (biotechnology and computer techniques, for example) that are applied to the discovery of new chemical entities. Pharmaceutical development, by contrast, covers all the activities subsequent to the preliminary selection of a new compound, including its further definition, refinement and formulation, and the extensive testing of any toxic, chemical, biological and metabolic effects in animals and humans.

In the past, most research in the pharmaceutical industry has taken a scatter-gun approach. The basic idea in this *conventional (screening) approach* to drug discovery is to start from new synthetic variations on familiar chemical compounds and to investigate their effects. This approach, however, is not always efficient. For example, America's National Cancer Institute screens 10 000 synthetic compounds each year as potential anti-cancer agents. During the eight years up to 1987, none has reached the market in the form of a new product (Wyke, 1987). Traditionally, drug firms were forced to cast around for new chemical entities and then test their effects on health problems. Two important results follow from such an approach: cost inefficiencies and 'me-too' products. While the trial-and-error approach can be very successful, it frequently takes a long time to find chemical substances that turn out to be cures for existing health problems. To improve the odds, drug companies started manipulating the chemical substances of known best-seller drugs. The result often is a series of 'me-too' products with marginal improvements in efficacy and side-effects. Since the 1960s about twenty beta-blockers and twenty non-steroidal anti-inflammatories have been launched on world markets. At the end of 1986 Merck launched the third H_2-antagonist (after Tagamet and Zantac) and more have been launched since.

An alternative approach to the traditional 'screening' methodology, the *rational drug discovery*, starts from diseases and through the understanding of these diseases tries to develop chemical substances that can modify (and hopefully cure) the causes of the disease. More specifically, this scientific methodology starts off with a hypothesis about the etymology of the *target disease*, and via a receptor or an enzyme, one tries to develop chemical substances that can selectively modify the targeted disease (Williams and Glenn, 1987). Sir James Black, the discoverer of beta-blockers and H_2-antagonists is considered to be one of the first proponents of this more rational drug discovery approach. This approach is becoming more feasible as our understanding of the body's biological and physiological processes improves. The integration of computer technology in drug invention has also been a contributing factor in the boom of rational drug development. Clearly, this rational drug discovery approach will create substantive opportunities for the integration of Research and Development and marketing. When the trial and error approach and its intrinsic stochasticity will be replaced by a more direct disease-targeting approach, the marketing inputs become relevant for Research and Development at a much earlier stage in the Research and Development process.

A third and complementary approach, *biotechnology*, is helping to take the rational approach to drug development another step forward. It can be viewed as essentially a back-to-nature method of drug research. Biotechnology itself is not a new concept, since techniques for manipulating such micro-organisms as yeast for human benefit have existed for thousands of years in applications like baking and brewing. The more recent use of this term identifies the dramatically different scale of intervention that is now possible using micro-organisms and organic molecules that have been modified using genetic engineering, or as it is more correctly termed recombinant DNA technology (rDNA). Recombinant DNA technology is a group of techniques that allow the direct manipulation of the molecule which makes up the genetic material, in the form of genes and chromosomes, of all living organisms (Fincham, 1983). From a practical point of view, this knowledge of the genetic code has also allowed the determination of the composition and structure of the proteins that are the end products of the stored genetic blueprint. Since proteins perform most of the necessary functions in any living cell, understanding them has been the key to unlocking a whole host of information about living processes.

Biotechnology has three main effects on the pharmaceutical industry. Firstly, the techniques involved can substitute for conventional methods of production, such as chemical synthesis and extraction from tissue, in the creation of new drug equivalent products. Secondly, biotechnology can be used to produce large amounts of scarce biological compounds, for example certain regulatory proteins. Finally, and perhaps in the long term most importantly, biotechnology yields basic knowledge about living cells on which future research can be based.

The advent of biotechnology has led to the creation and rapid growth of a whole new industry and has also had enormous effect on some existing sectors, and none more so than in pharmaceuticals. Pharmaceutical companies, with their vast experience of biological production methods, were uniquely suited to take advantage of these new techniques and to integrate them into their existing Research and Development systems (Figure 6.1).

While the impact of biotechnology on the pharmaceutical industry has been enormous, there are still a number of obstacles to be overcome. The use of genetically-derived proteins as drugs has a number of limitations, including one of administration. Since proteins are broken down in the stomach, these preparations must be injected. This problem is likely to be overcome in the not too distant future, but

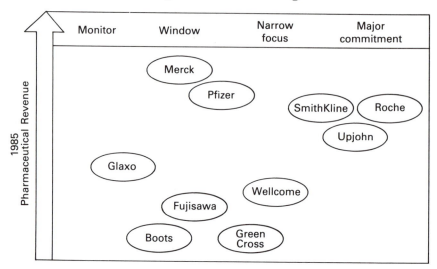

| Monitor | Window | Narrow focus | Major commitment |

Figure 6.1   Strategies to participate in biotechnology (ADL Spectrum, Jan. 1987)

more immediately it does present a problem for marketing proteins, one that is confounded by additional problems, such as the likelihood of side-effects. In addition, when these proteins are used as drugs for humans, they are subject to an array of government regulations concerning their testing and registration. The latter has been a good reason why many more monoclonal antibodies have been developed for diagnostic tests *in vitro* where less clinical testing is required, rather than therapy. An example of this is Eastman Kodak's test for blood cholesterol levels which forms a competitive product when marketed alongside new cholesterol-lowering drugs such as Merck's Lovastatin.

A more pressing problem for many pharmaceutical companies investing in biotechnology is the question of patents. New drugs without the financial incentives offered by patents are less commercially attractive. Since proteins are natural biological substances, it could be argued that their development and use cannot be patented by any single company. This problem has been highlighted by the legal battle between Wellcome and Genentech, the US biotechnology company, in London. The judge ruled that Genentech's patent for tissue plasminogen activator (TPA) used in the treatment of heart disease was not valid and that Wellcome was not required to pay royalties to the company if it wanted to make TPA by similar methods.

So the real breakthroughs for the pharmaceutical industry, as far as biotechnology is concerned, are unlikely to come from substituting rDNA for conventional drugs. Rather, biotechnology can allow researchers to identify specific proteins and then to produce them via rDNA techniques in sufficient quantities to allow their structure to be determined. Then using new, powerful computer graphic modelling techniques, suitable substitutes for the active part of the protein, or conversely antagonists, can be designed. These would then be made using conventional chemical synthesis which thus allows the company to patent all its efforts. Examples in this category include Merck's cholesterol-lowering agent, and rennin inhibitors now being developed to reduce blood pressure. Biotechnology is thus viewed as a tool for the rational attack of a specific health problem, rather than an alternative source of new products. In unlocking many of the fundamental biological mechanisms, biotechnology also provides a greater understanding of the underlying cause of many diseases, which will be the means by which these rational approaches to specific therapeutic problems will succeed.

The resulting potential drugs from the basic research stage might have a lot of desirable and undesirable effects on living organisms and the human body. To disentangle all these effects, and prevent disastrous uses of these synthetic compounds, a series of clinical trials and tests have been developed. Testing the compound on animals is required by health authorities before the potential drug can be tried out and tested on humans. Before the drug can be considered for acceptance by the appropriate health authority for marketing, a whole series of rigorous clinical trials on humans have to be accomplished and documented. More formally, the Research and Development process in the drug industry can be conceptualized as a six-stage process. (The outline of this process takes the USA as an example.)

6.2.1   Stage 1: Basic research

This stage consists of the synthesis and the extraction of active substances. It also includes the investigation of the biological influences of natural or synthetic substances.

As with basic research in other fields, a high chance factor is associated with this stage in the process. This phase involves the interaction of a wide range of scientific disciplines, including organic and physical chemistry, pathology, pharmacology, toxicology, biology, bacteriology and microbiology, amongst others.

Basic research is very expensive because a large number of projects are necessary to generate a small number of leads worthy of further investigation. It is difficult to put a time frame on basic research. It is currently estimated that on average 10 000 chemical compounds have to be investigated for every successful new-product introduction (Humer, 1987).

6.2.2   Stage 2: Preclinical pharmacology

In this phase of the Research and Development process the successful substances from basic research are tested on animals. This phase includes the testing of the pharmacological activities of the chemical compounds and their toxic and adverse effects.

On average, 10 000 projects in basic research generate ten projects to be tested in the preclinical phase. This phase is much less expensive than the basic research phase and can take up to three years.

At the end of the preclinical pharmacology stage, the company is required to file an investigatory new drug application (IND). By imposing this process the government, in the form of the Food and Drug Administration (FDA), controls the research process by avoiding the testing on humans of drugs that are too toxic. Similar systems apply in Europe and Japan.

6.2.3   Stage 3: Clinical testing: phase 1

In the first phase of clinical testing the chemical substances that have passed the preclinical pharmacology stage (approximately 50%) are tested for their essential pharmacokinetic parameters and to establish tolerance levels in patients. In this phase, the first tests on healthy humans are performed to check the absorption, distribution, metabolism and elimination of the molecules in the human body. About 60% of the tested drugs pass this stage.

6.2.4   Stage 4: Clinical testing: phase 2

Tests in this phase of the Research and Development process are designed to confirm the pharmacological properties of the drug proven for animals. This stage involves posology tests and the drug is tested against placebos. Again about 60% of the drugs tested in this phase pass the hurdle.

6.2.5 Stage 5: Clinical testing: phase 3

This is the last phase before submitting the drug to the FDA as a new drug application (NDA). In phase 3, the emphasis is on the efficacy and safety of the drug as compared to placebos and reference drugs.

The drug is also tested among a range of human volunteers (varying in age, sex, etc.) and several reference drugs are used as points of comparison.

This third phase can take longer than phases 1 and 2 of the clinical testing and is usually more expensive. On the average about 60% of the drugs tested in phase 3 are submitted as NDAs to the FDA. Between 50% and 60% of the drugs submitted to the FDA obtain approval and can be launched.

6.2.6 Stage 6: Clinical testing: phase 4

Research continues even after the drug has been commercialized. These phase 4 studies have two main objectives: to check the presence of any undesirable side-effects and to improve knowledge of the product.

Drug approval by the appropriate government body does not free the pharmaceutical company from its responsibility for adverse side-effects of the drug. Certain side-effects, in fact, can only be discovered in very rare cases or after a long period of time. Phase 4 clinical trials try to discover these eventual negative side effects of the drug.

These clinical trials are also directed at improving the posology of the drug and improving its usage conditions. These tests are sometimes performed by individuals outside the company without the company's knowledge. For example, phase 4 studies by hospital doctors have vastly improved the usage of anti-cancer chemotherapy.

Phase 4 studies can also result in the discovery of new applications for an existing drug, for example, the extension of the indications for metronidazole, the anti-arrhythmic activity of amiodaron, lactation inhibition by bromocryptine, secondary prevention of heart infarcts by beta-blockers, etc.

Phase 4 studies are also performed by drug companies to gain market acceptance by the prescribers. Although a by-product of phase 4 studies, they are important in the actual marketing of new drugs or for the discovery of new indications of existing drugs.

Figure 6.2 is a representation of a typical Research and Development pipeline necessary to bring one successful product on the market.

Years	Cost/project($MM)		No. of projects

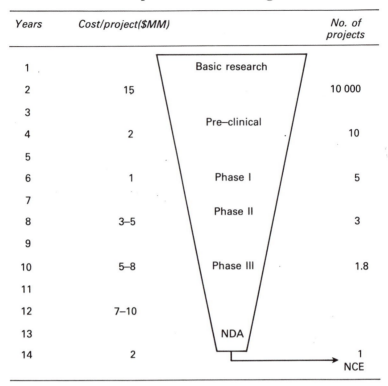

Years	Cost/project($MM)		No. of projects
1		Basic research	
2	15		10 000
3			
4	2	Pre–clinical	10
5			
6	1	Phase I	5
7		Phase II	
8	3–5		3
9			
10	5–8	Phase III	1.8
11			
12	7–10		
13		NDA	
14	2		1 NCE

Figure 6.2   The traditional Research and Development pipeline (Erickson, 1987)

6.3 RESEARCH AND DEVELOPMENT STRATEGY

Research and Development strategy is primarily concerned with the allocation of scarce resources, such as capital, specialized labour, research facilities and time, to a particular set of Research and Development projects. While any Research and Development strategy will also involve decisions on other issues (such as the licensing in and out of certain projects, the basic organization of the Research and Development function, etc.), it is the question of project selection during the Research and Development process that presents a major challenge in a pharmaceutical company.

The objective of Research and Development strategy is to maximize the chances of discovering breakthrough products within the constraint of scarce resources. It is extremely difficult to develop breakthrough products, especially with the trial-and-error approach and even with the more rational approach. The genius and rigour of the Research and Development people, serendipity, luck, and the synergy between Research and Development, registration and marketing are the key inputs to generate unique and successful new products. Efficient use of Research and Development funds is a matter of a well thought through and appropriately implemented Research and Development strategy.

An effective and efficient strategy implies an evaluation system that could eliminate, very early on, all projects that were destined to become market failures (type I error) and simultaneously avoid eliminating those projects that were destined to become market successes (type II error). This is shown in Figure 6.3.

The type I error could be reduced to zero by *eliminating all projects* and the type II error could be avoided by *keeping all projects.* Each of these solutions is unrealistic. If all projects are eliminated there is no Research and Development output, while keeping all projects would imply unlimited resources. A trade-off has to be imposed between these two extremes. Type I errors carry out-of-pocket expenses, potential litigation and morale problems for the Research and Development department, as well as, eventually, a poor image for the company. Type II errors, given the very low success probability of projects, are associated with huge opportunity costs of forgone profits. A trade-off based on an emphasis on avoiding type I errors will lead to a risk-averse, conservative Research and Development pipeline that will rarely result in breakthroughs. Putting the emphasis on reducing the type II errors will result in a more risky Research and Development approach with

		Decision	
		Go on	Stop
If introduced	Success	OK	Type II error
	Failure	Type I error	OK

Figure 6.3   The Research and Development problem

more failures but with a possibility of developing real breakthroughs. Within the limited Research and Development budgets, most companies emphasize the type II error in the early phases of the Research and Development process and the type I error in the development phases of the Research and Development process.

Even the most carefully selected methods cannot guarantee the selection of only those projects that will survive the rigorous testing undergone during development and that will subsequently go on to be successful products in the market place. Many potential new compounds – and estimates here suggest that this figure can be as high as 99.9% (NEDO Report, 1987) – have to be abandoned either early on, for reasons such as chemical instability or lack of efficacy, or during the testing phase, because of factors like toxicity, side-effects or limited efficacy.

In general, two key indicators are relevant in an assessment of a project by a pharmaceutical company: first, the *technical criteria* on which the project is to be judged, and second, the project's evaluation in terms of the *potential market*.

In general, the technical criteria for judging any particular project are the technical expertise and experience of the company, and the technical risk of the project.

The two market criteria that must be taken into account in the selection of research projects are the attractiveness of the potential market for the project, and the marketing expertise of the company.

Ideally, a company would like to invest in projects in which it has the strongest Research and Development experience and for which the risk is lowest, combined with an attractive potential market and the potential to capitalize on existing marketing expertise. To make a reasonable trade-off between these four factors, they have to be fully understood.

6.3.1 The technical dimension

The *technical Research and Development expertise* of the company can be described in terms of the type of technology used in the project and the technical expertise available in the department. The resources that a Research and Development department has at its disposal, including skills, techniques and equipment, as well as trained personnel, must also by necessity affect the degree of technical risk that the selection of any given project will involve. For example, although a project may require new basic research insights, if the company already has some unique experience in related domains, the risk may be considerably reduced. A biotechnology project might be very risky for a company with no expertise in that area, whereas it might be only a medium risk for a company with a successful record in other biotechnology areas. Arthur D. Little, in an analysis of the technical risk of Research and Development projects for different drug companies, makes the distinction between low-risk projects, which are those that involve developing products similar to existing ones (another H_2 antagonist, for example), and those that are high risk. If a project requires going back to the drawing board to find a suitable research lead, then it must be considered higher risk.

Although the technical dimension of the company and the technical risk of the project are inextricably entwined, there is also, for any given project, an independent innate level of technical risk that is due solely to the overall difficulty of the research problem that the project is seeking to solve. For example, for any company assessing a project that seeks to generate a major new treatment for a complex biological problem like cancer, that project will have a higher technical risk compared to another looking at, for example, heart disease, which is a better understood condition. This will be true no matter what the relevant technical expertise the company has in either area.

As illustrated in Figure 6.4, Research and Development projects can be classified into four categories depending on their technical aspects.

The innovator projects, new technology based on company expertise,

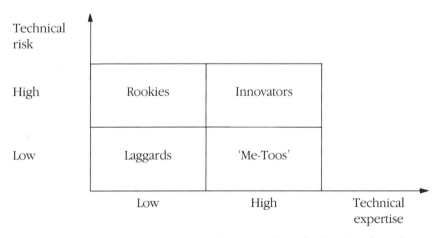

Figure 6.4   Categories of drugs according to technical risk and technical expertise

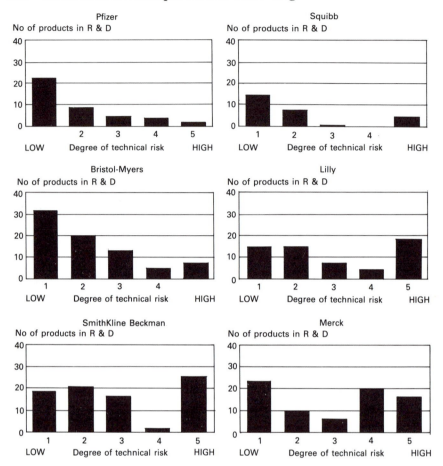

Figure 6.5   Research and Development portfolios, 1986 (ADL *Spectrum*, Feb. 1987)

have potentially high pay-offs in the long run by generating quantum-jump products. The laggard projects are undesirable because their technology is ageing and other companies probably have more expertise in those technologies. 'Me-too' projects are the result of risk-averse or defensive short-term attitudes which will produce products close to existing competitors. Rookie projects are the long-term future of the company and the key missing link here is the experience that one hopes to build up in the future to allow them to become innovators.

Comparison of different companies' Research and Development portfolios in terms of technical risk, as shown in Figure 6.5, reveals

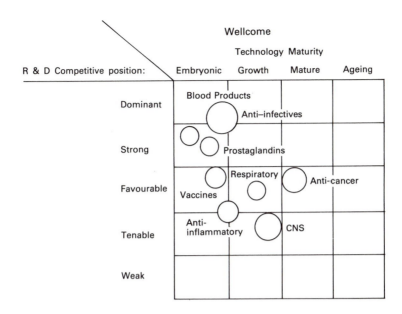

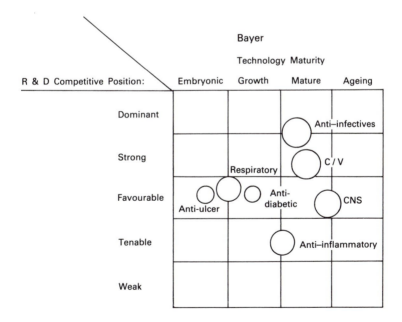

Figure 6.6 Research and development portfolios, 1985 (A. D. Little Inc.)

interesting differences. The comparison of, for example, Pfizer's portfolio with that of Smith Kline Beckman or Merck indicates rather
different types of Research and Development profiles. Where the
former's projects are rather conservative, SKB and Merck have projects
in all categories with a more pronounced emphasis on risky projects.

In addition to a comparison of Research and Development portfolios,
it is also interesting to assess the competitive profiles of different
companies in terms of technical maturity and relative competitive
position of projects in each therapeutic area (Figure 6.6). A company
such as Wellcome has the profile of a Research and Development
innovator, with a large proportion of projects in the embryonic or early
growth stages. The company's inherent competitive strength and technical expertise in the areas being covered tend to compensate for the
technical risk involved. Bayer, in contrast (Figure 6.6), has a more
conservative profile, accentuating maturing or ageing technologies
(Erickson, *ADL Spectrum*, February 1987).

Another way of looking at a company's Research and Development
portfolio from the point of view of the stages of development of the
project is illustrated in Figure 6.7. An analysis of those projects that are
in the preclinical pharmacological stages, clinical stages, or actually
launched gives a clearer picture of the global Research and Development strategies being considered by different companies. For
example, Hoechst has a large number of projects in the very early stages
of Research and Development but mostly in areas such as cardiovascular pharmaceuticals where its competitive position and technical
competence are strong. In contrast, Sandoz is selecting more research
projects in areas where it has little previous experience or established
expertise.

The shift in a company's Research and Development strategy to
concentrate on the selection of projects in areas of relative strength can
be seen by looking at its competitive profile over time (Figure 6.7). For
example, over two years Warner Lambert has cut back on those projects
in areas where it was perceived as being weak to concentrate on new
projects in the cardiovascular, anti-cancer and neotropic central nervous system (CNS) areas where it is in a strong competitive position.

6.3.2 The market dimension

Turning now to the second dimension that should be considered in the
selection of new projects, the market, the company must balance any

examination of a project in terms of technical criteria with an assessment of its overall market potential, both in terms of the marketing expertise of the company and the attractiveness of the potential market.

In the same way that the technical dimension of a company will affect the project's relative technical risk, a *company's marketing expertise* is very relevant in deciding on which Research and Development projects to support. Syntex, for example, used to be primarily involved in marketing to specialist doctors, such as dermatologists, obstetricians and gynaecologists. The development of NSAI Naprosyn was a high-risk project in terms of marketing, since it required a total change in the marketing approach and a substantial increase of the sales force to cover a totally new target-market of prescribers, that is, general practitioners (Clarke, 1983).

The selection of a research project is also dependent on the *attractiveness of its potential market*. To determine the market attractiveness of a research project is a difficult yet crucial task. Research for the sake of research and scientific recognition, as well as publications in scientific journals, cannot be the key decision variable in deciding to start or continue a research project for a commercial company. To quote Dr P. Roy Vagelos (Chief Executive Officer of Merck & Co.)

'The discovery that an enormous amount of research can be carried on for profit is surely one of the most revolutionary economic discoveries of the last century,' wrote the distinguished economist Sumner Slichter in the 1950s. To me, the key words are for profit. Turning the thought around, it would be equally meaningful to say that without profit an enormous amount of research and development *cannot* be carried on (Vagelos, 1987).

Conceptually, market attractiveness is composed of two critical factors, the size of the potential market and the degree of unmet therapeutic need. An analysis of the current relative positions of the major therapeutic areas on the basis of these two criteria is shown in Figure 6.8.

For totally new project areas, forecasts of the potential market size can be especially tricky. For example, at the time of the research into H_2 antagonists, the intended market was the relatively small antacid market. This assessment of the potential market, however, failed to identify the fact that although the number of patients using antacids was small, the real potential market was the total number of patients with gastric

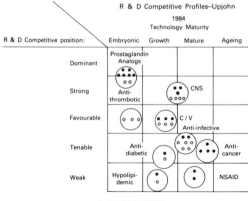

R & D Competitive Profiles–Upjohn
1984

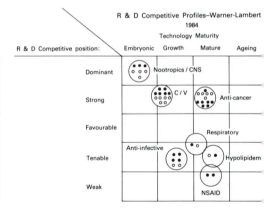

R & D Competitive Profiles–Warner-Lambert
1984

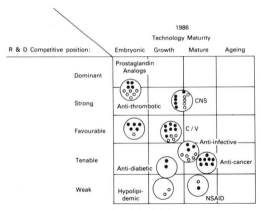

1986

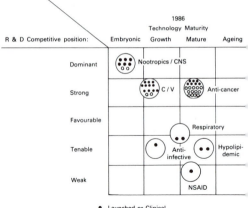

1986

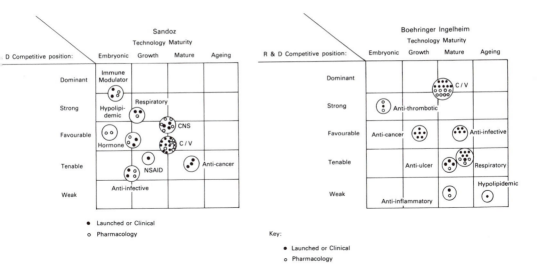

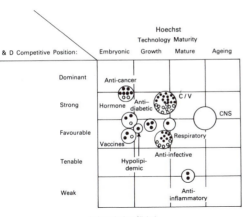

Figure 6.7 Research and Development competitive profiles, 1986
(A. D. Little Inc.)

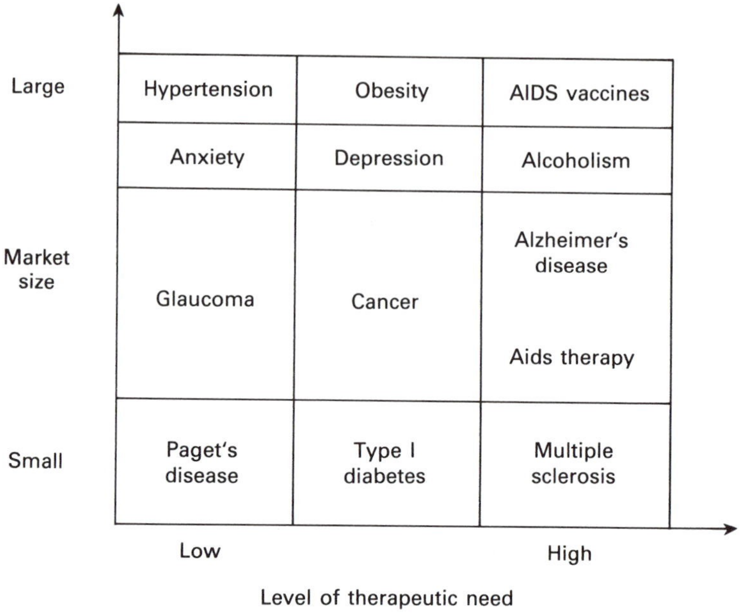

	Low		High
Large	Hypertension	Obesity	AIDS vaccines
	Anxiety	Depression	Alcoholism
Market size	Glaucoma	Cancer	Alzheimer's disease
			Aids therapy
Small	Paget's disease	Type I diabetes	Multiple sclerosis

Level of therapeutic need

Figure 6.8   Market opportunity (A. D. Little Inc., June 1988)

ulcers, and eventually those with stomach problems. This hidden market was enormous, but for most of these patients the existing products on the market were so inadequate that they did not use them at all. Once developed, drugs such as Tagamet and Zantac created their own market worth, amounting to about £2.3 billion in 1987. In this case, the failure to predict the potential market was due to the fact that the project had never been accurately assessed in terms of the unmet therapeutic need.

Among current research projects, there is uncertainty surrounding the market size for human growth hormones. Is their market to be the area of pituitary disorders, or could they also cover unmet therapeutic needs in fractures, burn healing and osteoporosis prevention? The market for a large number of biotechnology products is also rather difficult to predict. Tissue plasminogen activator (TPA) is the subject of very attractive market projections, but it could fall short or alternatively exceed them once Genentech's biotechnology-derived version, Activase, reaches the market (Wyke, 1987).

Problems in finding a large enough market for a particular project can often lead to a project being abandoned even though there is a clear therapeutic need. There is growing public awareness of these so-called orphan drugs, in which companies who have the research leads to do so, fail to develop drugs for patients with rare conditions because the final market size is too small to justify the investment. Government intervention in the form of Orphan Drug Acts, such as that already available in the USA, will aim to overcome much of this problem by providing financial incentives for companies to develop drugs that have been defined as having orphan status.

These evaluation factors, technical and market indicators, once as-sessed, can then be integrated by means of the concept of an *expected net present value* of the project (ENPV). This ENPV is a financial criterion that allows the manager for each project to calculate the value today of a stream of present and future costs and revenues weighted by the probability of success of the project. More specifically, for a project i:

$$\text{ENPV}_i = \sum_{t=1}^{T} \frac{P_i(R_t - C_t)}{(1 + \mu)^t}$$

where:

Σ: summation sign;
T: expected economic life of the new product that will be marketed based on project i;
P_i: probability of success of project i;
R_t: revenues of the project (and later the product) in period t;
C_t: costs of the project (and later the product) in period t;
μ: rate of return that is required by the company.

Projects can then be compared according to their ENPV, where higher ENPVs are preferred. When the ENPV method is used, the required rate of return (μ) must be selected in advance of making the calculations, because this rate is used to discount the expected return and costs in each year. The choice of the appropriate rate of return is a difficult matter. The *expected internal rate of return* (EIRR) method avoids this problem. This EIRR is the rate that equates the ENPV to zero, that is, it equates the expected present value of the returns to the expected present value of the costs. Projects can then be compared according to their EIRR, where higher EIRR are preferred to lower EIRR. This EIRR is sometimes called the expected project rate of return.

6.4   RESEARCH AND DEVELOPMENT PRODUCTIVITY

Productivity is usually defined as the output/input ratio of an activity. It is a measure of how efficiently the inputs (the resources used) have been able to generate outputs. High productivity levels are indicators of efficient operations, that is, maximum output for minimum inputs. Research and Development productivity is of crucial importance for the profitability of the pharmaceutical industry.

Table 6.1   Leading pharmaceutical companies' world sales and Research and Development activity, 1985

Company	Million $		
	Pharmaceutical sales	Pharmaceutical Research and Development expenditure	Research and Development as % of sales
Merck	2750	305	11
Hoechst	2320	340	15
Ciba-Geigy	2200	340	15
Amer Home Prods	2050	95	5
Pfizer	1960	160	8
SmithKline Beckman	1850	235	13
Glaxo	1850	170	9
Eli Lilly	1785	250	14
Takeda	1700	150	9
Hoffmann-La Roche	1600	390	24
Sandoz	1550	220	14
Bayer	1450	310	21
Johnson & Johnson	1440	215	15
Boehringer Ingelheim	1350	215	16
Bristol-Myers	1335	185	14
ICI	1150	145	13
Upjohn	1100	225	20
Schering-Plough	1050	140	13
Squibb	1050	130	12
Beecham	920	90	10
Average	1625	215	13

Source: Erickson, *ADL Spectrum*, February 1987.

6.4.1 Inputs

The inputs into the Research and Development process are very capital-intensive. In 1985, the top twenty pharmaceutical companies spent an average of 13% of sales income on Research and Development (Table 6.1). Three companies, Bayer, Hoffmann-La Roche and Upjohn spent more than 20% of their prescription sales on Research and Development. In 1985 the top twenty companies accounted for approximately half of the worldwide spending of $8.5 billion on the Research and Development of pharmaceuticals (Erickson, 1987).

Over time Research and Development costs have increased substantially as Figure 6.9a illustrates for the UK; the drug industry is one of the top Research and Development spenders. As indicated in Figure 6.9b, the pharmaceutical industry has the highest Research and Development investment ratio as a percentage of cash flow of the major science-based industries in the USA.

The Research and Development costs for a new drug have risen dramatically over time. Schwartzmann (1975) estimated these costs at $1.5–2 million in the late 50s and at $20–22 million in the late 60s. Current estimates put the average cost of a wholly new drug at more than $100 million, fifty times more than thirty years ago. This figure is estimated to be the minimum for a drug company to spend to maintain a serious presence in the pharmaceutical industry (Rigoni *et al.*, 1985).

Three specific reasons can be identified to explain the cost increases of Research and Development in the drug industry. First, the increased rigour of government regulation of new drug approvals has increased the need and cost of testing. As illustrated in Figure 6.10, between 1960 and 1982 the average development time for new chemical entities (NCE) almost quadrupled in the UK. Secondly, the depletion of the stock of usable biological knowledge has increased the cost for further Research and Development investigations. Thirdly, the therapeutic transition from Research and Development for acute therapies to chronic and long-term therapies has increased the need for drug-testing over a longer period of time which is therefore more expensive.

6.4.2 Outputs

A number of indicators can be used to measure the output of Research and Development in the drug industry, for example, the number of patents, the number of new chemical entities (NCEs) and, in the USA, the numbers of investigatory new drug applications (INDs) and new

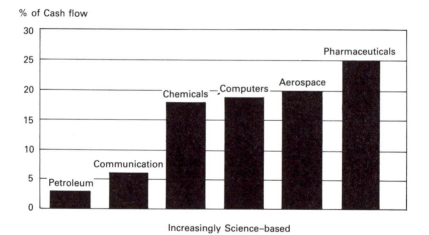

	R & D expenditure at current prices £m	R & D as % gross output
1984	490	13.7
1983	431	13.1
1982	360	12.1
1981	296	11.2
1980	251	11.5
1975	79	7.3
1970	30	6.6
1965	12	4.2
1960	8	3.8
1953	3	2.4

Notes: †All figures relate to R & D expenditure (including R & D capital spending) on prescription medicines, proprietaries and veterinary research incurred in the UK
*Figures have been adjusted by a retail price index and hence may include relative price effects

Figure 6.9   Expenditure on Research and Development by pharmaceutical companies (A. D. Little Inc., estimates)

drug applications (NDAs) being submitted to the Food and Drug Administration (FDA). According to a recent study by Barral (1987), more than 95% of all new products developed in the drug industry between 1975 and 1986 originated in nine countries (USA, Japan, West

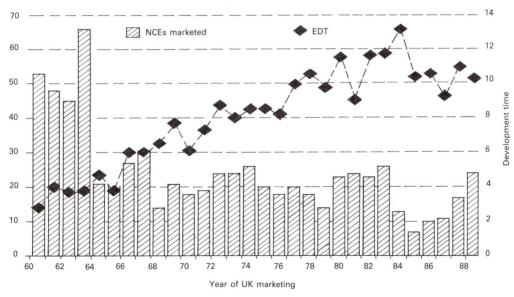

Source: Center for Medicines Research, 1990

Figure 6.10   Increase in development times for NCEs marketed in the UK, 1960–82 (Ravenscroft and Walker, 1983; updated, Centre for Medicines Research, 1990)

Germany, France, Italy, Switzerland, UK, Belgium and Sweden). The leader (USA), and Japan, generated almost half of all new products brought onto the market in the period from 1975 to 1986.

An independent study by Von Reis-Arndt (1987) focusing on new chemical entities (Figure 6.11), illustrates how the output of Research and Development has fallen over time. Several reasons have been cited for this decline.

1. Since the cost per Research and Development project has risen so quickly, companies now tend to select their projects more carefully. Those projects whose expected outcomes are less certain are dropped more rapidly than before.
2. A plateau in the level of commercially viable biological knowledge has been reached. The easy drugs have all been developed!
3. The greater rigour of the development and testing requirements have greatly lengthened development times for new drugs and reduced the output.

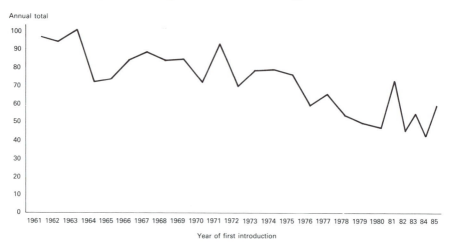

Figure 6.11   Annual totals of NCEs, 1961–85 (Von Reis-Arndt, 1987)

Not only the quantity but also the 'quality' of the new drugs coming out of Research and Development and onto the market is disappointing. In an extensive study of new product introductions between 1975 and 1986, Barral (1987) provides empirical evidence for the frequently mentioned problem of 'me-too' products in the pharmaceutical industry. The author studied all new drugs (new chemical molecules or biological entities) made available to the medical profession for the first time after 1 January 1975 (until the end of 1986) in a least one of the following seven countries: USA, Japan, UK, West Germany, Switzerland, France and Italy. By using the judgements of a number of experts (medical doctors, pharmacists, pharmacologists etc.) all new chemical entities and all new biological entities were evaluated in terms of their newness in chemical structure and their therapeutic improvements. As a result, all new products considered (610) were classified into four categories as indicated in Figure 6.12.

The new drugs embodying a therapeutic improvement or a new chemical structure were in a minority, thus confirming the 'me-too' syndrome in the Research and Development output of the drug industry. It is sometimes argued that this 'me-too' syndrome is caused by the fact that government doesn't discourage the marketing of 'me-too' drugs. By financial means (for example, low reimbursement percentages) or by non-approval for marketing, governments could drastically reduce the number of 'me-too' drugs introduced on the market. The

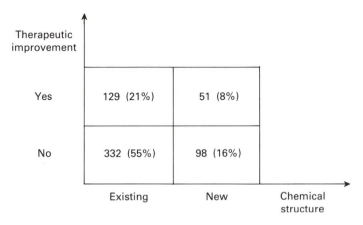

Figure 6.12   Attribution of new drugs (Barral, 1987)

problem with such a government policy would be that it would increase the riskiness of Research and Development projects. If all 'me-toos' were severely penalized, all but the front runners would be latecomers. In a number of cases companies start research projects to develop unique new products, but because of timing problems – that is, a competitor was faster in getting the product to the government approval stage – they end up with 'me-too' products. This is illustrated in Table 6.2.

This 'me-tooism' favours large drug companies, thus increasing concentration in the industry. Furthermore, the industry argues that, although they pursue research in areas that have already proved to be successful, the final outcome of the research might produce a valuable novel drug. Indeed, minor molecular variation on an existing product might produce dramatic differences in the end products. For example, thiazide diuretics for hypertension and oral hypoglaecemics for diabetes originated from minor modifications to the anti-microbial sulphanilamide. Moreover, the industry argues that these 'me-too' products will increase the competition among drugs and thus will probably reduce price levels. Finally, it can be argued that the classification of a product as a 'me-too' is rather arbitrary. Most products that are often considered as 'me-too' do differ, albeit slightly, from existing products. Eliminating these products will reduce the choice of drugs available to the prescriber.

Coupled with the increased Research and Development investments,

Table 6.2   UK patent filing dates to illustrate common pick-ups of scientific leads

Talampicillin (ampicillin derivative with improved oral absorption)	
– Company A priority date	9/6/71
– Company B priority date	15/6/71

Clavulanic acid (B-lactamase inhibitor for combination with penicillins)	
– Company A priority dates	20/4/74 – 11/12/74
– Company B priority date UK	7/2/75

Benzamides as anti-psychotic agents
– Company A and Company B dates within days of each other

B agonists as thermogenic drugs in obesity
– Company A and Company B dates within weeks of each other
– Company C also very close

Source: NEDO, 1987

the reduction in Research and Development output (in quantity and quality) has major implications for the drug industry.

First, higher costs and less output will lead to reduced profit levels. Second, increased concentration in the industry will continue because of the requisite ever-increasing Research and Development expenditures that exclude small-scale operations. If a research-based pharmaceutical company has to invest $100 million yearly in Research and Development in order to be viable, and given a Research and Development/sales ratio of approximately 14% for such companies, an annual turnover of about $750 million is implied for survival. To some extent the rational Research and Development approach and biotechnology might reverse this trend for the initial stages of Research and Development. Indeed, smaller Research and Development investments in biotechnology can be productive because the research can be aimed more directly at specific diseases. The development and testing of these biotechnology drugs will require large investments, and small companies developing them will have to rely on large companies for the testing and marketing. Thirdly, government regulatory bodies will be under pressure to reduce the long lead times necessary to evaluate new drug applications and/or extend their patent life. Fourth, the abundance of 'me-too' products will put more emphasis on non-product benefits to develop credible differential advantages, i.e., the creative marketing input will become more and more important in the pharmaceutical industry. Overall, however, the drug companies are paying for the very high premium that society places on the safety of the drugs it consumes.

To counterbalance the rather pessimistic view on declining Research and Development output, a majority of industry leaders are convinced that we are currently witnessing the second revolution in Research and Development output. The first revolution, 'the intercellular era', will be known to posterity for its discovery of anti-infective drugs. We are currently in the early stages of the second revolution, 'the intracellular era' based on new Research and Development technologies such as biotechnology, and a vastly improved biological knowledge of living organisms. The drug industry has great expectations for quantum-jump discoveries in the next few years in such areas as vascular diseases, cancer therapy, central nervous system therapies, Alzheimer's disease, new anti-depressants, ACE inhibitors, cholesterol-lowering agents, anti-viral agents, non-addictive anxiolytics, transdermal therapeutic systems, memory enhancers, weight control and hair restorers. In a survey of 227 leading biomedical scientists commissioned by Bristol-Myers, it was predicted that by the turn of the century cures would be available for AIDS, two out of three cancers, psychoanalysis would be severely reduced by new CNS drugs, and life expectancy at birth would be raised to over one hundred years for both men and women. The *Financial Times*, an astute observer, concluded its comment on this study, however, by remarking that 'no one presses [by the end of the century] a cure for the common cold' (Loshak, 1987).

6.5   MARKETING AND RESEARCH AND DEVELOPMENT

Consider this cautionary tale: once upon a time there was a leading pharmaceutical company in the final stages of developing a major new drug. Unfortunately the Research and Development director forbade his staff to talk to the Marketing Department – and the Marketing director reciprocated. One fine day the project was completed. The dossier was ready for submission; the tablets – three times per day – and packaging were finalized. The Marketing director's reaction, however, was not to accept the new product with thanks, but to turn it down as unmarketable: 'Twice per day or forget it!' was his reaction, which prevailed. Eighteen months later, new dossiers were ready for submission. The product turned out to be an enormous success and is currently in the top ten of ethical best-sellers worldwide. The delay, however, probably cost the company at least $300 million in unrealized profits.

During the recent visit to another pharmaceutical company by an interdepartmental group, the Research and Development project manager of the host company was discussing professional relations with the marketing member of the visiting party. Not realizing the status of her visitor, however, the project manager commented on the bad experiences she had had with her marketing department. 'Nowadays, we don't let them have any say at all before the registration dossier is ready for submission,' she said. Ironically, this same company had recently developed to registration submission a compound that one broker's analyst had described as 'a product in search of a market' (Ansell, 1987).

Mountains of evidence exist to show that, in general, one of the key factors of new product success is the degree of integration of Research and Development and marketing resources (Cooper, 1985; Crawford, 1983). Market-driven, as opposed to technology- (or Research and Development) driven new products have a significantly higher success rate. A market-driven process is a process by which marketing analyzes customer needs and discovers unsatisfied needs and market gaps, communicates those to Research and Development and works together with Research and Development in bringing the newly-developed product to the market. It does *not* imply that marketing takes over the Research and Development task. It simply points to the fact that marketing factors should be integrated during, and not only after, the Research and Development process.

Blending the marketing function with the Research and Development function is one of the most challenging tasks in any modern pharmaceutical company. The task is not unique to the pharmaceutical industry. High-tech industries all face similar problems integrating the marketing function into the development of new products; the continuous conflict between creative and account executives in advertising agencies is another instance of the same kind of problem. In most industrial goods companies, coordinating the Research and Development and marketing functions still has a long way to go.

The link between Research and Development and marketing is particularly difficult in the pharmaceutical industry for three fundamental reasons.

First, the still predominant *trial and error nature of basic research.*

Due to the limited knowledge of the functioning of the human body, targeting basic research at specific (unmet) therapeutic needs pin-pointed or defined by marketing is rather difficult. The development of Ultra Pampers, freeze-dried coffee, decaffeinated coffee, light beer, and the Apple Mackintosh PC, were all the results of close interactions between Research and Development and marketing. Both consumer and industrial goods research is more rational, based on advanced knowledge of the basic sciences of physics and chemistry, and the unsatisfied needs can be more clearly defined and specified by marketing. To the extent that basic research in the drug industry will become more 'rational', a systematic interaction between research and marketing will become more fruitful. The way Merck Sharp and Dohme came up with Mevacor and Vasotec is illustrative of the integration problems of marketing and Research and Development.

> Early on, we looked at those biomedical disciplines that we thought were going to be critical and concentrated on a small number of fields. About twelve years ago, for example, we selected key enzymes as targets. We felt that if we could affect the rate of activity of these enzymes, we had a crack at modifying disease processes, and we were right. Drugs such as Vasotec, for control of high blood pressure, and Mevacor, a cholesterol-lowering agent, grew out of this research (Vagelos, 1987).

A second, and compounding, factor that makes it difficult to integrate marketing requests and Research and Development activities is that *market testing* is very special in the drug industry. If in the development of freeze-dried coffee a test market points out some problems in the product no serious harm is done. If a new lung cancer drug has serious side-effects, permanent damage could be inflicted upon the human beings involved in the tests.

A third factor is the *relative dominance* of Research and Development over marketing in pharmaceutical companies, which doesn't contribute to a smooth integration of marketing in the Research and Development decision-making process.

In the pharmaceutical industry marketing has been traditionally involved in two aspects of the Research and Development process. First, marketing usually plays a role in defining the nature of the clinical studies undertaken in terms of the desired claim structure to be tested, in order to create a defensible differential advantage for the product when launched into the market place.

Most companies have set up project teams, re-grouping marketing, registration and clinical researchers, to guide and provide inputs for the clinical trial process. In some companies these teams get involved in the process as early as the preclinical phase. In other companies the project team only gets involved at phase 3 of the clinical trial process. The formal power of these groups differs greatly from company to company, ranging from providing 'I wish' recommendations to 'Stop-Go' power. Given the different market situations in different countries, 'I wish' teams are usually set up in the country subsidiaries of large multi-national companies to provide local inputs to the centralized Research and Development department. The further down the clinical trial process, the stronger the impact of the project team on specifying the way the process is run, until at phase 4 the marketing team usually takes over the responsibility for clinical trials. In fact, in most countries phase 4 is seen as the first stage in the marketing process to get opinion leaders to try the new drug and, as such, start the adoption process of the new drug.

Second, marketing also contributes to Research and Development by suggesting directions for Research and Development efforts to defend existing products by broadening claims, discovering evidence for new indications and creating new dosage forms and formulations. Given the reduced output rate of new products and the predominance of 'me-too' products, these defensive strategies have become vital for the continued profitability of pharmaceutical companies. It is sometimes claimed by industry specialists that as much as 20% to 25% of the Research and Development budgets of pharmaceutical companies are directed at such defensive strategies.

How much interaction is actually necessary between Research and Development and marketing? Three frequently encountered positions in the industry can be summarized as follows.

1. *Research and marketing activities have to be kept separate.* Dr Janssen, the world-renowned researcher from Janssen Pharmaceut-icals (now part of Johnson & Johnson), is a typical proponent of this thesis. According to this approach, research-oriented personnel tend to look at problems and possible solutions and so can open up new markets (as Janssen himself has done with, e.g., the imidazoles in mycology) and a scientific background is essential for the identifi-cation of superior products.

2. *Marketing and Research and Development have to work closely together* to avoid the development of new products that are not in

line with what the market wants and to suggest the most profitable opportunities. Therefore, marketing and Research and Development should together define the basic research programme of the company and marketing should be the driving force in this process.

3. This *intermediate solution* has been proposed by Merck Sharp and Dohme's chairman, Dr P. Roy Vagelos in the following terms: 'The interaction between research and marketing at Merck has always been close. But our head of Research and Development selects the fields in which he is going to concentrate. Once a product candidate or research area has been identified, he may invite the opinion of the marketers. But marketers can put a value only on what they know and understand. When you are in an entirely new field, you have to depend upon your research organization to look beyond what is currently available toward what may succeed in the future' (Vagelos, 1987).

Organizational theory (for example, Galbraith and Nathanson, 1978) suggests that the need for integration between Research and Development and marketing depends on two main parameters: *company strategy* and *environmental uncertainty*.

First, for companies that want to be leaders (innovators) in the market the need for integration is higher than for companies that are satisfied with being followers or reactors. A drug company that wants to get into totally new products, markets and technologies is likely to have a greater need for market information to reduce the risk of new product failure. Secondly, the greater the uncertainty in the environment, including ascertaining consumers' and prescribers' new-product requirements, emergence of new competitive forces in the market and new regulatory constraints on product performance and design, the greater the need for integration of the Research and Development and marketing efforts.

The need for integration varies from company to company because company strategies differ. The increased uncertainty in the environment of the drug industry, however, is similar for all companies and seems to point in the direction of a need for more integration.

The change in the basic research approach, going from a 'trial-and-error' to a more 'rational' research approach is another factor that seems to point to a need for more integration between Research and Development and marketing. This 'rational' approach provides the opportunity for more fertile interactions between marketing and basic research. When the development of new compounds is to some extent due to serendipity and luck (the 'trial-and-error' approach) the marketing inputs to Research and Development can only be effective at the later clinical trial stages. When Research and Development can be more targeted to particular diseases or therapeutic needs from the very start of the basic research, the marketing inputs become much more relevant at the early stages.

The extent to which the integration of both functional areas is actually achieved depends on a number of organizational and personality factors. Following Gupta, Raj and Wileman (1986), three specific factors have to be taken into account. First an *'ad hoc*-cratic' organizational structure is likely to encourage integration. Such a structure is characterized by little formalization, selective decentralization, mutual adjustment as a coordinating mechanism and decision power distributed among managers and non-managers. Secondly, *top management* plays a crucial role in the effectiveness of the integration. Encouragement of risk-taking from both Research and Development and marketing managers, establishing joint reward systems for Research and Development and marketing and promoting the need for their integration, will all result in more efficient and effective Research and Development-marketing integration. Thirdly, the degree of actual integration depends on the *socioeconomic and personality differences* between the marketing and Research and Development individuals involved. Can they work together, do they respect each other's points of view, do they understand each other's tasks, do they share similar objectives, etc.?

A number of practical guidelines have evolved from the Research and Development-marketing integration experiences in different companies. For integration to 'work' the following conditions are necessary, yet not sufficient.

Research and Development people have to understand the complexity of the marketing job and marketing people have to understand the complexity of the Research and Development job. Regular interaction between Research and Development and marketing people will make Research and Development people more sensitive to such marketing issues as segmentation and differential advantage. It will also help marketing people understand better the marketing inputs needed by the Research and Development department. Training Research and Development people in marketing and vice versa is crucial, and can be achieved in different ways, for example by having Research and Development people participate in marketing exercises or by transferring Research and Development people for a limited period of time to a marketing position. Similarly, marketing people should improve their knowledge of the Research and Development process, by formal training courses or by attaching them for limited periods of time to the Research and Development department. The latter is more difficult, given the highly technical nature of Research and Development activities. STRATPHARM (Corstjens and Demeire, 1988) is an example of a marketing simulation exercise, specifically designed for the pharmaceutical industry, which emphasizes the interaction between Research and Development and marketing. This business game is particularly useful for Research and Development people to understand the complexity of the marketing environment. For marketing people, STRATPHARM also provides the means for a better appreciation of the intricacies of the Research and Development task.

The physical distance between marketing and Research and Development departments in companies is another contributor to the malfunctioning of the two-way communication between them. Research has shown that communication is facilitated by reducing the (physical) distance between the protagonists. Bringing the departments closer together, physically or through regular meeting schedules, should improve their communication and create synergies beneficial for the Research and Development-marketing interface.

Marketers should reconsider and adjust their approach to generating (realistic) market forecasts for breakthrough new products, recognizing that this task is different from that of estimating opportunities in existing product areas for conventional products. The following extract from an internal document of a Research and Development vice president of a large drug company is fairly typical and illustrates the problem.

The market rationale for a basic research project derives, in part, from the medical need, i.e., how satisfactory is the current prophylaxis/therapy for the medical condition in question; and, in part, from the prevalence and character of the medical condition. In general, diseases for which the therapy leaves a lot to be desired (cancer, osteoporosis, Alzheimer's disease) have a strong medical need and those which are either chronic or very prevalent or both have a large potential market. Specifically, if we can find a safe and effective cure for cancer, the marketing folks will be able to sell it. It is usually true that the marketing research group has the responsibility for determining the market rationale. My experience suggests that marketing people are very good at estimating market potential for therapeutic areas in which the market is reasonably well established. They are less able to deal with markets for which no effective therapy exists. For example, I know of no one who correctly judged the size of the Tagamet market beforehand. It is important to listen to and interact constructively with the marketing function. In part, the quality of their judgements depends on the quality of scientific information received from Research and Development; we are responsible for defining the product profile.

The key problem seems to be in the area of providing market and marketing inputs for truly new product areas. The currently available new-product forecasting approaches are predominantly developed for products in established markets. This problem, however, is not unique to the drug industry. As illustrated by Najak and Ketteringham (1986), similar forecasting problems hindered the introduction of such break-through products as VHS-format video cassette recorders, 3M Corporation's 'Post-It' note pads, microwave ovens, Federal Express, athletic footwear by Nike and exercise machines by Nautilus Inc.

A possible remedy for improving such forecasts might be to create a marketing research section that specializes in analyzing the potential markets for new drug ideas coming from the Research and Development department, or suggesting such ideas to Research and Development. This section of the marketing research department would work very closely together with the basic research people. Over time such specialization might improve the accuracy of the forecasts and thereby improve marketing's contributions to potentially profitable Research and Development activities. Currently, market research people in the pharmaceutical industry are fully occupied in the manipulation of IMS statistics on current markets. They are not used to dealing with requests from Research and Development people to project market potentials for truly new products. They therefore have little experience and expertise in this area. Building a special marketing research group for dealing with these types of problem might be a step in the right direction.

Top management has to promote the Research and Development-marketing interaction and provide incentives for successful interdisciplinary groups. Creating this *company culture* can only be achieved with top management commitment. The interaction between Research and Development and marketing is not natural and therefore requires substantial coaching. Marketing people are generally not technically sophisticated, and when it comes to the nitty gritty of chemistry and biotechnology, they do not seek genuine dialogue with their research counterparts. They tend to administer research budgets rather than debate programme content. Research people become reticent to discuss their projects with marketing people because they feel they will not be understood, or that marketing will not be patient enough.

There should be some *stability* in the interdisciplinary (marketing, Research and Development and registration) teams giving them a sense of a common goal for which they will be responsible. For example, a project team could be set up at the preclinical stage and kept on until after the successful launch of the product on the market. Such project teams should act as business teams, i.e., they are responsible and accountable for bringing their portfolio of projects to fruition in the market place.

The marketing inputs in the Research and Development process have to be *as specific as possible.* Inputs such as 'there's an unmet therapeutic need for AIDS', or that 'Research and Development should develop a therapy for Alzheimer's disease, which will increase because of the ageing of the western world's population', are not only trivial but are also not at all helpful. Much more helpful are inputs on the desirable claim structure or the indications domain of a newly-developed compound.

Such inputs should be derived from careful analysis of the potential target customers' needs in view of obtaining substantial differential advantages when launching the product. *Conjoint analysis* is a method that could be used in this context. This technique views new products as bundles of characteristics and calibrates the extent to which customers may be willing to give up some level of performance on one characteristic to increase performance on another. From this procedure a preference structure is derived that represents the utility to the customer (or prescriber) of each level of each attribute.

To illustrate this technique, suppose Research and Development has come up with a new drug in the crowded anti-rheumatics field. Three product benefits that are important to the target customers have been identified by the marketing group: the dosage level (once, twice, or three times a day), the form of the product (suppository, tablet, or injection); and the indication of the drug (analgesic, anti-inflammatory, analgesic *and* anti-inflammatory). It would be important to bring the product with the best product benefits to the market. To apply conjoint

Table 6.3   Trade-off tables

(a) Dosage

Form	Once a day	Twice a day	Three times a day
Suppositories	4	6	7
Tablets	1	2	3
Injection	5	8	9

(b) Dosage

Indication	Once a day	Twice a day	Three times a day
Analgesic	3	6	7
Anti-inflammatory	2	5	8
Analgesic + anti-infla	1	4	7

(c) Formulation

Indication	Suppository	Tablet	Injection
Analgesic	6	3	9
Anti-inflammatory	5	2	8
Analgesic + anti-infla	1	4	7

analysis, three trade-off tables, as illustrated in Table 6.3, have to be completed by a representative sample of target customers (or pre-scribers). From Table 6.3 it follows that the once-a-day tablet form is the most-preferred combination, and the injection three times a day the least-preferred option. The via conjoint analysis derived utility values (Table 6.4) indicate that product formulation is the most important product benefit (utility range is the largest) and the indications factor is the least important.

Furthermore, the following useful inputs for Research and Development can be deduced from Table 6.4.

1. The utility of all possible new-product concepts can be derived and the desirability of these concepts can be rank ordered accordingly (Table 6.5).
2. Going from a suppository formulation to a tablet is not as much appreciated by the target customers as going from three times a day to once a day.
3. It is more important to continue research on bringing the dosage to a once-a-day level than to get evidence in clinical trials that the new drug is effective as both an analgesic and an anti-inflammatory drug.

Table 6.4   Numerical utilities for attributes

Dosage	once a day	0.8674	Utility Range
	twice a day	0.4376	0.7768
	three times a day	0.0905	
Formulation	suppository	0.3955	Utility Range
	tablet	1.0000	1.0000
	injection	0.0000	
Indication	analgesic	0.2908	Utility Range
	anti-inflammatory	0.4652	0.3487
	analgesic + anti-inflammatory	0.6395	

It should be very clear in the messages of top management and well understood by all functional areas in the company that enough flexibility has to be given to Research and Development, especially basic research, to permit room for *scientific dabbling*. Scientific dabbling by researchers is at the heart of creativity and should be a key priority in any pharmaceutical company. The biggest disaster for a drug company, and for the output of the drug industry as a whole, is to let marketing or any other non-Research and Development function in the company be in control of the Research and Development activity.

6.6   CONCLUSION

New research paradigms (e.g., the rational approach) and the ever-improving understanding of biological processes in the human body will provide a basis for more fruitful interaction between marketing and Research and Development. In the era of pure 'trial and error' (screening) research methodologies the synergy between Research and Development and marketing was severely limited because of the very stochastic nature of the Research and Development output. In those circumstances marketing could only intervene in the later stages of the development of new products. The rational Research and Development approach will allow marketing to contribute to the Research and Development process at a much earlier stage.

Overall, although the integration between marketing and Research and Development could be improved in the drug industry, such integration should not be taken to extreme situations that could paralyze the creativity of the research department. Ideally, marketing should help and stimulate the creativity of the researchers, and channel it in directions that will be fruitful for the long-run profitability of the company.

Table 6.5   Total utilities for new product concepts

			Utility	Rank order
		Analgesic	1.5537	11
	Supp	Anti-inflammatory (AI)	1.7281	9
		Analgesic + AI	1.9024	6
		Analgesic	2.1582	3
Once a day	Tablet	Anti-inflammatory	2.3326	2
		Analgesic + AI	2.5069	1
		Analgesic	1.1582	17
	Injection	Anti-inflammatory	1.3326	15
		Analgesic + AI	1.5069	12
		Analgesic	1.1239	19
	Supp	Anti-inflamatory	1.2983	16
		Analgesic + AI	1.4726	13
		Analgesic	1.7284	8
Twice a day	Tablet	Anti-inflammatory	1.9028	5
		Analgesic + AI	2.0771	4
		Analgesic	.7284	24
	Injection	Anti-inflammatory	.9028	21
		Analgesic + AI	.0771	27
		Analgesic	.7768	22
	Supp	Anti-inflammatory	.9512	20
		Analgesic + AI	1.1255	18
		Analgesic	1.3813	14
Three times a day	Tablet	Anti-inflammatory	1.5557	10
		Analgesic + AI	1.7300	7
		Analgesic	.3813	26
	Injection	Anti-inflammatory	.5557	25
		Analgesic + AI	.7300	23

REFERENCES

ADL (1987) Pharmaceuticals, *Spectrum*, February, pp. 1–13.

Ansell, J. (1987) Across the Great Divide: Research and Development and marketing cooperation, *Pharmaceutical Executive*, December, pp. 30–5.

Barral, E. (1987) *Douze ans de Resultats de la Recherche Pharmaceutique, 1975–86*, Prospective et Santé Publique, Paris.

Clarke, D. (1983) *Syntex Laboratories*, Harvard Business School, Case 0–584–033.

Cooper, R. (1985) Selecting Winning New Projects: Using the Newprod System, *Journal of Product Innovation Management*, March, pp. 38–44.

Corstjens, M. and Demeire, E. (1988) *Stratpharm*, Prism, Fontainebleau.

Crawford, C. (1983) *New Product Management*, R. D. Irwin, Homewood, Illinois.

Erickson, (1987), Pharmaceuticals, *Spectrum*, A. D. Little, February, pp. 1–13.

Galbraith, J. and Nathanson, P. (1978) *Strategy Implementation: The role of structure and process*, West, St Paul, Minnesota.

Gupta, A., Raj, S. and Wileman, D. (1986) A Model for Studying Research and Development – Marketing Interface in the Product Innovation Process, *Journal of Marketing*, April.

Little, A. D. (1987) Biotechnology products and technologies, *Spectrum*, January, pp. 1–7.

Little, A. D. (1988) Leadership in 2001, Technology and Markets, *A. D. Little Decision Resources*, June, p. 16.

Loshak, R. (1987) Daunting Investment Needed, *Financial Times*, October 1.

Najak, P. and Ketteringham, J. (1986) *Breakthroughs*, Rawson Associates, New York.

Ravenscroft, M. and Walker, S. (1987) *Innovation as Assessed by New Chemical Entities Marketed in the UK Between 1960 and 1982*, Paper presented at the July 1983 meeting of the British Pharmacological Society, NEDO (National Development Office), Pharmaceuticals, Focus on R & D, Economic Development Committee.

Rigoni, R., Griffiths, A. and Laing, W. (1985) *Pharmaceutical Multinationals: Polemics, perceptions and paradoxes*, IRM Multinational Report, No. 3, John Wiley, Chichester, January–March.

Tischler, R. and Denkenoter, K. (1966) Drug Research – Whence and Whether, in *Progress in Drug Research* (ed. E. Jucker), Basel, Switzerland.

Vagelos, R. (1987) Research and Development: Good Medicine for the World, *Across the Board*, The Conference Board, May, pp. 22–7.

Von Reis-Arndt, E. (1987) Ein Vierteljahrhundert Arzneimittelforshung: 1961–1985, *Pharmazeutische Industrie*, 49.

Williams, M. and Glenn, T. (1987) From Discovery to Marketing, *Pharmaceutical Executive*, May, pp. 37–8.

Wyke, A. (1987) Pharmaceuticals, *The Economist*, February 7.

FURTHER READING

Bezold, C. (1983) *Pharmaceuticals in the Year 2000*, Institute for Alternative Futures, New York.

Helms, R. (1975) *Drug Development and Marketing*, The American Enterprise Institute for Public Policy Research, Washington.

Sterman, A. (1988) Let's Talk: Better Research and Development/marketing communication, *Pharmaceutical Executive*, September.

SEVEN

Government and marketing

7.1 INTRODUCTION

Marketing is basically about the satisfaction of consumers' needs. In the pharmaceutical industry, however, the scope of marketing actions is significantly restricted by government regulations. This chapter is devoted to describing these government interventions in order to identify marketing problem and opportunity areas that result from these constraints.

The pharmaceutical industry provides products which have a profound impact on the health of our society. Therefore, governments all over the world play an important role in this industry. In general, the government has two roles in the pharmaceutical industry: as a contributor to the Research and Development activity of the industry and as a regulator of the industry. The Research and Development contributions of government in the drug industry cover a wide spectrum, from the research and development of anti-cancer, anti-epileptic, contraceptive, anti-infective (especially for the military) and anti-viral drugs, to the support of the development of new, fundamental knowledge via grants to universities and other research institutions. The Government also acts as a regulator of the industry. This role and its implementation varies significantly from country to country depending on the country's health care status, and standard of living. Governments basically regulate in four different ways to influence the drug industry: in the introduction of new products, in the pricing of drugs, in the trade in drugs, and in patents and trademarks.

After having discussed the dual role of the government, i.e. as a creator and a regulator, the main emphasis of this chapter will be on the four domains of government regulation.

7.2 RATIONALE FOR GOVERNMENT INTERVENTION

7.2.1 Government as a creator

Usually the drug industry perceives governments as the tough regulators of the industry. However, their contributions to the Research and Development activity of the drug industry should not be underestimated. As indicated in Figure 7.1 the US federal government has invested more in medical Research and Development than the private medical industry between 1950 and 1980. Although it is not obvious what is included in these Research and Development figures, it is clear that governments contribute substantially to the improvement of medical health. More specifically, they contribute to the Research and Development of the drug industry via three major routes. First, by providing research grants (e.g. National Institute of Health and the National Science Foundation) to universities and medical schools, they provide the fuel necessary for original basic research which will be useful to the drug industry. This basic research provides the improved biological and medical understanding which is often a vital input to the Research and Development process of drug companies.

Secondly, the government invests directly in the Research and Development for new drugs. Because some diseases are not attractive to research for drug companies (low incidence in the population, high

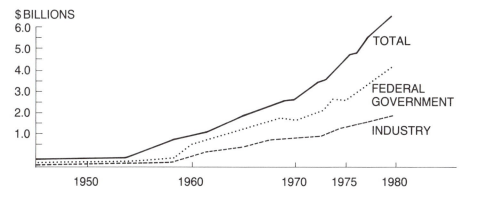

Figure 7.1   Total national contribution to medical Research and Development 1949–1980 (USA) (Bezold, 1983)

liability risks, high Research and Development investments relative to the market, high risk in the Research and Development), governments themselves invest in those areas, e.g. anti-epileptic drugs, the original contraceptive therapies and orphan drugs. Sometimes, the urgency of finding cures for certain diseases (e.g. AIDS virus, cancer) leads governments to invest in the development of new drugs to accelerate the normal Research and Development process of drug companies.

Thirdly, governments are active in the testing (clinical trials) phase of the Research and Development process. For example, drug companies are not always very motivated to continue heavy investments in clinical trials for off-patent drugs.

It goes without saying that in most Eastern Bloc countries, the government is still the producer (or importer) of drugs and as such completely controls the whole industry.

7.2.2 Government as a regulator

Since the actual health status in any country is, to some extent, a function of the drugs available on the market, the government, as the protector of the health of all members of its constituency, has an important regulatory role to play in the drug industry.

Extremists could argue that the demand and supply forces of the free market would suffice to regulate the market. In the final analysis, it is true that unsafe products will become market failures, that price competition will bring down the price level of drugs to their real consumer benefit level and that unproven claims for a drug will be discovered by consumers and as such penalize the originator. Unfortunately, there are important time lags involved in the adjustment process of demand and supply and these time lags might cost human lives. Furthermore, demand and supply forces might unevenly favour those patients who can afford expensive therapies to the neglect of those who cannot. Demand and supply forces in the context of profit-maximizing drug companies might result in the neglect of low incidence or less profitable health problems. Most of these problems are not quite as devastating, for example, for the soap industry as they are for the drug industry, where human lives are at stake.

Free market forces and price competition might also result in a situation where cheap copies of expensively-researched drugs might drive down the profitability of the drug industry to a level that is

Table 7.1 Trade balance of the developed countries 1970–1980/83 (Exports less imports, incl. Eastern bloc, excl. China)

Positive balance ($m)	1980/83 Average	Change from 1970	Negative balance ($m)	1980/83 Average	Change from 1970
1. USA	+1372	+1037	14. Czechoslovakia*	−2	−14
2. Switzerland	+1176	+925	15. Ireland	−8	−3
3. UK	+1075	+821	16. Israel	c.−43	−35
4. Germany	+945	+629	17. Spain	−59	−8
5. France	+718	+632	18. Finland	−67	−35
6. Hungary*	+195	n.a.	19. New Zealand	−75	−51
7. Denmark	+140	+123	20. Australia	−85	−40
8. YUGOSLAVIA	+111	+118	21. Norway	−100	−79
9. Netherlands	+71	+41	22. South Africa	−102	−82
10. BELGIUM	+60	+115	23. Greece	−107	−61
11. Italy	+17	+6	24. Portugal	−111	−88
12. SWEDEN	+14	+51	25. Austria	−126	−89
13. POLAND*	+13	+23	26. Canada	−245	−173
			27. Japan	−852	−702
			28. Soviet Union*	−1110	n.a.

* average 1982/83
Countries in CAPITAL LETTERS have changed from a negative trade balance in 1970 to a positive balance in 1980/83.
Source: Redwood, 1988.

insufficient to fund the heavy Research and Development investments necessary to develop 'quantum-jump' new products.

As a result of all these forces, most sensible participants in the drug industry accept the principle of government regulation in their industry. Not surprisingly, however, they don't all agree on the specific regulations imposed on the industry. More accurately, they all disagree with the specific regulations; not necessarily for the same reasons.

Globally speaking, government regulation in the drug industry has a dual role. On the one hand, government should restrict some activities of drug companies, e.g. unproven claims in promotional activities and unsafe products. On the other hand, government should stimulate Research and Development activities by drug companies to develop new products which will improve the health of society. Balancing these two types of intervention is the main challenge of government regulation in the drug industry.

Moreover, since governments are the principal purchasers of pharmaceuticals in a large number of developed countries, they are particularly concerned about prices and profits in the drug industry, especially in periods of recession.

Finally, governments often wish to stimulate pharmaceuticals as an important wealth-producing and exporting sector of the economy to reduce its trade deficit in pharmaceuticals (Table 7.1).

In Tables 7.2 and 7.3 a summary of the forms of government intervention in the pharmaceutical industry (1981) is shown which indicates the heterogeneity of government regulations around the world.

Table 7.2   Government action on the drug industry in developed countries

Country	Safety of new product regulated	Imports activity restricted	Prices control	Patent system for products and processes
USA	Yes	Perhaps	No	Both
UK	Yes	No	Yes*	Both
France	Yes	Yes	Yes	Both
West Germany	Yes	No	No	Both
Japan	Yes	Yes	Yes	Both

* Indirectly, via profit controls
Source: OECD, 1985.

Table 7.3   Government regulations 1982

Type of action	Countries taking such action
Controls over introduction of new product	All countries
Control over drug prices	All developed countries, except USA, Germany, the Netherlands and South Africa
Tariffs and quota restrictions	No developed – many developing countries
Non-tariff restrictions to imports	Common
Qualification of tariff protection	Canada, many developing countries
Promotion of local industry	Some developed – many developing countries

Source: *The Pharmaceutical Industry*, Economists Advisory Group, 1985, p. 15.

7.3   INTRODUCTION OF NEW PRODUCTS

In all countries drug companies have to submit extensive clinical and toxicological data to government bodies before a drug is allowed to be launched on the market. Safety of the drugs is the key priority, but evidence on the efficacy, manufacturing and packaging quality and modes of administration are also key parameters often investigated by governments in the drug-approval process. The process of drug-approval is rather tough in almost all countries and the USA, Canada and Japan are thought to be particularly severe. In most countries, the government intervenes at two stages in the Research and Development process. First, before the drug can be tested on humans, i.e., after the preclinical testing, governments reserve the right to stop or delay further testing in humans. In the USA this government intervention is formalized via the IND (Investigational New Drug Application) submission for approval. Secondly, the government has the right to stop or delay the large-scale marketing of a new drug after the third clinical trial phase via, e.g., the NDA procedure (New Drug Application) in the USA.

These hurdles set by governments have become more rigorous and more time consuming because of the discovery of important side-effects in some drugs that had been introduced on the market. The Thalidomide disaster of 1960 and the more recent problems with Oraflex (in Europe: Opren) are just two examples. Because of such tragedies some anxiety has developed in society with respect to pharmaceutical products. This has created an environment which encourages official vigilance and provides potential gains in the image of politicians to make the new product acceptance procedures even tougher. Furthermore, improved biological and pharmacological knowledge have resulted in more thorough testing procedures leading to longer development cycles. The experience of a number of companies is that, whereas in 1970 approximately 50% of total Research and Development resources were spent on development, by 1983 this figure had risen to 70%. Development expenditures per unit of research have more than doubled. The longer development periods have also resulted in significant reduction in the effective patent lives of drugs.

The problem for the government, however, is rather complicated. Firstly, drugs are almost all, by definition, toxic to some extent. Often, the efficacy of a drug is positively correlated with its toxicity levels. How much toxicity should one tolerate to gain efficacy? Secondly, the negative side-effects might be devastating for specific groups of patients (sometimes minorities, e.g., pregnant women) and not significant for other groups. Should such drugs be allowed on the market? Thirdly, sometimes in the case of an important health problem in society, e.g. a potential AIDS epidemic, should the introduction of a unique drug be postponed for thorough testing? Governments have accepted AZT, the Wellcome drug for AIDS, in the record time of a few months, skipping the usual minimum clinical trials. Fourthly, given the strict approval criteria set by government and potential litigation problems, pharmaceutical companies, in anticipation of a possible rejection of a new drug, might drop further testing of some potential quantum-leap drugs as soon as they discover some side-effects in a small proportion of the clinical trials. Such an attitude could lead to the premature abortion of important new drugs.

The heterogeneity of the acceptance procedures of governments across the world leads to rather undesirable situations. The USA was the forty-first country to introduce lithium, a valuable manic-depressive psychosis drug and the fifty-first country to introduce Rifampicin, an important anti-tubercular drug (James, 1977). How can one quantify the loss to the welfare of the US consumers from this postponement of introduction?

The acceptance procedure for generics is being relaxed in a lot of countries. The Waxman-Hatch Act (1984) in the USA allowed generic drug manufacturers to file abbreviated new drug applications (ANDAs).

Instead of the usual extensive new drug applications (NDA) procedure, generic drugs only have to demonstrate bio-equivalency to already approved drugs. This process also reduces the time lost in extensive administrative procedures for generic drugs. Revision of the NDA regulations in 1985 also reduced the review time for new drug applications in the USA.

The Japanese new drug acceptance process has been slightly relaxed for foreign manufacturers and made more difficult for local firms thereby forcing the latter to go for international markets. Foreign firms may now obtain manufacturing approval directly from the Japanese Ministry of Health and Welfare, rather than working through a Japanese importer.

Some efforts have been made within Europe to reach a uniform European pharmaceutical legislation. National procedures for approval of drugs have been progressively harmonized in the EEC over the last twenty years. Several EEC directives, which are legally binding, regulate the conditions and time limits for drug-taking and the conditions for the manufacture and control of drugs. Since 1977, testing data are mutually accepted. Since 1979, drug companies may approach each member state separately for drug approval or use a multi-state application procedure through the Committee for Proprietary Medicinal Products (CPMP). Unfortunately, the opinions of the CPMP concerning the grounds for refusal, suspension or acceptance of a marketing authorization are not binding on member states and do not replace national decisions. From 1979 to 1985, only forty-one registration applications were received by the CPMP. Of the thirty-seven applications received by September 1984, ten came from nine different US companies, eight from three Danish companies, three from three German companies, three from three Swedish companies and one each from a UK, a Dutch and a Swiss company (SCRIP, 1985, No. 1044, p. 5). At the national level, France, Germany and to a greater extent Italy are thought to be less demanding than other EEC countries. In Europe, Great Britain, the Netherlands, Switzerland and the Scandinavian countries, are considered to be tougher.

The World Health Organization (WHO) has also tried to promote common standards in manufacture and trade through the WHO Certification Scheme on the quality of pharmaceutical products moving in international commerce.

Arguing for international harmonization of new drug approval procedures among developed countries, sharing scientific and social values, should presumably be as readily accepted as 'motherhood and apple pie'. Why is it progressing so slowly? Maybe the sensitivity to safety issues is different across these countries, or perhaps postponing such harmonization is a tool for certain countries to favour local manufacturers, for example by demanding local replication of clinical tests. (Rigoni *et al.*, 1985)

7.4 PRICING OF DRUGS

In the prescription drug industry pricing used to play only a secondary role for the prescriber and the user. Novelty, therapeutic advantage and effective sales promotion played a much more crucial role in determining the success of prescription drugs. The increased importance of generics, however, has made the drug markets, or at least some of their segments, more price-sensitive. For the drug company, of course, the price of a drug, i.e. its margin, is vital for its profitability.

The prices of new drugs and drug price increases are controlled by government in most countries either through direct price controls, reimbursement schemes or both, or through control of corporate profits of pharmaceutical companies. Except for the USA, Canada, Germany, the Netherlands and South Africa, most governments control the prices at which prescription drugs are sold. Germany and the Netherlands operate negative lists which exclude certain classes of drugs from national reimbursement schemes, thereby indirectly controlling the prices of drugs. Elsewhere price control systems range from controlling return on investment on supplies to the National Health Service (e.g. UK) to controlling the mark-up pricing structure based on production cost (e.g. France); to controlling prices with reference to prices in the home market of the company or assorted baskets of other international prices.

Because of the ageing population and the inelastic demand for pharmaceutical products, governments in the developed world have seen health costs increase beyond their ability to meet them. Since, in most countries the government pays a major part of the health bill and since drugs represent a significant share of this bill, governments have a direct interest in keeping the drug prices under control. Each country, however, has a unique pricing mechanism. Figure 7.2 provides an overview of these pricing schemes for the EEC countries.

The overview of the reimbursement schemes in operation in Europe, as illustrated in Table 7.4, indicates the heterogeneity of these policies across countries.

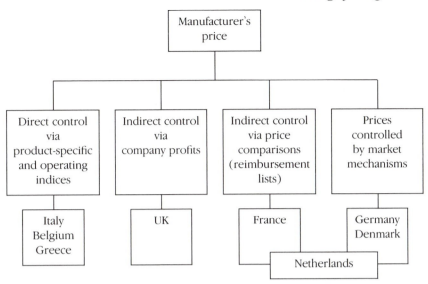

Source: Martens, 1988

Figure 7.2   Approaches to pricing of new pharmaceuticals in the EEC

The British government does not set prices for individual drugs, but puts a ceiling on the drug company's profit on sales to the National Health Service, i.e., it controls the total return on capital employed on the company's product line. In 1983, the industry's target rate of return was reduced from 25% to 17% and a price freeze was instituted. Later, it restricted the promotional expenditures of drug companies and restricted the drugs for which the National Health Service was prepared to pay.

Because of the heterogeneity of price controls across different European countries, an opportunity has been created for parallel imports. It has been argued that, at the wholesale level, drug prices vary by a factor of three between the least and the most expensive countries. Drugs are relatively cheap in Belgium, France and Italy, relatively expensive in Denmark, Germany and the Netherlands, with the UK and Ireland in an intermediate position. Price controls tend to hold down the prices of older drugs, but these older drugs are frequently replaced by new, more effective and more expensive drugs. This change in the product mix makes it more difficult for governments to restrict drug costs as a percentage of the health bill.

Table 7.4 Comparison of reimbursement systems in operation in Europe

Country	% Population covered	Method of reimbursement		Beneficiaries		Reimbursable drugs		Reimbursement structure			Reimbursement level	
		Direct	Mixed	Subcat	All	Select	All	% Retail price	Fixed amount	Mixed	Subcat	All
Belgium	82	X		X		X		X			X	
France	98		X		X	X		X			X	
UK	100	X		X		X			X			X
Ireland	37		X	X		X				X		X
Italy	100	X			X	X				X	X	
Netherlands	68		X		X	X				X		X
W. Germany	90	X			X	X			X			X
Denmark	100		X		X	X		X			X	
Finland	100		X	X		X				X		X
Norway	100		X	X		X				X		X
Sweden	100	X		X		X		X				X

Source: Haayer-Ruskamp and Dukes, 1986

In Japan the government, faced with the highest consumption of drugs per capita in the world and a significant ageing of the population, has lowered drug prices by 50% between 1981 and 1986, with another 10% price cut in 1987. It has also raised the cost of treatment for the elderly and for members of health insurance schemes.

In the USA there are no price controls. By encouraging competition among patented and generic drugs, the US government has been able to dampen price increases in recent years. A comparison of price indices per dosage unit between the USA, Japan and Europe is shown in Table 7.4.

7.5 TRADE IN ETHICAL PHARMACEUTICAL DRUGS

Except for the developing world, tariffs and import quotas are rarely applied to pharmaceuticals. Safety and price controls, however, may block trade in favour of local products. To limit the importance of foreign imports, national governments have set up non-tariff barriers such as the requirement of local duplication of clinical trials. Pricing, reimbursement controls and foreign ownership limitations have been used, especially in Europe, to discriminate against imports. Japan has been particularly tough to enter for non-Japanese pharmaceutical companies. Redwood (1987) cites the SMON case, a side-effects disaster that appears to have affected only Japanese patients. Currently, however, these Japanese discriminatory practices are slowly disappearing.

Some countries, on the contrary, have provided incentives and subsidies to attract foreign pharmaceutical companies to invest in local pharmaceutical manufacturing and Research and Development. The Irish pharmaceutical industry has been developed based on such incentive systems.

Because of different price control systems in neighbouring countries, a special form of trade, 'parallel imports', causes headaches for drug companies. For example, in the EEC, Germany, the Netherlands and the UK are countries in which some drug prices are significantly higher than in Belgium, France and Italy. As a result, wholesalers in e.g. the Netherlands might buy those drugs in e.g. Belgium. The Dutch wholesaler might then sell his drugs cheaper to the Dutch pharmacist than the local supplier. In some countries, e.g. West Germany, part of the benefit is passed on to the consumer. In other countries, e.g. the UK, both the wholesaler and the pharmacist increase their margins without passing on the benefits to the consumer.

Such a system, of course, creates problems for the suppliers. As for example one EEC study puts it: 'the sales of an American drug company in Europe might come from their warehouse in Belgium.' In the context of free movement of goods in the EEC, parallel imports are clearly legitimate. However, for a drug company to finance its expensive Research and Development activity to generate new drugs, it needs an adequate rate of return. The higher price in one country might be necessary to compensate for the low price, forced by too stringent price controls, in another country. Parallel imports might result in a too low rate of return for drug firms to invest heavily in Research and Development. On the other hand, why should e.g. the Dutch consumer (or government) pay substantially more for some drugs than their French counterparts?

Table 7.5 illustrates the seriousness of parallel imports, in this case for West Germany.

The one clear winner of parallel imports must be the transportation business.

Table 7.5   Examples of extreme prices differences, involving West Germany

Trade name in West Germany	Form sold	Size sold	Price in DM	Lowest foreign price (DM)	Percentage price differential
Tonoftal	Cream	30g	19.85	1.99 (Italy)	997.5
Tavor 2.5mg	Tablet	20tb	15.01	1.62 (Italy)	926.5
Traumanase ft	Dragee	20dr	19.66	2.29 (Italy)	858.5
Volon 8mg	Tablet	10tb	25.40	3.13 (Italy)	811.5
Anuno 100mg	Supp.	10sp	20.95	2.83 (Italy)	740.3
Volon A 40mg	Ampul.	3am	50.25	7.00 (Italy)	717.9
Tebonin	Liquid	100ml	25.00	3.61 (Italy)	692.5
Visken	Drops	30ml	21.91	3.40 (Italy)	644.4
Darebon	Tablet	30tb	26.10	4.06 (Spain)	642.9
Bellergal	Dragee	100dr	25.43	4.23 (Spain)	601.2
Adelphan Es	Tablet	50tb	20.70	3.46 (Spain)	598.3
Adelphan Es	Tablet	50tb	20.70	3.51 (France)	589.7
Tebonin	Liquid	30ml	11.10	1.89 (Italy)	587.3
Darebon	Tablet	30tb	26.10	4.46 (France)	585.2
Zyloric 100mg	Tablet	50tb	28.18	4.93 (Italy)	571.6

Source: Haayer-Ruskamp and Dukes, 1986.

7.6   PATENTS AND TRADEMARKS

Patent laws provide innovators with monopoly rights on a product or process for a limited period of time. They are incentives for innovation. Trademark laws give manufacturers ownership of a symbol such as a brand name, without exclusive rights to the product or process. They are an incentive for maintenance of product quality. Since trademarks have virtually indefinite lives, a strategy that uses the patent period to transfer the value of the patent onto the trademark may enable a manufacturer to continue to enjoy the benefits of a patent beyond the patent expiration. Since in the drug industry the prescriber is confronted with complicated, risky products to prescribe, the trademark and the company name are important vehicles to reduce the risk involved in prescribing a drug. These company names and trademarks are crucial in the drug industry. As opposed to frequently purchased consumer goods, where the brand names play a role in terms of awareness and habit formation, in the drug industry the company name and trademarks are, in addition, true risk-reduction mechanisms. Company and trademark loyalty are crucial factors in the success of any pharmaceutical product. As such, even after a patent is expired, brand loyalty towards the trademark of the original drug is an important barrier to entry to competitors in the pharmaceutical industry. The stock of the prescribers' information created through the experience with drug companies and existing brands creates a major hurdle for newly entering brands to overcome. This brand loyalty towards the patented drug's trademark and the drug company can explain the continued market dominance of some drugs beyond patent expiration.

In Table 7.6 this strong foothold of patented drugs after patent expiration is illustrated.

Although the increased impetus given to generics by the US government will probably increase their market share *vis-à-vis* the off-patent drugs, the resilience of the off-patent drugs is quite impressive due to the importance of company and trademark loyalty of the prescribers. Hospital drug usage is less influenced by this brand loyalty phenomenon because the hospital decision-maker must internalize the economic consequences of his (or her) drug selection.

Patents are available in most developed countries. The European Patent Convention offers protection to both products and processes for twenty years from the date of filing. Except for Greece, Sweden, Switzerland and some other non-EEC countries, this twenty-year patent

Table 7.6 Patent expiration, competition and market position

Brand Name	Manufacturer	Year of patent expiration	Market size* ($ millions)		Number of competitors		Loss of market share from patent expiration to 1979 (%)	
			Drug store	Hospital	Brands	Generics	Drug store	Hospital
Atarax	Roerig	1976	16.5	14.2	1	5	2.1	1.7
Compazine	SmithKline	1976	9.4	4.4	0	2	1.2	1.1
Darvon	Eli Lilly	1972	14.6	3.2	3	19	9.5	25.1
Diuril	Merck	1974	14.7	0.9	0	5	7.4	9.5
Doriden	CIBA, USV	1971	8.8	0.5	0	6	2.1	0
Gantanol	Roche	1976	5.1	0.5	0	2	0	0
Librium	Roche	1976	54.7	4.5	3	17	7.2	9.0
Placidyl	Abbott	1975	4.3	0.4	0	0	0	0
Pro-Banthine	Searle	1970	4.6	1.0	0	10	1.8	9.6
Robaxin	Robins	1973	4.5	1.2	2	20	4.7	22.9
Tandearil	Geigy	1973	6.5	0.3	0	0	0	0
Thorazine	SmithKline	1970	21.6	13.4	2	5	9.5	28.2

*Market size in the year before patent expiration
Source: Stratman and Tyebjee, 1981.

life is accepted in Western Europe*. Similar provisions hold in the USA and Japan. Canada has a restrictive patent system and compulsory licences may be awarded to the local producers. In Third-World countries the system is rather ambiguous because patents are either non-existent, or of short duration, and are often difficult to enforce. The twenty-year patent protection offered in most countries is actually less comprehensive than expected. The patent protection is granted at a very early stage of development. It is generally said that effective duration of a patent (i.e. when the drug is on the market) is currently approximately ten years (Chew *et al.*, 1985) and decreasing. In the USA, the Waxman-Hatch Act (1984) recently extended the lifespan of initial patents to make up for delays caused by the Food and Drug Administration (FDA) in the approval of new drugs. Holders of post-1982 patents may apply for patent extensions of up to five years.

The strength of the effective patent position and its legal enforcement are crucial factors in the development of the pharmaceutical industry. Countries with weak patent laws (e.g., Italy before 1978, Spain, Portugal and Greece) have a rather weak national pharmaceutical industry. Patent protection was a necessary condition for the Japanese pharmaceutical industry to develop after 1976.

7.7 OTHER INTERVENTIONS

The government intervenes in other ways in the industry. For example, it controls manufacturing process and facilities standards as well as laboratory facility standards.

In some countries the government has gone much further in their regulation of the marketing activities of drug companies. In the UK for example, the government has established a system within their PPRS (Pharmaceutical Price Regulation Scheme) to limit drug companies' marketing expenditures. This regulation stipulates that a drug company can only spend a prespecified percentage (in 1988 6%) of the total sales of their prescription drugs on marketing expenditures (sales force, journal advertising, etc.). In addition, £50 000 is allowed for each of the top three products of the company, £40 000 for the next three products, £30 000 for the next three products and £20 000 for the next fourteen products. Such regulations go to the heart of the marketing activities and are driven by the fact that pharmaceutical companies are perceived to overspend on marketing as compared to their Research and Development investments and their profit levels.

* Italy did not protect drugs in any way from 1939 to 1978.

In most countries, governments push prescribers and distributors towards more economical drug therapies. Generic substitution by pharmacists (legal in the USA and Canada) and checking on doctors' prescribing behaviour (i.e. does he or she prescribe too many expensive drugs?) in most European countries are examples of such initiatives. In Germany and in the Netherlands, in particular, under pressure of the sick funds, economic prescribing has been pushed very far and has resulted in a powerful generics business.

7.8 THE COST OF REGULATION

Government regulation is intended to protect the consumer from potentially unsafe products. In a large number of countries, it also tries to control the prices of products for which the demand is inelastic and for which prescribers are rather brand loyal. Simultaneously, governments have to provide incentives to drug manufacturers, in terms of attractive margins and patents, to induce them to invest in Research and Development activities to generate new 'quantum-jump' drugs which will improve the health of the government's constituents.

Clearly, these objectives of government regulations are not all compatible with each other. Restricting the price levels of drugs and the rather elaborate time-consuming new product approval procedures which consume patent life do not help to stimulate drug companies to increase their Research and Development investments. It also might delay the introduction of important new products which could improve the health of patients. Peltzman, for example, concluded that the 1962 Amendments to the Food and Drug Act in the USA, which sharply increased the severity of American regulations, had reduced consumer's net benefits in the US by $250–300M per year by the early 1970s (Peltzman, 1977). It is often argued that the FDA has had the following influences on the industry.

1. Increased development times for new drugs.
2. Increased average development cost for drugs.
3. Concentrated Research and Development into major companies.
4. Increased ratio of development to research costs.

On the positive side, it has reduced the number of 'me-too' products, improved the research efficiency and avoided the introduction of less safe drugs on the market.

Another major hurdle for drug companies to deal with, which complicate their marketing strategies, is the fact that government regulations are not uniform across countries. In order to ensure that the costs of the Research and Development are recovered, it is almost imperative for a company to market a new product in as many countries as possible. Given the heterogeneity of the national regulatory requirements, drug companies have to make separate applications to each of the national authorities. Since these do not place a uniform emphasis on the various requirements, companies tend to seek to satisfy the most rigorous of the individual countries' tests from the outset. This inevitably adds to the costs of meeting the requirements of the regulatory authorities and delays the introduction of the new product. This heterogeneity in regulations reduces the possible economies of scale for drug manufacturers and creates an environment in which parallel imports and other trade distortions exist.

In his inaugural lecture at the University of Groningen, Dr M. Dukes (1985) clearly illustrates the perverse effects of government regulation of the pharmaceutical industry:

I would characterize the main consequence of fragmented policy as gross waste – waste of money, waste of knowledge, of effort and of lives. The world in which we live is not, by and large, getting the drugs that it needs, even where they exist. Let us assume that I, a multinational, succeed in developing a superior beta-blocker, a true godsend to the patient with high blood pressure which, unlike its predecessors, will not cause him to become fatigued and will not aggravate his asthma. Once I am satisfied that I have established its safety and efficacy in accordance with the current state of the art my patent protection may still, with luck, have twelve years to run. Introduction to anything like a world market will however entail convincing up to a hundred different national drug regulatory agencies and nearly as many different price regulatory bodies; in assessing my drug, a few of these agencies will be courageous or efficient; a very few will be both; the rest will wait to see what the others do. A lot of countries will not be able to afford my drug; but I dare not cut my price to them, for if I do some parasitic parallel importer from Europe will soon be on the spot to buy up the local stocks and destroy my turnover in the wealthier markets which would normally pay my overhead costs. What all this in practice means is that the bulk of the return on my Research and Development investment will have to be obtained hastily, before the generic manufacturers and middlemen take over, by hammering my sales message into physicians serving perhaps only the 5% most affluent of the world population until they prescribe my product. I shall have to convince them despite the fact that most of them have only a meagre grounding in drug therapy. So I shall have to shout, ring bells, simplify, exaggerate, take them to dinners and on cruises to gain their attention; all in all I shall have to spend on that process a multiple of what I spent on research. And in the meantime, perhaps even for the next generation, my new drug, whatever its merits, weighed down by all these expenses, will be quite out of reach of the other 95% of the world's people. With any luck I shall have earned a good return on my investment; but I shall not have done a fraction of the good with my drug which I might have done. (Dukes, 1985)

7.9   MARKETING IMPLICATIONS

It could be projected that successful marketing is also becoming a political exercise. It seems clear that there will be a growing need in the drug industry to master the art of dealing not only with prescribers, hospitals, wholesalers, pharmacists and final consumers, but also with the regulatory agencies.

The first task relates to the registration of new drugs and the price and/or reimbursement negotiations with the government. One easy way out of this problem is to pass it on completely to the registration department. However, marketing can and should play a supporting role. In this context it is crucial for marketing people, or at least a subgroup of marketing people, to broaden their view on who their customers are. Marketers are used to creating perceptions, preferences and satisfactions in target-buyers and prescribers. Because other parties such as regulatory agencies play a crucial role in the marketing of drugs, marketers should also try to treat these agencies as target-customers. Trying to understand how these regulators work and how to influence them will be more and more important in the future. For example, the Merck, Sharpe and Dohme approval for Mecavor was achieved in the near-record time of nine months. Most companies wait an average of thirty months for US approval; Merck's average is less than nineteen months. This is a crucial differential advantage (the time saved is saved integrally as longer effective patent life) for MSD that is based on the close cooperation of Research and Development, registration and marketing people and on their understanding of how the FDA works and what is required of drug companies submitting new drug applications. The same is true for negotiations of reimbursement percentages that are negotiated in most countries around the world. A 5% increase in reimbursement is probably worth a couple of market share points. In developing countries, this need for understanding the legislative and regulatory processes is probably even more crucial.

Of course, marketers are conscious of this problem. What is more often lacking, however, is a systematic approach to treat it as an issue almost as important as segmentation or positioning of their products. It is, in a way, very similar to the problem with competitive analysis. Marketing people feel they know their competition and lack the need for systematic and careful analysis of their competition.

The increased harmonization of government interventions especially in Western Europe (EEC) will pose a second challenge for pharmaceutical companies. The implication of such harmonization must be more global marketing strategies and tactics. Reinforced by economies of scale and price pressures, more harmonized government regulating of the drug industry must force pharmaceutical companies to think on a worldwide scale. A move towards strategic alliances (e.g., Hoffman-La Roche and Glaxo for Zamtac in the USA; Abbott and Eli Lilly commercializing substances from Takeda and Yamanouchi), more uniform product assortments and pricing policies will become a *conditio sine qua non* for pharmaceutical companies in the 1990s. Such global strategies have to be locally implemented in terms of segmentation, product formulation and distribution policies to adjust to idosyncratic local situations. 'Think globally, act locally' seem to be the buzzwords for the near future. It will imply an even more delicate balance between headquarters pushing for globalization, and subsidiaries pushing more for local adjustments.

In the context of the further move towards a single European (EEC) market a number of harmonization mechanisms will be accelerated (but probably not completely accomplished)* among the member states, including harmonization of patent legislation, standardization of product information, Pan-European mechanisms for registration, pricing transferences and reduction of incentives for local production. Naturally, such policies point towards further concentration of the drug industry. More standardization of the governmental interventions will make it more difficult for smaller national companies to compete with the larger companies. Further mergers and strategic alliances will be

---

*The EEC's Single Market Legislation, which aims at free trade between member states, also includes (Article 36) certain exceptions, in particular the protection of health and life of humans. This Article 36 could be used by member states to slow down the move for a single European Market in 1992.

the logical outcome of the move towards more uniform government regulations in the Western world. Non-European companies will have incentives to form joint ventures with European drug companies to avoid the expected new barriers to enter the single European market from outside.

The expected acceleration of governmental push for generics and the fact that a large number of top drugs will run out of patent will pose a third challenge to pharmaceutical companies. These developments will reinforce the importance of the overall company image, trademarks and brand names as a means of reducing the inroads of generics. It will also have important implications for pricing of out-of-patent drugs. How far should the price of the original drug come down to reduce the impact of generics? Finally, it will also lead to more large pharmaceutical companies entering the generics market themselves, under their name or a new name.

REFERENCES

Bezold, C. (1983) *Pharmaceuticals in the Year 2000*, Institute for Alternative Futures, New York.

Chew, R., Smith, G. and Wells, N. (1985) *Pharmaceuticals in Seven Nations*, Office of Health Economics, London.

Dukes, M. (1985) *Pharmaceuticals: Take another look*, Inaugural lecture, University of Grownigen.

Haayer-Ruskamp, F. and Dukes, M. (1986) *Drugs and Money*, World Health Organization.

James, B. (1977) *The Future of the Multinational Pharmaceutical Industry to 1990*, Associated Business Programmes, London.

Martens, R. (1988) *Strategic Groups in the European Pharmaceutical Industry*, Unpublished doctoral thesis, University of Antwerp.

OECD (1985) *The Pharmaceutical Industry*, OECD, Paris.

Peltzman, S. (1977) *Regulation of Pharmaceutical Innovation*, American Enterprise Institute of Public Policy Research, Washington.

Redwood, H. (1987) *The Pharmaceutical Industry: Trends, problems and achievements*, Oldwicks Press, Felixstowe.

Reekie, D. (1981) *Price Comparisons of Identical Products in Japan, The United States and Europe*, Office of Health Economics.

Rigoni, R., Griffiths, A. and Laing, W. (1985) *Pharmaceutical Multinationals: Polemics, perceptions and paradoxes*, IRM Multinational Report, No. 3, John Wiley, Chichester, January–March.

Stratman, E. and Tyebjee, T. (1981) Trademarks, Patents and Innovations in the Ethical Drug Industry, *Journal of Marketing*, Summer, pp. 71–81.

EIGHT

Strategic marketing review

8.1 INTRODUCTION

The development of marketing strategies in the pharmaceutical industry calls for regular reviews of the status and the performance of those strategies. Strategy formulation without control and evaluation is a rather academic exercise. In this chapter a conceptual framework and a checklist is proposed to guide such a strategic marketing review (SMR).

8.2 THE CONCEPT OF A STRATEGIC MARKETING REVIEW

It is important to understand the distinction between a marketing plan, a marketing audit and a strategic marketing review.

A 'Marketing Plan' is a *yearly* exercise in which the implementation of the marketing strategy is detailed. It is mainly concerned with the specification of the *marketing mix* (i.e., sales force, pricing, advertising, distribution, mailings, samples, conferences, etc.) needed to achieve the yearly goals. The main responsibility for the marketing plan is with the *product manager.*

A 'Marketing Audit' is a comprehensive analysis of the whole marketing system, including the *marketing strategy*, the *marketing tactics* and the *marketing organization.* It is done far less frequently than a marketing plan and less frequently than a strategic marketing review. It is often advisable to let *outside consultants* be responsible for marketing audits. Marketing audits are often undertaken as a result of a crisis or extraordinary situation.

The 'Strategic Marketing Review' (SMR) is focused on the *marketing strategy* of the company (or the division) and usually the marketing manager of the company is responsible for its completion and nature/contents. It takes place less frequently than the setting of marketing plans but more frequently than marketing audits. More specifically, a strategic marketing review is a *periodic, systematic and objective analysis* of a company's *strategic marketing decisions* to enable top management to accomplish two tasks.

1. To evaluate *past* strategic marketing decisions.
2. To provide a basis for *future* strategic marketing decisions.

A number of elements in this definition have to be emphasized. First, the analysis has to be *periodic*, e.g. once every two years. The exact periodicity of the SMR depends on size of the company, the changes in their markets, technology and competitive environment. A SMR is *not* aimed at solving a particular problem (e.g. poor performance) but to provide *regular* feedback on the status of the marketing strategy of the company and to plan marketing strategies for the future.

In general, three obstacles inhibit the systematic use of strategic marketing reviews. First, the need for a strategic marketing review might not be perceived during 'normal times'. Second, marketing management may perceive strategic marketing reviews as a threat and as such they sometimes have to be instigated by top management. This situation may complicate the gathering of data and the objective execution of the review. At the extreme, reviews can be perceived as Machiavellian tools to open up problem areas and to identify weaknesses or errors rather than as a tool to identify strengths and opportunities. And finally, the cost of properly executed strategic marketing reviews, in an industry where efficiency and cost effectiveness are more and more important, is a further disincentive. The SMR is vulnerable to cost-cutting because it can be dropped without any immediate, visible, negative effects on profitability. Two types of costs are generally associated by the industry with an SMR, use of management time and out-of-pocket expenses. Even if the SMR is executed by outsiders, scarce management time for interviewing and data-gathering is consumed by the SMR. The out-of-pocket expenses include the fees for outside consultants or for the internal reviewers and the data-gathering costs. However, although the actual cost of a SMR is high the first time it is put in place, subsequent reviews are easier and less expensive to execute because a system has already been developed and only needs updating.

In the pharmaceutical industry two types of strategic marketing reviews are currently encountered. First, strategic marketing analyses which take place when the company is faced with a particular problem or crisis. Secondly, in situations when headquarters get involved, usually by means of a combination of outside consultants and headquarters specialists, to review on an *ad hoc* basis their subsidiaries (e.g. country operations). The trend towards regular strategic marketing reviews is slow in some companies and non-existent in others. Two important reasons underlie the desirability of strategic marketing reviews, even for successful operations: first, success can create complacency and laxity and, secondly, the marketing environment is changing and competitive activity is intensifying.

The SMR should be *systematic*, comprehensive and rigorous. A standard set of procedures should be developed to cover the important dimensions of a marketing strategy. By imposing a common framework for the SMR for all strategic business units (SBUs) comparability across SBUs is possible, which will be vital to enable management to allocate resources across the different SBUs. It will also make the organization less dependent on individuals if they leave the company or move jobs.

The *objectivity* of the SMR is an important requirement to provide top management with an impartial view. This means that the managers of each SBU should not be responsible for the SMR on their own SBU. Obviously, they will have to be involved in the data collection and the analysis phase, but they should not be responsible for completing the SMR on their own SBU. Outside consultants can play an important role provided they have an understanding of the intricacies of the pharmaceutical industry. The consultant's role can be crucial, especially for the initial SMR. For subsequent executions of the SMR, the outside consultant could act as a referee to ensure objectivity of the analysis.

Four stages can be distinguished in the SMR

Stage 1: Planning for the review.
Stage 2: Product-market assessment.
Stage 3: Assessing strategic performance.
Stage 4: Strategic options for the planning horizon.

In the planning phase the objectives and periodicity of the review have to be specified and the unit of analysis determined. The first part of the actual review provides the relevant data and analyses to make a diagnosis of the strengths, weaknesses, opportunities and threats (SWOT) of the product. This information is used to evaluate strategic performance and to formulate clear strategic objectives, which are then in turn elaborated upon in a proposed action plan for the relevant planning horizon. These four stages will now be discussed in detail.

8.3 STAGE I: PLANNING FOR THE REVIEW

Before the actual review takes place three key issues have to be resolved: the objectives of the review, the periodicity of the review and the unit of analysis of the review.

8.3.1 The objectives of the review

A SMR without clear objectives is a recipe for 'paralysis via analysis'. The SMR usually has two objectives: to *assess past and current performance* and to recommend an *action plan for future* strategic marketing decisions.

By carefully analyzing past strategic marketing decisions, and the resulting performance, an SMR should develop an accurate appreciation of the appropriateness of past and current strategic marketing decisions. By integrating future market and competitive trends in the analysis the SMR should also include a precise set of recommendations for future strategic marketing decisions.

This diagnosis and these recommendations are principally developed in terms of the key strategic marketing decisions, i.e. resource allocation across strategic business units; target market selection; and differential advantages for the products analyzed in the SMR. The implementation of these decisions in terms of field force, journal advertising, mailings, samples, conferences, etc., is the domain of the marketing plan.

In what follows the emphasis will be on the use of a SMR to plan future marketing strategies. Clearly, the SMR can equally well be used to assess past and current marketing strategies.

8.3.2 The periodicity of the review

Ideally, the SMR should be done every two years. Costs and time are the main obstacles against an annual SMR. A two to three year SMR horizon is usually more practical. The key point in this context is that a SMR is not done on an *ad hoc* basis or to deal with a specific problem, but regularly as an integral part of the development of a company's strategy.

8.3.3   The unit of analysis of the review

A SMR can be performed at a number of levels in the organization. It can be done at the level of the pharmaceutical division of a company at the world-wide level, at the level of the pharmaceutical division at the level of a subsidiary, at the level of a therapeutic group or product-market combination at the world-wide or subsidiary level. The key issue here is that the unit of analysis should be chosen such that it corresponds to some level of decision-making responsibility for marketing strategy. If this is not the case, then the relevance of the diagnosis and the implementation of the recommendations become of a somewhat academic nature. The fundamental motivation behind a SMR is to improve strategic marketing decisions and not the creation of reams of analyses without decision-making implications.

In what follows, the product (brand) market is used as the basis for developing the SMR. This implies that several reviews might have to be done for products that are positioned in different markets. The definition of the market is rather arbitrary, yet necessary. Managerial judgement has to specify market boundaries that are neither too broad nor too narrow in their definition. A product that is aimed at innovators and adopters would probably not be treated as two separate product-markets. Similarly a migraine product that can be used prophylactically or for acute treatment can be handled as one product-market. Conversely, a product that is positioned for two totally different indications, e.g. aspirin as a pain killer and as a coronary prevention drug, should probably be treated as two different product-markets. A good starting point is the use of those current market definitions as employed by the strategic marketing department.

8.4   STAGE 2: PRODUCT-MARKET (PM) ASSESSMENT

The objective of the product-market assessment module of the SMR is to provide the decision-maker with an inventory of the key inputs necessary to evaluate the current strategy and to develop strategies for the future.

8.4.1   Key data

1. First introduced worldwide.
2. First introduced in the country of the subsidiary (CS).
3. Registration date of indications in the CS.

4. First marketing of indications in the CS.
5. Dates of introduction of new forms/packs.
6. Patent expiration.
7. Current presentations.
8. Current prices and discounts per presentation.

The objective of this section is to provide the history of the PM. Given the turnover in personnel, it is important to have a record of this information which is independent of the person currently responsible for the PM.

The list of eight key items of data is by no means exhaustive; however it provides an indication of the type of information necessary.

8.4.2   Market definition

In this section a justification has to be provided for the market definition used throughout the SMR. Although it can often be somewhat arbitrary, such definition should be *practical*, *relevant* and *measurable*. It should be practical in the sense that someone is responsible for the strategic product decision for that market. Its relevance relates to the fact that although any market can be broken down into sets of smaller, more homogeneous markets, a relevant market is the one that is worthwhile (in terms of growth or profitability or size) for the company to pursue. The key facts about the market should be measurable to ensure control and evaluation of the strategic performance. Managerial judgement will be needed and should be trusted, yet could be challenged. The explicit incorporation of the market definition in the SMR is precisely to force the managers to think about this problem and to state explicitly their assumptions leading to the precise market definitions.

8.4.3   Key market indicators

The objective here is to establish the key statistics about the attractiveness of the market as defined above.

The following table (Table 8.1) is suggested. The sales statistics indicate the importance of this market for the company. The total promotional spend as a percentage of total sales is used as an indicator of the profitability of the market. A high promotional spend implies less profitability, yet it is also indicative of the difficulty experienced in entering this market by new competitors. An eleven-year rolling time horizon is suggested, i.e. five years in the past and five years into the

Table 8.1   Key market indicators

	t−5	t−4	t−3	t−2	t−1	t	t+1	t+2	t+3	t+4	t+5
Market value ($)											
Growth of market value ($)											
Market value/total pharm											
Market value (%)											
GP market value (%)											
RX (No. written)											
No. of patients treated											
Total promotional Spend/Total market value (%)											

future. This should enable management to assess the past and future attractiveness of the market. Clearly, the future projections are not known with certainty and therefore the assumptions underlying these forecasts have to be made explicit in the report.

8.4.4   Patients

The behaviour of the patients is analyzed in this section, focusing on the following issues.

1. *Size* of patient pool and patient *categorization.*
2. *Perceptions* and *expectations* of the patients of the available therapies.
3. Role of the patient in the therapy (decider, influencer, user).

Basically, the issues uncovered in this section should allow the marketing strategist to understand better the perceptions, attitudes and behaviour of the patients.

8.4.5   Customers

The complex interaction between different customer groups is unravelled in this section. It includes the analysis of prescribers, influencers, referrals, support people and adoption/diffusion processes. Prescribers span the whole range of general practitioners, specialist doctors and hospital prescribers. Influencers include patient organizations, government agencies, word of mouth among prescribers, etc. The referral process is very important for the marketing strategist to under-stand. It provides a flow chart of the different stages the patient goes through before he or she gets the therapy. For example, for an immuno-suppressant drug used in renal transplants the referral process might look as shown in Figure 8.1.

In addition to the basic flow chart, the relative importance of each element in the chain has to be determined. What is the percentage of patients with renal problems that see a General Physician? Of these patients what percentage is referred to a nephrologist? The complete

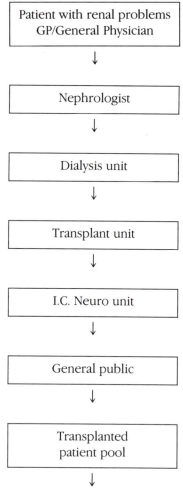

Figure 8.1   The referral process for an immuno-suppressive drug used in renal transplants

picture of the referral process is a vital input to the strategic marketing decisions.

The *adoption sequence* of a drug therapy is equally important in developing a marketing strategy. The academic – hospital – GP adoption sequence is most typical for drugs. Other sequences, for example from major transplant units to minor transplant units, are possible and have to be made explicit if they exist.

The role of *supporting staff* is often overlooked in the drug industry, although they might be very important in developing successful marketing strategies. In this category one could include nurses, receptionists, hospital and retail pharmacists and laboratory staff.

8.4.6 Segments

First, the current segmentation system (or lack thereof) has to be specified and justified. Secondly, alternative segmentation schemes should be proposed and evaluated in the following terms.

1. Homogeneity with respect to the needs within the segment.
2. Economic viability.
3. Identifiability.
4. Selective reachability.

For each segment identified, a set of key indicators has to be specified.

1. Size and growth rate for the planning horizon.
2. Major competing products.
3. Promotional intensity (heavy, medium, light).
4. Prescriber type and the key benefits being looked for.

This information can be summarized in a table as, for example, Table 8.2.

8.4.7 Competition

The following seven competitive issues should be clearly analyzed.

1. Identify competitors and competing brands.
2. Market share evolution of competitors and competing brands.
3. Brand switching matrix, for example as shown below (Table 8.3).
4. Relative importance of the product(s) to the competitor(s). This could be approximated by estimating the share of this product's sales in the total sales of the competitor.

Table 8.2 Analysis of segmentation descriptions

Segment descript.	No. of RX units	RX Value	Percent of market	Growth rate	Competing products (market/ share)	Promotion cost (high/med/ low)	Prescriber type	Key benefit prescriber is seeking
A								
B								
.								
.								
.								
N								

Table 8.3 Brand switching

t\t+1	A	B	C	....	N
A			.30*		
B					
C					
.					
.					
.					
N					

*30% of prescribers of Product A in period t,
prescribe Product C in period t + 1.

5. Areas of vulnerability of the competitor(s).
6. Areas where the product is vulnerable to the competitor(s).
7. Expected new competitive products (with expected launch dates).

The analyses of these seven issues should provide the marketing strategist with a clear view of the competitive threats and opportunities.

8.4.8 Differential advantages

In this section the core differential advantages of the products on the market and those expected to come on the market in the near future have to be specified. More specifically, the following issues have to be addressed per segment (as identified in 8.4.6).

1. How are the competing products perceived by the customers and on which dimensions are these products perceived to be unique? Semantic scales, perceptual maps, or if these tools are not available the sales force, product managers and marketing managers' opinions have to be used to generate the perceived profiles of the products competing in the market.
2. How sustainable are the differential advantages of all the competing brands?
3. Are there any new products in the pipeline (the company's or its competitors') that have a differential advantage for the future?

8.4.9 Environment

Important anticipated changes in the environment during the strategic planning horizon have to be made explicit. Such environmental changes might, for example, include government policies, customer education, pressure from generics, consumer groups' pressure, pricing and parallel importing, etc.

This section should not be perceived as a necessary annex to the review but as an integral part of the analysis with potentially important strategic marketing implications.

The first part of the SMR therefore provides the inputs necessary to evaluate performance and to develop the marketing strategy for the product for the planning horizon. At the end of the product-market assessment, a clear statement of the target market(s) and the differential advantage (DA) for the product market have to be determined and justified. Depending on the situation, the product and the available segments, several options are available. The final decision of which targetmarket(s) and DA(s) will be pursued will depend on the role this product will have to fulfil in the product portfolio of the company and the resulting company resources available for the product. This decision is more fully addressed in Stage 4 of the SMR, the strategic objectives.

8.5   STAGE 3: ASSESSING STRATEGIC MARKETING PERFORMANCE

Strategic marketing planning is an output-oriented activity. The product-market performance should be measured and compared to targets set at the beginning of the planning cycle. Measurement is critical in developing a market-driven business orientation.

Performance evaluations can be internal or external. The internal performance evaluation is based on the targets set for the *PM* within the company. External performance evaluation is based on more global and broadly defined targets. Each of these will be discussed in turn.

8.5.1   Internal performance benchmarks

The most common type of objectives used by pharmaceutical companies are set in terms of profits, growth and market share. The ultimate 'bottom line' test of PM performance is profitability, which reflects the market viability of the PM and its ability to compete. Profits can be measured in absolute or in relative terms. ROI (return on investment) is probably the most commonly used profit indicator. It refers to the efficiency and the effectiveness of the PM's strategy, i.e., the extent to which the scarce resources invested in the PM have been used to generate value. Profitability objectives are sometimes difficult to use in

Table 8.4   Orion's planned versus actual performance

	Budgeted	Actual	Variance
Revenues			
Sales (ADD)*	10 000	9 900	−100
Price per ADD	$10	$11	+$1
Revenues	$100 000	$108 900	+$8 900
Total market size (ADD)	100 000	90 000	−10 000
Share of market (ADD)	10%	11%	+1%
Costs			
Variable cost per ADD	$3	$3.5	+$0.5
Contribution per ADD	$7	$7.5	+$0.5
Total contribution	$70 000	$74 250	+$4 250

* ADD: Average daily dosage

the pharmaceutical industry at the (country) subsidiary level. Indeed, because of the complexities of the transfer pricing systems dictated by headquarters, real profits are often ambiguous. Often, in those subsidiaries, sales, market share and growth criteria are the only viable performance indicators.

Growth objectives as measured by the evolution of sales, market shares and profits are good indicators of the current and long-term business health of the PM. Market share objectives focus the attention on the PM's competitive position.

Comparing the actual performance with the target is a crucial aspect of the SMR in assessing the extent to which the PM fulfilled its mission. This comparison should also lead to an explanation of the causes of the discrepancies between planned and actual performance. These rationalizations are crucial inputs for the next phase of the SMR.

Deviations from the planned performance can be attributed to a variety of causes. To assign specific responsibilities pinpointing these causes is a crucial task of strategic marketing control. A control system, called Variance Decomposition, can be instrumental in this context (Hulbert and Troy, 1977). Assume that for a particular product-market (say Orion) the figures of Table 8.4 are last year's results.

Overall, Orion's actual contribution exceeds the planned target (+$4,200). However, this globally positive result gives no information about the cause. For example, it hides the fact that actual market size was smaller than hoped. The Variance Decomposition method provides a logical framework to analyze the composition of the total PM performance. In this framework the overall performance of a PM can deviate from the planned performance for three major reasons: (1) incorrect forecast of the *market size*; (2) incorrect planned *market share*; and (3)

Table 8.5   Variance decomposition

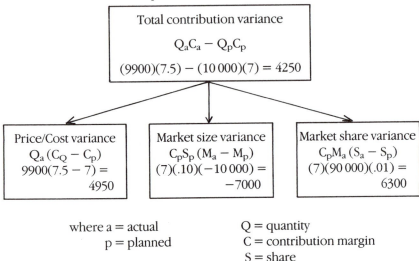

where a = actual
      p = planned

Q = quantity
C = contribution margin
S = share
M = market size

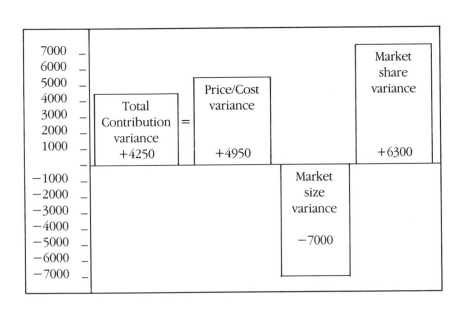

incorrect *price* cost forecast. More formally, this decomposition can be derived as in Table 8.5.

The real problem in the performance of Orion, which is hidden in the positive overall assessment, is due to a poor market size forecast. The price cost variance is positive especially due to the significant price increase of 10%. Market share performance is very good, but is completely offset by the overly optimistic forecast of the size of market.

This Variance Decomposition procedure utilizes the key strategic variables of contribution, market share and market size as a framework for strategic marketing control.

8.5.2 External performance benchmarks

The PM performance could also be evaluated based on industry-wide benchmarks. Of course, market share is a criterion that compares the PM performance to that of the direct competitors. One could, however, go further by comparing the PM's performance to the performance of similar businesses in general. Almost invariably, managers are able to rationalize any performance of their PM. Objective benchmarks would indeed be very useful to overcome this problem. The PIMS (Profit

Table 8.6   The PIMS data base

Industry classification	Percent of sample
Consumer products (including pharmaceuticals)	
	27%
Capital equipment	16%
Raw materials	13%
Components	23%
Industrial supplies	14%
Service and distribution	7%
	100%

Total businesses in sample = 2800

Geographical location	*Size of corporation* (Total Sales)	
	Over $100MM	Under $100MM
North American based	55%	35%
Foreign	10%	0%
	65%	35%

Table 8.7 Limited information model for a therapeutic group (1987)

Factors	Estimate of a normal ROI by category of impact		Impact of* factor on estimate of ROI (%)
		This business	
1 Market share index	:		3.1
Market share (%)	:	30.0	
Relative market share (%)	:	57.0	
2 Relative quality	:	90.0U	7.5
3 Unionization (%)	:	0.0	0.0
4 New product sales/sales (%)	:	0.0	0.0
5 Research and Development expenditure/ sales (%)	:	0.5	−0.2
6 Marketing expenditure: sales (%)	:	12.0	−4.9
		Competitive position and action	7.1
7 Investment intensity index	:		4.1
Investment/sales (%)	:	29.0	
Investment/value added (%)	:	29.3L	
8 Value added: sales (%)	:	99.0U	1.9
9 Operating effectiveness	:	184.8	15.5
10 GBV of P&E: Investment (%)	:	58.6	1.7
GBV of P&E/sales (%)	:	17.0	

11 Receivables: investment (%)	:	44.8	1.7
Receivables/sales (%)	:	13.0	
12 Capacity utilization (%)	:	100.0	6.2
		Capital and production structure	31.3
13 Real market growth rate (% p.a.)	:	2.0	−0.6
14 Industry concentration (%)	:	83.0	1.0
15 Number of immed. customers = 50% sls	:	3870.0U	−1.5
16 Purchase amount immediate customers	:	4.0	3.5
		Environment and customer features	2.4
		Total impact	40.7
		Average ROI, all PIMS businesses	21.5
		Estimated ROI, this business	62.2

L: Lower limit
U: Upper Limit
GBV: Gross Book Value
P&E: Plant and Equipment

Source: Strategic Planning Institute, Private communications.

* The individual impacts are determined by comparing the actual value for a business variable against its mean in the PIMS Data base.

Impact of Market Strategy) approach permits management to do just that. The PIMS method provides performance guidance from the collective experience of a diverse sample of businesses. In 1986 this sample represented over 2800 strategic business units contributed by more than 250 companies (Table 8.6).

This confidential data base, created by General Electric and the Strategic Planning Institute, spans 15 years of experience and provides a whole series of performance indicators at the level of the strategic business unit (e.g., therapeutic groups). Some large pharmaceutical companies participate in the PIMS project.

The PIMS PAR ROI report is especially useful in the context of performance evaluation. This report indicates for a specific SBU an estimate of the pretax return on investment normal for SBUs that are comparable in terms of their market attractiveness and competitive strength. Moreover, the same report also provides a comparison of the specific SBU with its strategic peers in terms of thirty-two strategic factors. Finally, the PAR (Profit Assessment Report) report also indicates the relative profit impact of each of those thirty-two strategic variables.

PIMS also provides a more succinct report, the Limited Information Model (LIM). This simplified version of the PIMS PAR report focuses on sixteen key variables that have an impact on the profitability of SBUs. Table 8.7 is an actual example of such a LIM study for a therapeutic group for a specific pharmaceutical company which cannot be identified for confidentiality reasons. The LIM report shows a comparison of a particular therapeutic area of a pharmaceutical company X (this business) and the average SBU in the PIMS data base for the sixteen significant strategic variables. According to the LIM report this particular therapeutic area for company X should show a ROI of 62%, almost triple the ROI of the average PIMS SBU. The company in question can now compare the actual ROI with this predicted ROI. The predicted ROI (62.2%) is a useful benchmark for performance evaluation by the management of company X because it represents what ROI the average manager of the 2800 SBUs of the PIMS sample businesses would obtain if he or she were put in charge in that particular therapeutic group for company X. Finally, the LIM report also provides management with indications of how to improve their current profitability. For example, the LIM report suggests that if the high marketing expenditures (impact figure of −4.9) were reduced, *ceteris pariobus*, the ROI could be significantly increased.

In general, performance evaluation of strategic marketing decisions will always be complicated by the fact that the actual performance of a PM is not only determined by the appropriateness of the strategic marketing decisions but also by the implementation of those decisions (i.e., the marketing mix). As pointed out by Bonoma (1984), and illustrated in Table 8.8, quality of the implementation of the marketing strategy influences the evaluation of the strategic marketing decision.

8.6 STAGE 4: STRATEGIC OPTIONS FOR THE PLANNING HORIZON

8.6.1 The strategic objectives

To determine the strategic objectives for all of the company's product *market contribution* a portfolio analysis must be carried out. Two well-established approaches to this analysis, the Boston Consulting Group (BCG) Approach and the Composite Portfolio Approach were discussed in detail in Chapter 3. In this particular case the Composite Portfolio Approach is proposed as it is felt to be more comprehensive and better adjusted to the idiosyncrasies of the pharmaceutical industry. The analysis can be done based on current (or past) market and product information to *assess the current (or past) performance* or it can be done on the basis of future product and market information to *develop strategies for the future planning horizon.*

The market attractiveness indicators proposed for the SMR are as follows:

1. Market size.   +
2. Market growth.   +
3. Cost of entry/participation.   −
4. Segment opportunities.   +
5. Unmet market need.   +
6. Price sensitivity.   −
7. Number of competitors.   −

The pluses and minuses refer to the positive or negative relationships between the factors and the overall market attractiveness. The bigger the market size the more attractive the market. Conversely, the higher the cost of entry and participation (i.e., marketing spend as a percentage of sales) the less attractive the market.

The competitive strength is approximated with the following factors.

1. Differential advantage (DA).   +
2. Degree of sustainability of the DA   +

Table 8.8   The marketing strategy/implementation trade-off

**Marketing
implementation**

	Appropriate	**Inappropriate**
Excellent	*Success* The profits, markets share and growth objectives are met.	*Rescue or ruin* Good implementation may mitigate poor strategy and give management time to correct it, but good execution of poor strategy may hasten failure.
Poor	*Trouble* Poor implementation hampers appropriate strategy; management may conclude wrongly that the strategy was inappropriate.	*Failure* Cause of failure is hard to diagnose because poor strategy is masked by poor implementation.

Marketing strategy

Source: Bonoma, 1984.

3. Marketing expertise.   +
4. Research and Development and regulation expertise.   +

For each of the product-market combinations an index for market attractiveness (MA) and competitive strength (CS) has to be developed. Therefore, weights have to be given to the respective indicators of the MA and the CS dimensions. Subsequently, each product-market combination has to be scored on each of the indicators and a weighted average index has to be computed. This index will then allow the analyst to put each product-market combination in the composite portfolio map as illustrated in Table 8.9.

Depending on the position of the PM in the portfolio chart a number of strategic options are available (as discussed in Chapter 3). Depending on the market attractiveness, the competitive strength and the available resources in cash, Research and Development and marketing these strategies can vary from heavy investment to divesting.

Table 8.9 The calculation for the position of a PM in the composite portfolio

Market attractiveness (MA)

	1	2	3	4	5	6	7	8	9	10	Weight	Score
Size of market		X									1.5	3
Growth of market							X				2.0	14
Cost of entry/ participation							X				2.0	14
Segment opportunities			X								1.0	3
Unmet market need					X						1.5	7.5
Price sensitivity		X									1.0	2
Number of competitors			X								1.0	3
											Index	46.5

Competitive strength (CS)

	1	2	3	4	5	6	7	8	9	10	Weight	Score
DA					X						4.0	20
Quality of evidence						X					2.0	16
Marketing expertise					X						2.0	16
Medical expertise			X								2.0	6
											Index	52

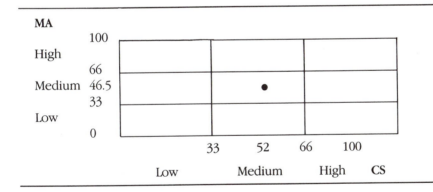

It is important to note here that the strategic objective derived from the composite portfolio is not just to decide to invest heavily, but to indicate *how* and *where* to invest and *what* the aim of the heavy investment will be. Such a statement as 'Invest heavily in PM X to gain market share' is still too vague. The strategic objective should state what the target market share is and how this target will be achieved. Will it be through converting prescribers for competing products, or will it be through moving the product from a second-line therapy to a first-line

Table 8.10   The strategic sales objectives

	t	t + 1	t + 2	----	t + n

Sales
Sources of sales
(e.g., existing patients,
    new patients etc. per
    segment)					

Growth per year Market share in segment 1 Market share in segment 2 Market share in segment 3 Market share in segment n					
Marketing investment					
Medical investment					

therapy, or will it be to increase the average number of patients per current prescriber, or will it be to move from the innovative prescribers to the adopters and laggards, and so forth? The strategic objective should send a precise message to the PM manager as to what his set of objectives will be for the planning horizon. The strategic objective should not specify the marketing-mix efforts necessary to accomplish the objective. The latter is the task of the yearly marketing plan rather than the objective of the SMR.

The strategic objective statement should also point out the risks involved in the stated objectives and a contingency plan should be developed to deal with the possible risks.

Increased generic substitution and changes in government intervention are some examples of what might be potential risks to be taken into account.

Finally, the strategic objective should be summarized in quantified objectives as illustrated in Table 8.10.

8.6.2 Action plan

The implementation of the strategic objectives is the responsibility of the product-market manager by means yearly marketing plans. However, to achieve the strategic objectives set forth in the SMR for the planning horizon of the next three to five years, a number of actions have to be planned over that three to five year horizon which would not be covered in the yearly marketing plans. These actions typically relate to clinical trials and market research studies that are necessary to achieve the strategic objectives and to evaluate the performance of the strategy.

For example, for a migraine drug the strategic objective of increasing market share by developing the market of migraine patients that are currently not using a therapy and by developing new potential indications for the drug might look as shown in Table 8.11.

Table 8.11   The options for enlarging the market for migraine drugs

Action	Cost	Responsibility	Start	Deadline
1. Set up a market research study to profile the migraine patient that doesn't use any drug.	$200 000	Head of market	Jan. 90	March 91
2. Establish a large educational programme for these non-user migraine patients.	$1 000 000	Migraine product manager	June 91	March 92
3. Arrange migraine educational programme for GPs and junior hospital doctors aimed at non-user migraine patients.	$600,000	Migraine product manager	March 90	June 91
4. Complete pilot studies in new indications (e.g., vertigo).	$20 000	Medical director	Jan. 90	June 90
5. Set up full clinical trials in new indications if pilot studies are positive.	$100 000	Medical	Oct. 90	Mid 92

8.7   A CONCLUDING NOTE

The first key to a successful SMR is that it should be *action-oriented*, either to diagnose the current strategic marketing position or to make strategic marketing decisions for the future or both. Decisions are needed, however difficult they are to make. As illustrated in Table 8.12, each step in the SMR should result in a decision.

Second, the objective of the SMR is not to generate more data as a means of avoiding difficult decisions. Although a number of subjective inputs are necessary, this does not invalidate the review. What is needed

Table 8.12   Overview of the strategic marketing review

State of the SMR	Outcome/conclusion
Stage 1: Planning for the SMR	
Objectives	Performance and strategic options
Periodicity	Every X years
Unit of analysis	Definition of the strategic business unit
Stage 2: Product market assessment	
Key data	Product history – key facts
Market definition	Clear delineation of the market
Key market indicators	Relative importance of the market to the company
Patients	Perceptions, attitudes and behaviour of the patients
Customers	The relative importance of different customer groups in the market
Segments	Target segment(s)
Competition	Competitive threat and opportunities
Differential advantage	DA in each target segment
Environment	Key environmental factors
Stage 3: Strategic performance	
Inside the company	Variance decomposition
Globally	PIMS
Stage 4: Strategic options for the planning horizon	
(A) Strategic objective	
Portfolio	Strategic options
(B) Action plan	
Action plan	Short and medium-term actions

is to exercise professional judgement, rather than to sweep tricky issues under the carpet. One can always argue that more information is needed to reach decisions. This stalling tactic, however, causes delays and a sterile decision-making environment. Only *important data* that can contribute to better decision-making should be included. Data are abundant in the industry, probably too much so; what is needed is decision-oriented information.

Thirdly, the SMR has to be seen in an *evolutionary way*. The first time it is done it will require a lot of time and effort. Subsequent SMRs, however, should build on the first one and therefore should be faster and easier to accomplish. The ultimate goal is to develop a standardized procedure that can be easily updated and adjusted to changes in the company, the products and the general environment.

REFERENCES

Bonoma, T. (1984) *Managing Marketing: Test, cases and readings*, Free Press, London.

Hulbert, J. and Troy, N. (1977) A Strategic Framework for Marketing Control, *Journal of Marketing*, April, pp. 12–20.

FURTHER READING

Shoeffler, S., Buzzell, R. and Heavy, D. (1974) Impact of Strategic Planning on Profit Performance, *Harvard Business Review*, March–April, pp. 137–45.

NINE

Implementation of marketing strategy: the marketing mix

9.1 INTRODUCTION*

Once the target market(s) have been selected and the differential advantage determined, the marketing-mix elements have to bring this strategy to the relevant set of customers. Three major type of marketing-mix elements have to be specified: pricing, communication and distribution. Each of these has its specific role to play in turning the marketing strategy into successful results in the market place.

Pricing is a key variable that contributes to the profitability of the products, and that communicates a quality dimension about the product. Generics, government regulations, and third party pressures have made the price variable of vital importance to the pharmaceutical industry in recent years. Several means of *communication* exist in the pharmaceutical industry including the sales force, symposia, journal advertising and mailings. Their relative importance varies over the product life cycle. Since they absorb substantial resources in large pharmaceutical companies, efficiency and effectiveness of these communications media are crucial factors to consider in an industry where margins are under pressure. *Distribution* patterns are changing and the increased power of the members of the pharmaceutical distribution

---

* The author is preparing a sequel to the current book which will focus on the marketing-mix tactics in the pharmaceutical industry. This current chapter is therefore more of an overview of marketing-mix issues rather than an in-depth analysis.

channels will cause pharmaceutical companies to pay more attention not only to the logistics of moving their products from the producer to the final consumer but also to the maturation of their distribution channel members. Samples and clinical trials phase 4 are also important marketing-mix elements for any drug company. All of these issues will now be discussed in some detail.

9.2   PRICING

For a long time price was not a crucial competitive weapon in prescription drug warfare. The price of a drug was usually set as high as possible within the limits set by similar products and/or the government.

Increased generic competition, abundance of 'me-too' products and stricter government control on prices (directly or indirectly) and the increasing importance of managed health care systems in some countries (e.g., US) have reshaped the importance of price as a tactical tool to implement marketing strategies.

9.2.1   General pricing rules

Three types of pricing rules exist: differential pricing, competitive pricing and product line pricing (Nagle, 1987). *Differential pricing* basically implies pricing a product at different levels for different versions of the product (original or generic) or for different customers (quantity discounts for large purchases) or for special occasions (price promotions) or for different countries (geographic pricing). *Competitive pricing* rules include limit pricing, experience curve pricing, and price signalling. Limit pricing refers to a pricing strategy that aims at deterring entry of new entrants. Reducing the price of an original drug in anticipation of a generic introduction by the competition is an example of limit pricing approach. If the cost of a drug to the manufacturer depends strongly on the volume of sales, a relatively low price can be set in anticipation of high volume sales in the future. Generics pricing and pricing of some antibiotics can be classified in this category. Setting a price at a high level to signal the exceptional differential advantage of the product is a strategy used for new breakthrough drugs (price signalling). *Product line pricing* implies that the price of a product is not only a function of the product itself and its competitive position in the market but also of its synergistic effects with other products in the company's product line.

9.2.2   Pricing new pharmaceutical products

The initial pricing decision for a new drug is crucial because it will position the product on the market relative to the competing drugs. It will also determine the product's profitability, obviously in the short run, but it will also have important implications for the longer-term profitability because it will be very difficult to increase the price later. Market forces or government price control will limit price increases in later phases in the product life cycle. The actual price of a new pharmaceutical product will depend to a large extent on its differential advantage. Straight 'me-toos' will have to accept lower prices than innovative new drugs. To quantify the market's price sensitivity a tool like trade-off analysis can be extremely useful. The following example will illustrate its use in the pricing of new drugs.

Table 9.1   Attributes of a hypertensive drug

CNS Side-effects
- 1   Relatively (as compared with other hypertensives) low
- 2   Similar to other hypertensive drugs

Absorption by body
- 1   Not affected by meals
- 2   Affected by meals

Dosage regime
- 1   Once a day
- 2   Twice a day
- 3   Three times a day

Mode of action
- 1   New
- 2   Traditional

Renal flow
- 1   Increase renal blood flow
- 2   No change in renal blood flow
- 3   Decrease renal blood flow

Four price levels are envisaged
- 1 $0.25 per daily dosage
- 2 $0.50 per daily dosage
- 3 $0.75 per daily dosage
- 4 $1.00 per daily dosage

Suppose a company has to decide on the price of a new hypertensive drug. The important attributes which will determine the price of the drug are: dosage regime, CNS side effects, absorption by the body, renal flow and mode of action as indicated in Table 9.1 (a stylized version of Montemayer, 1987).

In total 288 possible combinations of these attribute levels are possible ($2 \times 2 \times 3 \times 2 \times 3 \times 4$), where one attribute combination might be a hypertensive which decreases renal blood flow, similar CNS side-effects to other hypertensive drugs, absorption affected by meals, once-a-day, traditional mode of action at $0.75 per daily dosage. Through statistical techniques (fractional factorial design) the total number of relevant combinations can be reduced from 288 to sixteen (Green *et al.*, 1978).

These sixteen drug profiles are then presented to a representative sample of the new drug's target market (e.g., general practitioners). Based on their rankings (from most preferred to least preferred) over the sixteen drug profiles, the relative importance of the attributes can be derived via a statistical technique called conjoint analysis. The results can be presented as follows in Figure 9.1.

From these results it appears that the 'renal blood flow' is the most important characteristic (utility spread is 34) in this product category for the members of the target market. Price is the second most important attribute (utility spread is 15). It also follows from this analysis that the target market is willing to prescribe a drug that is significantly more expensive if it could increase the renal blood flow. Similarly, changing the dosage regime from three times a day to once a day ($+8$) would more than compensate for a price increase from $0.25 to $0.75 ($-7$).

Furthermore, trade-off analysis can help the manager get a feeling for sales and market share effects of different pricing tactics: Suppose that currently three products (A, B and C) are on the market and that a new competitor is considering introducing a new product (D). The profiles of the respective products are shown in Table 9.2.

The predicted market share for scenario 1 is derived as shown in Table 9.2.

Integrating the profit implications with the market share predictions will help the company to decide on the optimal price for the new drug D.

The pricing of new drugs also has to be seen in the international context. A common practice, especially in Europe, is to introduce the product first in countries that have a favourable attitude towards the company (e.g., the home base country) and/or that have a relatively favourable drug pricing system (i.e., high price countries). Subsequent introduction of the product in other less favourable or lower price countries could then still ensure relatively high prices by referring to the initial markets which could be used as a standard. Increased harmonization of prices within the EEC and the threat of parallel imports might dramatically change this practice.

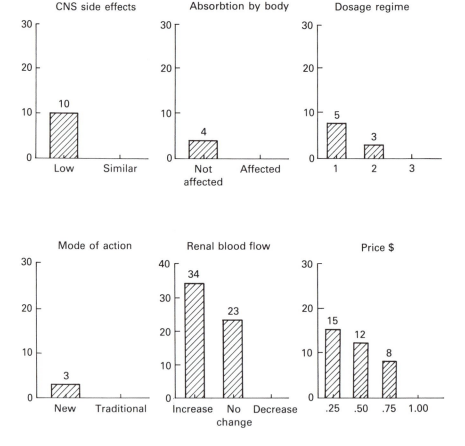

Figure 9.1   The importance of attributes

Table 9.2 Trade-off analysis

	A	B	C	D (New product)
CNS side effects	Similar	Low	Similar	Similar
Absorption by body	Affected	Affected	Not affected	Affected
Dosage regime	2 × a day	3 × a day	1 × a day	1 × a day
Mode of action	Traditional	Traditional	New	New
Renal blood flow	Decrease	No change	No change	Increase
Price				
Scenario 1	.25	.50	.75	.25
Scenario 2	.25	.50	.50	.50
Scenario 3	.25	.50	.50	.75
Scenario 4	.25	.50	.50	.50
Predicted market shares				
Scenario 1	10.6	26.6	27.2	35.6
Scenario 2	10.8	27.1	27.7	34.4
Scenario 3	11.1	27.8	28.4	32.7
Scenario 4	11.7	29.2	29.9	29.2

Table 9.2a Predicted market share for scenario 1

Brands	Utility	Predicted Market Share
A	$0 + 0 + 3 + 0 + 0 + 15 = 18$	$18/169 = 10.6$
B	$10 + 0 + 0 + 0 + 23 + 12 = 45$	$45/169 = 26.6$
C	$0 + 4 + 8 + 3 + 23 + 8 = 46$	$46/169 = 27.2$
D	$0 + 0 + 8 + 3 + 34 + 15 = 60$	$60/169 = 35.6$
	169	

9.2.3 Pricing out-of-patent drugs

All prescriptions drugs will face the generics' threat sooner or later. When the patent life runs out, the original drug has three possible options: to reduce its price, to introduce a 'fighter' generic brand or to stay put. The first option reduces the attractiveness of the generic to the prescribers, but simultaneously, to some extent, gives more credibility to the generic by admitting that the differential advantage of the original drug over the generic is marginal. This policy aims at maintaining the sales volume of the original drug by giving up some of its margin. The actual price reduction will strongly depend on two factors: the quality and credibility of the generic and the brand loyalty to the original drug.

The introduction of a fighter generic by the original drug manufacturer is becoming, at least for some companies, more and more popular. This two-pronged defensive approach aims at marginalizing 'foreign' generics while keeping the original brand untouched. The key problem with this approach is that it might lead to increased cannibalization of the original brand, not only by foreign generics but also by the own generic. It might also lead to confusion for the prescriber by having two company brands ('the original' and the 'generic') on the market. Some pharmaceutical companies try to avoid this problem by creating a new company (and a new company name) for launching generic products. Staying put and not changing the price of the original drug and not introducing a fighter generic is an approach adopted by some pharmaceutical companies that as a matter of principle don't want to give credibility to generics by entering themselves or by giving in by terms of reducing the price of the original brand. The original brand can be protected by marketing communication (e.g. sales force effort), but some sales loss will be hard to avoid. This third approach aims at capitalizing on brand and company loyalty.

9.3 COMMUNICATION

Communicating with the company's target markets is a crucial element in the tactical marketing puzzle confronted by pharmaceutical companies. Usually, the pharmaceutical company disposes of a number of powerful means of communication, including the sales force, journal advertising, mailings, conferences and symposia.

Given the nature of pharmaceutical products, personal communication with prescribers is a key success factor in the industry. The sales force muscle of drug companies is and will be, together with the quality of their products, the most important factor in obtaining successful product penetration and product profitability.

9.3.1 Communication and the product life cycle

In Table 9.3, the relative importance of the different means of communication across the product life cycle stages is illustrated. Generally speaking, the importance of all of the media declines over the product life cycle, thereby emphasizing that the success or failure of a pharmaceutical product is determined in the early stages of the life cycle. The importance of the pre-launch phase has also to be emphasized. Indeed, even before the product is actually launched the target-market has to be prepared for the product's introduction: the sales force has to be trained and has to start spreading the gospel of what is to come. Journal advertising and mailings are also useful to prepare for successful launches by informing the target audience of what is to come. Conferences and symposia are actually most important at the pre-launch phase of the product's life cycle.

Table 9.3 Communication and the product life cycle

	Pre-launch	Intro	Growth	Maturity	Decline
Sales force	3	1	2	4	5
Journal advertising	3	1	2	4	5
Mailings	3	1	2	4	5
Conferences and symposia	1	2	3	4	5

In Table 9.4, the importance of the different means of communication per stage in the product life cycle is illustrated. After the pre-launch stage the sales force dominates the other media in the introductory and the growth stage of the product. Later in the product's life the more impersonal, mass media become more important, also because they are less expensive.

Table 9.4 Communication at each stage in the product life cycle

	Pre-launch	Intro	Growth	Maturity	Decline
Sales force	2	1	1	2	—
Journal advertising	4	3	2	3	—
Mailings	3	4	3	1	1
Conferences and symposia	1	2	4	4	—

9.3.2 Communication tasks

The way to communicate with the target market and the communication message depends on the type of product involved. A distinction can be made between four types of products, depending on the involvement of the prescriber in the product category and on the decision process he or she goes through in making the prescription decision (Vaughn, 1980).

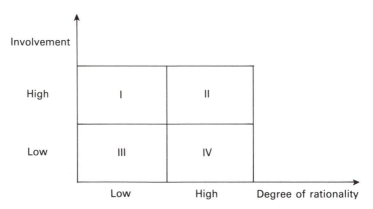

Figure 9.2   Products categorized by doctors' involvement and decision-making

The involvement dimension represents the level of prescribing risk, uncertainty about the innovation and the prescriber's clinical interest. For some product categories the prescription decision is based on rational arguments, whereas for some other product categories less rational approaches (e.g., company and product loyalty, impact of the product on the patient's self-image, habit) are prevalent.

The resulting four types of product categories have implications for the communication message and media.

1. *Reassure/legitimize.* Symposia and group presentations are crucial to provide peer group support and personal assurance for the prescriber. Journal advertising and other print media should provide more emotional support for the prescriber.
2. *Inform.* Specialized detailing, hospital presentations and clinical symposia are important vehicles to try to convince the prescribers of the added value of the product. Advertising with long copy format

and argumentation should be used to convince the prescribers who are interested in additional informations.

3. *Generate feeling.* The prescriber is not very interested in detailed information about this type of product. Simple messages via third-order detailing, journal advertising, and promotional activities seem most appropriate here.

4. *Habit formation.* Reminding the prescriber with simple messages is important for these types of products. Direct mailing, journal ads and other less expensive media should frequently be used for this product category.

Most pharmaceutical prescription products fall in the second ('inform') category and the task of the manager is to guide the prescriber through a set of stages described in the 'Hierarchy of Effects' approach (Figure 9.3).

Figure 9.3 The hierarchy of effects

The awareness stage

Most prescribers are aware of most new pharmaceutical products, at least those put on the market by large pharmaceutical companies. The key task at this stage is to achieve not only passive awareness, but 'top of mind' awareness. Prescribers have a limited capacity to process information and limited memory space. Coupled with the proliferation of new (mostly 'me-too') products and new product extensions, gaining 'top of mind' awareness often requires the use of heavy marketing artillery. Conferences, symposia, journal advertising and detailing effort are used in this context. Currently, promotional activities aimed at the final consumer are coming in vogue. The Mickey Mantle (ex-baseball star) promotional campaign by Ciba-Geigy for Voltaren in the US seems to have generated substantial 'top of mind' awareness not only for prescribers but also for patients.

Phase 4 clinical trial activities also contribute to generate 'top of mind' awareness with opinion leaders.

The interest stage

When confronted with a specific health problem of a patient the prescriber usually considers very few therapeutic alternatives. To enter this evoked set of alternative products is an important step to build a market position for a drug. Information about the benefits of the product are very important at this stage. The sales force, combined with supportive journal advertising and samples are crucial communication media at this stage.

The preference stage

Personal communication by the sales force is absolutely necessary to convince the prescriber to use a particular drug. The emphasis at this stage is the real differential advantage of the product.

The availability stage

Making sure the product is available at the point of purchase for the consumer can be improved by superior logistic systems, and good relationship with the wholesalers, drugstores and pharmacies. In a number of countries the role of the pharmacist is becoming very important, especially in the context of generic substitution. Sales force visits to pharmacists, samples, promotions and attractive margins for drug retailers are becoming more and more the rule rather than the exception.

The trial stage

Here clinical trials, phase 4 and samples are the key marketing instruments to induce the prescriber to try the product. In this context, sales force effort directed at opinion leaders and hospital prescribers can be instrumental in gaining effective penetration of the market.

The repeat stage

'Does the product live up to its expectations?' is the key issue at this stage. Furthermore, prescribers that are actually using the product are also sensitive to further information to reinforce their beliefs about the product benefits. Therefore, selective sales force, journal advertising and mailings are still important at this stage of the hierarchy. These satisfied prescribers and patients will also be important vehicles via their own 'word of mouth' to contribute to the success of products.

The importance of the final consumer (or patient) as a communication target is becoming more and more important, especially in the US as illustrated in Table 9.5.

Similarly, HMO formulary committees, hospital administrations, purchasing agents and DRG receivers are becoming increasingly important communication targets for prescription drugs.

Table 9.5 Recent promotional programmes for a variety of prescription products oriented towards consumers

Year	Product/Indication	Company
1981	Pneumonia vaccine	Merck
1982	Hepatitis B vaccine	Merck
	Consumer programme	Pfizer
1983	Rufen versus Motrin	Boots
1983–85	FDA moratorium on DTC advertising by product name	
1984	Menstrual cramps	Syntex
	Quit smoking	Merrell Dow
1985	Painful leg cramps	Hoechst–Roussel
	Quality of life	Squibb
1986	Genital herpes	Burroughs Wellcome
	Allergy sufferers	Merrell Dow
1987	Diabetes/recipes	Roerig Pfizer
	Arthritis/angina	Pfizer
	Tavist-1	Sandoz
1988	Ulcers	Smith Kline & French
	High cholesterol	Merck

Source: K. McRoberts, 1988, p. 54.

9.3.3   How much to spend on communication?

A crucial question confronting drug companies, is and will be, how much should be spent on these different means of communication? How many reps? How should the reps be allocated over the products in the company's portfolio? How much should be spent on journal advertising, mailings, conference? Given that for a typical large pharmaceutical company these communication expenditures can run up to 15% to 20% of sales, the efficiency of the communication media is a crucial issue.

Companies often take a pragmatic view with respect to these type of allocation decisions. 'We know we might be spending 50% too much, but we don't know which 50%', is an often-heard frustration about advertising investments. Over time companies have come to adopt one of following approaches:

1. *Percentage of sales*: depending on the stage in its product life cycle magical percentages of sales have evolved as the basis for communications investments.
2. *Competitive parity*: given what our competitors are doing, and they cannot all be wrong, let's keep up with them and match their communication expenditures.
3. *Affordable method*: our current and expected profitability will indicate what we can afford to spend on communication.
4. *Objective and task method*: to obtain our objectives of sales, market share and profitability, we think we should invest specific amounts on the means of communication.

Often, the actual decision rule is some combination of the above methods. To improve these decisions, a relatively new method, which could be called 'turbo driven intention', has in recent years been used successfully by a number of large pharmaceutical companies, including Syntex, Ciba-Geigy, Glaxo and Bristol Laboratories.

This particular method starts from the premise that managers will make decisions that are in line with their intuitions. The approach starts out from an S-shaped response function as illustrated in Figure 9.4 in the case of the field force. Similar curves can be used for the other communication media.

This rather general S-shape implies that for any product even with no field force effort there will be some sales (S_0). A minimum field force effort (F_1) is necessary to make an impact. If more field force is allocated

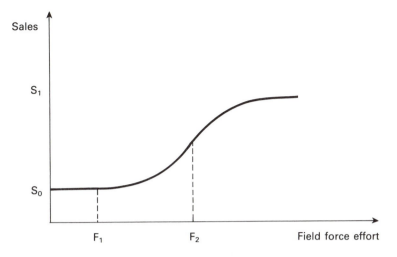

Figure 9.4 Field force response function

to a product sales will rise fast up to a point (F_2) from where the field force impact on sales will still increase but at a decreasing rate. Finally, whatever the field force effort for a product, sales can never exceed a saturation sales level S_1. In more formal terms this curve can be expressed as:

$$S = S_0 + (S_1 - S_0)\left[\frac{FF^\alpha}{\beta + FF^\alpha}\right]$$

where: S = sales
S_0 = minimum sales
S_1 = maximum sales
FF = field force effort (expressed in e.g. number of reps, or in terms of number of rep. contacts).

The four parameters of the model (S_0, S_1, α and β) will then be estimated, based on the manager's intuition. Suppose a company wants to decide how many reps to put on a specific product for next year. The managers familiar with the product and its market position will be asked five questions to calibrate the parameters of the field force response function.

They will be asked to think about next year's situation for their product, and then consider the following possibilities.

1. What will be the sales if no field force effort is allocated to our product?
2. What will be the sales if one half of the present effort is allocated to our product?*
3. What will be the sales if the same effort as at present is allocated to our product?
4. What will be the sales if there was a 50% greater effort allocated to our product?*
5. What will be the sales if there was a saturation level of sales effort?

Usually, several individuals, familiar with the product, will be asked to respond to these questions separately. Afterwards, the answers are compared and discussed and one aims to reach a reasonable level of consensus. This interactive process can be time-consuming. On the positive side, it forces managers to quantify their intuitions and to defend their opinions in the open. Furthermore, it will get managers very involved in the process and it will increase the acceptability of the resulting solutions.

The consensus results will then be used to estimate the parameters of the sales force response function in the following way.

Question 1 gives an estimate of S_0.
Question 5 gives an estimates of S_1.
Questions 2 and 4 provide two equations in two unknowns (α and β) and can be solved with some simple algebraic manipulations.
Question 3 is used as a reference condition.

Once the response curve is specified, contribution and cost figures can be added to the sales estimates and optimal sales force efforts can be determined via a sensitivity analysis.

A Harvard Business School case on Syntex provides the following example in the context of determining the optimal sales force for the company and for allocating the sales force over Syntex's major products. (Syntex case study, 1983).

Product, sales and marketing managers provided the inputs for the market response to varying field force levels for the seven top Syntex

---

*Here any two levels of field force effort can be used, as long as they are sufficiently reasonable to the manager that he or she can respond to the questions.

Table 9.6 Product response input

	No calls	One half	Present	50% more	Saturation
Naprosyn	47	68	100	126	152
Anaprox	15	48	100	120	135
Norinyl 135	31	63	100	115	125
Norinyl 150	45	70	100	105	110
Lidex	56	80	100	111	120
Synalar	59	76	100	107	111
Naslide	15	61	100	146	176

Source: Syntex, 1983.

products (Table 9.6). Forty-seven refers to the consensus opinion of Syntex managers that if the following year no field force effort was assigned to Naprosym it would reach a sales level of 47% of the previous year's sales level.

Based on these inputs the sales response functions for the seven products were calculated and subsequently, taking into account the profit margins of the seven products, the sales force level that would maximize profits was derived. Simultaneously the optimal allocation of the sales force over the seven products was derived (Table 9.7).

Table 9.8 clearly indicates the significant modification of the sales force size and its allocation over the seven products as compared to their previous year situations.

Table 9.7 Optimal sales force policy

Allocation to	Optimal number of reps	Presen-tations	Sales in dollars	Gross profit	Net profit
Naprosyn	265	975 964	309 378 624	250 906 061	236 176 981
Anaprox	183	671 467	41 111 928	26 023 851	15 890 188
Norinyl 135	82	302 049	24 380 000	20 406 060	15 847 593
Norinyl 150	42	153 412	39 374 664	32 956 594	30 641 320
Lidex	52	193 052	43 396 008	26 731 943	23 818 433
Synalar	33	120 383	14 876 068	9 163 659	7 346 852
Nasalide	94	344 004	16 813 808	10 088 285	4 896 636
Total	751	2 760 331	489 331 100	376 276 454	334 618 003

Source: Syntex, 1983.

Table 9.8   Previous year sales force policy

Allocation to	Number of reps	Presen- tations	Sales in dollars	Gross profit	Net profit
Naprosyn	97	357 853	202 001 792	163 823 451	158 422 789
Anaprox	143	527 581	36 500 000	23 104 501	15 142 337
Norinyl 135	53	195 443	20 113 592	16 835 077	13 885 480
Norinyl 150	24	88 818	35 992 408	30 125 646	28 785 224
Lidex	27	101 123	36 894 000	22 726 706	21 200 582
Synalar	30	110 351	14 600 000	8 993 601	7 328 195
Nasalide	57	210 225	10 471 728	6 283 037	3 110 363
Total	433	1 591 394	356 573 520	271 892 018	247 874 969

Source: Syntex, 1983.

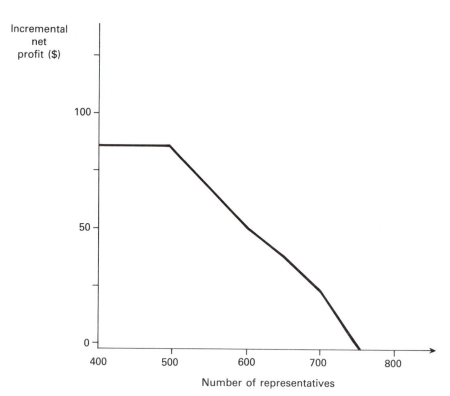

Figure 9.5   Incremental net profit per rep added at optimally deployed representative levels

Sensitivity analysis can then be done to find out the responsiveness of profits to various suboptimal levels of the sales force as illustrated in Figure 9.5.

This approach, although very insightful, has to be complemented by additional strategic and tactical considerations. For example, in the Syntex case, the optimal sales force level (751 reps) implied an increase of the sales force by more than three hundred reps. Training, availability, supervision and management of such an increase was not taken into account in the model. In the final decision the company increased the field force size but not as dramatically as the model suggested. The model's contribution was to suggest to management that a substantial increase in the sales force was called for and would be profitable. It also indicated that a reshuffling of the sales force might be considered in the direction suggested by the model.

Similar methods can be used to design territories (Zoltners and Sinka, 1988), and to evaluate the effectiveness of several marketing-mix elements simultaneously, e.g., field force, journal advertising and mailings.

9.4 DISTRIBUTION

The ultimate aim of all marketing is to place the manufactured drugs in the hands of consumers. This means the organization of efficient channels of distribution, and each company must decide how this process is best achieved and what resources will be required to do it.

Distribution channels exist to move the products from the manufacturer to the consumer. Because of the gaps that exist between the output of the manufacturer and the desired inputs for the consumer a number of tasks have to be fulfilled by distribution firms. First, because of the geographical concentration of the manufacturer and the geographical dispersion of the consumers, the distribution system *decentralizes* the manufacturers' product offerings. As a result it reduces the *delivery time* necessary to fill the customer's orders. In France, for example, pharmacists can get deliveries four times a day from their wholesalers. Second, the distribution system also adjusts the optimal manufacturer's *lot size* (large packages) to the consumer's lot size (small package). Third, the distributor acts as an *assortment* builder for the final consumer by assembling products from all manufacturers in one point of sale.

To make sure any product (assortment) is available to the consumer at the right time (delivery time), at the right place (market decentralization), in the right units (lot size), different configurations of intermediaries exist in different countries. These differences are partly due to history, tradition, economic reasons of efficiency and effectiveness and legal constraints.

A general distribution channel is illustrated in Figure 9.6.

The typical distribution channel includes a wholesaler and a retailer (pharmacist or drug store or drug chain). The relative importance of the different elements of the channel configuration varies significantly across countries. In Japan the dispensing prescriber is still important, whereas in Europe and the US the role of the dispensing prescriber is rather marginal. In the US HMOs are much more important than in Europe.

A pharmaceutical company has to work with the distribution system that is in place in the country of interest. Building its own distribution network is far too expensive and too time-consuming.

The distribution variable in the marketing mix is rather special: it is difficult to change, i.e., a long-term commitment, not under as much control of the manufacturer as its price or communication variables.

Recent changes in the distribution channels open up new challenges for pharmaceutical companies.

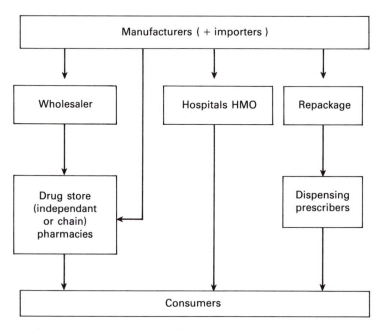

Figure 9.6 A general distribution channel

1. *The increased importance of drug retailers*, via generic substitution laws in some countries. In addition to the prescriber, drug retailers will become strong gatekeepers in the prescription drug industry. Furthermore, the tendency of pharmaceutical companies to try to convert prescription drugs into OTC products will also make the drug retailer a more vital link in the product's way to the final customer.

2. *Information technology*. Improved information technology at the wholesale and the retail level will create opportunities for pharmaceutical companies to improve their relationships with the trade via computer links in the transfer of orders, invoicing, and inventory management. This might also create the opportunity to create differential advantages for drug manufacturers with their trade partners in the distribution channel.

3. *Concentration* in the distribution systems in most countries. In a number of countries, e.g., the US, the concentration in the trade will result in enhanced negotiating power for the wholesales and drug chain stores.

9.5   A CONCLUDING NOTE

The best strategies will fail if not adequately implemented. Managing the sales force, the other communication media and the distribution channel, and setting appropriate prices in line with the needs of chosen target-markets to amplify the product's differential advantage, is the task of operational marketing and product managers. In a changing pharmaceutical world with a changing prescriber population, increased importance of the final consumer and the pharmacist, generic competition and increased government regulation and harmonization, the marketing implementation problems will require new skills of marketing and product managers. More attention will have to be given to setting optimal prices in a context of more transparent prices across countries and the increased generics competition. More analytical skills will be needed to assess the appropriate allocation of resources to the sales force, journal advertising, mailings, samples and communication. Pressure on drug margins will inevitably result in a more cost-conscious approach to the overall marketing costs of pharmaceutical products. The increasing power of drug distributors will require drug manufacturers to adjust their marketing policies accordingly: communication directed at drug retailers and the management of the manufacturer's relationships with his or her vital channel partners.

REFERENCES

Clarke, D. (1983) *Syntex Laboratories*, Harvard Business School, Case 0–584–033.

Green, P., Tull, D. and Albaum, G. (1978) *Research for Marketing Decisions*, Prentice Hall, Englewood Cliffs, NJ.

McRoberts, K. (1988) Direct to Consumer New Route for Ethical Drug Marketeers, *Pharmaceutical Executive*, November.

Montemayer, M. (1987) The Use of Conjoint Analysis in Forecasting and Price Elasticity for a New Pharmaceutical Entry – A Multicountry Market Research, in *Pricing and Forecasting in the Pharmaceutical Industry*, ESOMAR, pp. 115–36.

Nagle, T. (1987) *The Strategy and Tactics of Pricing*, Prentice Hall, Englewood Cliffs, NJ.

Vaughn, R. (1980) How Advertising Works: A Planning Model, *Journal of Advertising Research*, **20** (5), October, pp. 27–33.

Zoltners, A. and Sinha, P. (1988) Salesforce Byte: Computer-aided Territory Design, *Pharmaceutical Executive*, October, 50–6.

FURTHER READING

Corstjens, J. (1990) *Advertising Strategy*, Heinemann, London.

Hardy, K. and Magath, A. (1988) *Marketing Channel Management*, Scott, Foresman and Co., Glenview, Illinois.

Lilien, G. and Kotler, P. (1983) *Marketing Decision Making: A Model Building Approach*, Harper and Row, New York.

Little, J. (1970) Models and Managers: The Concept of a Decision Calculus, *Management Science*, April, pp. 466–85.

Vaughn, R. (1986) How Advertising Works: A Planning Model Revisited, *Journal of Advertising Research*, **26** (1).

Wind, Y. (1982) *Product Policy: Concepts, Methods and Strategy*, Addison-Wesley, Reading, Mass.

Index